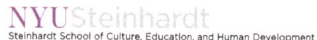 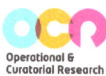 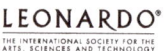 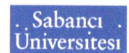 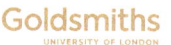

LEA is a publication of Leonardo/ISAST.

Copyright 2014 ISAST
Leonardo Electronic Almanac
Volume 20 Issue 2
April 15, 2014
ISSN 1071-4391
ISBN 978-1-906897-32-1
The ISBN is provided by Goldsmiths, University of London.

LEA PUBLISHING & SUBSCRIPTION INFORMATION

Editor in Chief
Lanfranco Aceti lanfranco.aceti@leoalmanac.org

Co-Editor
Özden Şahin ozden.sahin@leoalmanac.org

Managing Editor
John Francescutti john.francescutti@leoalmanac.org

Art Director
Deniz Cem Önduygu deniz.onduygu@leoalmanac.org

Editorial Board
Peter J. Bentley, Ezequiel Di Paolo, Ernest Edmonds, Felice Frankel, Gabriella Giannachi, Gary Hall, Craig Harris, Sibel Irzık, Marina Jirotka, Beau Lotto, Roger Malina, Terrence Masson, Jon McCormack, Mark Nash, Sally Jane Norman, Christiane Paul, Simon Penny, Jane Prophet, Jeffrey Shaw, William Uricchio

Cover
Deniz Cem Önduygu

Editorial Address
Leonardo Electronic Almanac
Sabanci University, Orhanli – Tuzla, 34956
Istanbul, Turkey

Email
info@leoalmanac.org

Web
» www.leoalmanac.org
» www.twitter.com/LEA_twitts
» www.flickr.com/photos/lea_gallery
» www.facebook.com/pages/Leonardo-Electronic-Almanac/209156896252

Copyright © 2014
Leonardo, the International Society for the Arts,
Sciences and Technology

Leonardo Electronic Almanac is published by:
    Leonardo/ISAST
    211 Sutter Street, suite 501
    San Francisco, CA 94108
    USA

Leonardo Electronic Almanac (LEA) is a project of Leonardo/ The International Society for the Arts, Sciences and Technology. For more information about Leonardo/ISAST's publications and programs, see http://www.leonardo.info or contact isast@leonardo.info.

Leonardo Electronic Almanac is produced by
Passero Productions.

Reposting of this journal is prohibited without permission of Leonardo/ISAST, except for the posting of news and events listings which have been independently received.

The individual articles included in the issue are © 2014 ISAST.

LEONARDO ELECTRONIC ALMANAC, VOLUME 20 ISSUE 2

Interference Strategies

BOOK EDITORS
LANFRANCO ACETI & PAUL THOMAS

EDITORIAL MANAGER
ÇAĞLAR ÇETİN

The Leonardo Electronic Almanac acknowledges the institutional support for this book of

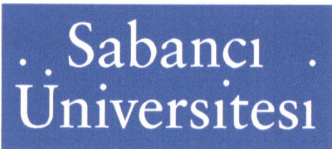

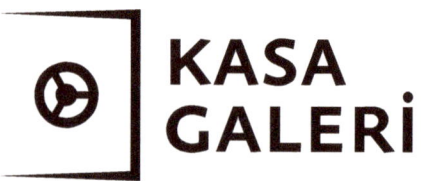

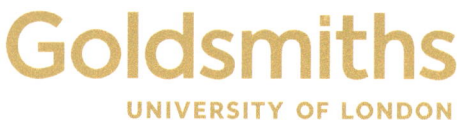

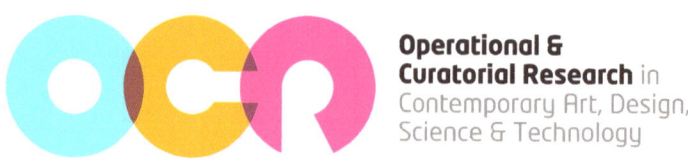

The publication of this book is graciously supported by

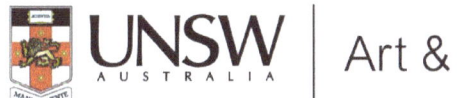

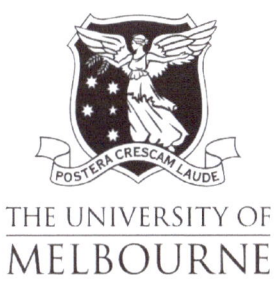 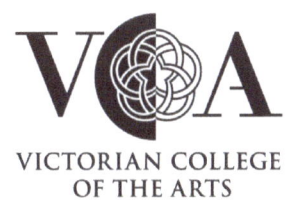

The book editors Lanfranco Aceti and Paul Thomas would especially like to acknowledge Su Baker for her continual support of this project and Andrew Varano for his work as conference organiser.

We would also like to thank the Transdisciplinary Imaging at the intersection between art, science and culture, Conference Committee: Michele Barker, Brad Buckley, Brogan Bunt, Edward Colless, Vince Dziekan, Donal Fitzpatrick, Petra Gemeinboeck, Julian Goddard, Ross Harley, Martyn Jolly, Daniel Mafe, Leon Marvell and Darren Tofts.

CONTENTS

Leonardo Electronic Almanac
Volume 20 Issue 2

10   **INTERFERENCE STRATEGIES: IS ART IN THE MIDDLE?**
Lanfranco Aceti

13   **INTERFERENCE STRATEGIES**
Paul Thomas

16   **THE ART OF DECODING: *n*-FOLDED, *n*-VISIONED, *n*-CULTURED**
Mark Guglielmetti

26   **THE CASE OF BIOPHILIA: A COLLECTIVE COMPOSITION OF GOALS AND DISTRIBUTED ACTION**
Mark Cypher

36   **CONTAMINATED IMMERSION AND THOMAS DEMAND: THE DAILIES**
David Eastwood

50   **GESTURE IN SEARCH OF A PURPOSE: A PREHISTORY OF MOBILITY**
Darren Tofts & Lisa Gye

60   **HEADLESS AND UNBORN, OR THE BAPHOMET RESTORED INTERFERING WITH BATAILLE AND MASSON'S IMAGE OF THE *ACEPHALE***
Leon Marvell

CONTENTS

72   **IMAGES (R)-EVOLUTION: MEDIA ARTS COMPLEX IMAGERY CHALLENGING HUMANITIES AND OUR INSTITUTIONS OF CULTURAL MEMORY**
Oliver Grau

86   **INTERFERENCE WAVE DATA AND ART**
Adam Nash

96   **INTERFERING WITH THE DEAD**
Edward Colless

114   **MERGE/MULTIPLEX**
Brogan Bunt

122   **A ROBOT WALKS INTO A ROOM: GOOGLE ART PROJECT, THE NEW AESTHETIC, AND THE ACCIDENT OF ART**
Susan Ballard

132   **TOWARDS AN ONTOLOGY OF COLOUR IN THE AGE OF MACHINIC SHINE**
Mark Titmarsh

146   **TRANSVERSAL INTERFERENCE**
Anna Munster

INTRODUCTION

Interference Strategies: Is Art in the Middle?

If we look at the etymological structure of the word *interference*, we would have to go back to a construct that defines it as a sum of the two Latin words *inter* ((in)between) and *ferio* (to strike), but with a particular attention to the meaning of the word *ferio* being interpreted principally as *to wound*. Albeit perhaps etymologically incorrect, it may be preferable to think of the word interference as a composite of *inter* ((in)between) and the Latin verb *fero* (to carry), which would bring forward the idea of interference as a contribution brought in the middle of two arguments, two ideas, two constructs.

It is important to acknowledge the etymological root of a word not in order to develop a sterile academic exercise, but in order to clarify the ideological underpinnings of arguments that are themselves summed up and characterized by a word.

This book, titled *Interference Strategies*, does not (and in all honesty could not) provide a resolution to a complex interaction – that of artistic interferences – that has a complex historical tradition. In fact, it is impossible, for me, when analyzing the issue of interference, not to think of the Breeches Maker (also known as Daniele da Volterra) and the coverings that he painted following a 1559 commission from Pope Paul IV to 'render decent' the naked bodies of Michelangelo Buonarroti's frescoes in the Sistine Chapel. That act, in the eyes of a contemporary viewer, was a wound inflicted in between the relationship created by the artwork and the artist with the viewer ((intentio operis and intentio auctoris with intentio lectoris)), as Umberto Eco would put it. Those famous breeches appear to be both: a form of censorship as well as interference with Michelangelo's vision.

Interference is a word that assembles a multitude of meanings interpreted according to one's perspective and ideological constructs as a meddling, a disturbance, and an alteration of modalities of interaction between two parties. In this book, there are a series of representations of these interferences, as well as a series of questions on what are the possible contemporary forms of interference – digital, scientific and aesthetic – and what are the strategies that could be adopted in order to actively interfere.

The complexity of the strategies of interference within contemporary political and aesthetic discourses appears to be summed up by the perception that interference is a necessarily active gesture. This perception appears to exclude the fact that sometimes the very existence of an artwork is based on an interfering nature, or on an aesthetic that has come to be as monoconsonant to and, hence, interfering with a political project.

Interfering artworks, which by their own nature challenge a system, were the artworks chosen for the exhibition *Entartete Kunst* (1937). The cultural and ideological underpinnings of the National Socialist German Workers' Party could solely provide an understanding of aesthetics that would necessarily imply the definition of 'degenerate art' produced by 'degenerate artists.' Art that was not a direct hymn to the grandeur of Germany could not be seen by the Nazi regime as anything else but 'interfering and hence degenerate,' since it questioned and interfered with the ideal purity of Teutonic representations, which were endorsed and promoted as the only aesthetics of the National Socialist party. Wilhelm Heinrich Otto Dix's *War Cripples* (1920) could not be a more critical painting of the Body Politic of the time, and of war in general, and therefore had to be classified as 'degenerate' and condemned to be 'burnt.'

Art in this context cannot be and should not be anything else but interference; either by bringing something in between or by wounding the Body Politic by placing something in between the perfectly construed rational madness of humanity and the subjugated viewer. An element that interferes, obstructs and disrupts the carefully annotated and carefully choreographed itinerary that the viewers should meekly follow. In this case interference is something that corrupts, degenerates and threatens to collapse the vision of the Body Politic.

In thinking about the validity of interference as a strategy, it was impossible not to revisit and compare the image of Paul Joseph Goebbels viewing the *Entartete Kunst (Degenerate Art)* exhibition to the many images of pompously strutting corporate icons and billionaires in museums and art fairs around the globe, glamoring with pride over the propaganda, or –better – over the broadness that they have commissioned artists to produce.

Today's contemporary art should be interfering more and more with art itself, it should be corrupted and corrupting, degenerate and degenerating. It should be producing what currently it is not and it should create a wound within art itself, able to alter current thinking and modalities of engagement. It should be – to quote Pablo Picasso – an instrument of war able to *interfere*: "No, painting is not done to decorate apartments. It is an instrument of war for attack and defense against the enemy." [2]

If art should either strike or bring something is part of what has been a long aesthetic conversation that preceded the Avant-garde movement or the destructive fury of the early Futurists. In this particular volume the issue of art as interference and the strategies that it should adopt have been reframed within the structures of contemporary technology as well as within the frameworks of interactions between art, science and media.

What sort of interference should be chosen, if one at all, remains a personal choice for each artist, curator, critic and historian.

If I had to choose, personally I find myself increasingly favoring art that does not deliver what is expected, what is obvious, what can be hung on a wall and can be matched to tapestries. Nor can I find myself able to favor art that shrouds propaganda or business under a veil with the name of art repeatedly written in capital letters all over it. That does not leave very much choice in a world where interference is no longer acceptable, or if it is acceptable, it is so only within pre-established contractual operative frameworks, therefore losing its 'interference value.'

This leaves the great conundrum – are interferences still possible? There are still spaces and opportunities for interference, and this volume is one of these remaining areas, but they are interstitial spaces and are shrinking fast, leaving an overwhelming Baudrillardian desert produced by the conspirators of art and made of a multitude of breeches.

Interference Strategies: Is Art in the Middle?

If we look at the etymological structure of the word interference, we would have to go back to a construct that defines it as a sum of the two Latin words *inter* (in between) and *ferio* (to strike), but with a particular attention to the meaning of the word *ferio* being interpreted principally as *to wound*. Albeit perhaps etymologically incorrect, it may be preferable to think of the word interference as a composite of *inter* (in between) and the Latin verb *fero* (to carry), which would bring forward the idea of interference as a contribution brought in the middle of two arguments, two ideas, two constructs.

It is important to acknowledge the etymological root of a word not in order to develop a sterile academic exercise, but in order to clarify the ideological underpinnings of arguments that are then summed up and characterized by a word.

This book, titled *Interference Strategies*, does not (and in all honesty could not) provide a resolution to a complex interaction - that of artistic interferences - that has a complex historical tradition. In fact, it is impossible, for me, when analyzing the issue of interference, not to think of the Breeches Maker (also known as Daniele da Volterra) and the coverings that he painted following a 1559 commission from Pope Paul IV to 'render decent' the naked bodies of Michelangelo Buonarroti's frescoes in the Sistine Chapel. That act, in the eyes of a contemporary viewer, was a wound inflicted in between the relationship created by the artwork and the artist with the viewer (*intentio operis* and *intentio auctoris* with *intentio lectoris*), as Umberto Eco would put it. Those famous breeches appear to be both: a form of censorship as well as interference with Michelangelo's vision.

Interference is a word that assembles a multitude of meanings interpreted according to one's perspective and ideological constructs as a meddling, a disturbance, and an alteration of modalities of interaction between two parties. In this book, there are a series of representations of these interferences, as well as a series of questions on what are the possible contemporary forms of interference - digital, scientific and aesthetic - and what are the strategies that could be adopted in order to actively interfere.

The complexity of the strategies of interference within contemporary political and aesthetic discourses appears to be summed up by the perception that interference is a necessarily active gesture. This perception appears to exclude the fact that sometimes the very existence of an artwork is based on an interfering nature, or on an aesthetic that has come to be as non-consonant to and, hence, interfering with a political project.

Interfering artworks, which by their own nature challenge a system, were the artworks chosen for the exhibition *Entartete Kunst* (1937). The cultural and ideological underpinnings of the National Socialist German Workers' Party could solely provide an understanding of aesthetics that would necessarily imply the defini-

INTRODUCTION

tion of 'degenerate art' produced by 'degenerate artists.' Art that was not a direct hymn to the grandeur of Germany could not be seen by the Nazi regime as anything else but 'interfering and hence degenerate,' since it questioned and interfered with the ideal purity of Teutonic representations, which were endorsed and promoted as the only aesthetics of the National Socialist party. Wilhelm Heinrich Otto Dix's *War Cripples* (1920) could not be a more critical painting of the Body Politic of the time, and of war in general, and therefore had to be classified as 'degenerate' and condemned to be 'burnt.'

Art in this context cannot be and should not be anything else but interference; either by bringing something in between or by wounding the Body Politic by placing something in between the perfectly construed rational madness of humanity and the subjugated viewer. An element that interferes, obstructs and disrupts the carefully annotated and carefully choreographed itinerary that the viewers should meekly follow. In this case interference is something that corrupts, degenerates and threatens to collapse the vision of the Body Politic.

In thinking about the validity of interference as a strategy, it was impossible not to revisit and compare the image of Paul Joseph Goebbels viewing the *Entartete Kunst* (*Degenerate Art*) exhibition [1] to the many images of pompously strutting corporate tycoons and billionaires in museums and art fairs around the globe, glancing with pride over the propaganda, or - better - over the breeches that they have commissioned artists to produce.

Today's contemporary art should be interfering more and more with art itself, it should be corrupted and corrupting, degenerate and degenerating. It should be producing what currently it is not and it should create a wound within art itself, able to alter current thinking and modalities of engagement. It should be - to quote Pablo Picasso - an instrument of war able to *inter-ferio*: "No, painting is not done to decorate apartments. It is an instrument of war for attack and defense against the enemy." [2]

If art should either strike or bring something is part of what has been a long aesthetic conversation that preceded the Avant-garde movement or the destructive fury of the early Futurists. In this particular volume the issue of art as interference and the strategies that it should adopt have been reframed within the structures of contemporary technology as well as within the frameworks of interactions between art, science and media.

What sort of interference should be chosen, if one at all, remains a personal choice for each artist, curator, critic and historian.

If I had to choose, personally I find myself increasingly favoring art that does not deliver what is expected, what is obvious, what can be hung on a wall and can be matched to tapestries. Nor can I find myself able to favor art that shrouds propaganda or business under a veil with the name of art repeatedly written in capital letters all over it. That does not leave very much choice in a world where interference is no longer acceptable, or if it is acceptable, it is so only within pre-established contractual operative frameworks, therefore losing its 'interference value.'

This leaves the great conundrum - are interferences still possible? There are still spaces and opportunities for interference, and this volume is one of these remaining areas, but they are interstitial spaces and are shrinking fast, leaving an overwhelming Baudrillardian desert produced by the conspirators of art and made of a multitude of breeches.

INTRODUCTION

In this introduction I cannot touch upon all the different aspects of interference analyzed, like in the case of data and waves presented by Adam Nash, who argues that the digital is in itself and *per se* a form of interference: at least a form of interference with behavioral systems and with what can be defined as the illusory realm of everyday's 'real.'

Transversal interference, as in the case of Anna Munster, is a socio-political divide where heterogeneity is the monster, the wound, the interfering and dreaded element that threatens the 'homologation' of scientific thought.

With Brogan Bunt comes obfuscation as a form of blurring that interferes with the ordered lines of neatly defined social taxonomies; within which I can only perceive the role of the thinker as that of the taxidermist operating on living fields of study that are in the process of being rendered dead and obfuscated by the very process and people who should be unveiling and revealing them.

With Darren Tofts and Lisa Gye it is the perusal of the image that can be an act of interference and a disruption if it operates outside rigid interpretative frameworks and interaction parameters firmly set via *intentio operis*, *intentio auctoris* and *intentio lectoris*.

It is the fear of the unexpected remix and mash-up that interferes with and threatens the 'purity' and sanctimonious fascistic interpretations of the aura of the artwork, its buyers, consumers and aesthetic priests. The orthodoxical, fanatic and terroristic aesthetic hierarchies that were disrupted by laughter in the Middle Ages might be disrupted today by viral, a-morphological and uncontrollable bodily functions.

My very personal thanks go to Paul Thomas and the authors in this book who have endeavored to comply with our guidelines to deliver a new milestone in the history of LEA.

As always I wish to thank my team at LEA who made it possible to deliver these academic interferences: my gratitude is as always for Özden Şahin, Çaglar Çetin and Deniz Cem Önduygu.

Lanfranco Aceti
Editor in Chief, Leonardo Electronic Almanac
Director, Kasa Gallery

REFERENCES AND NOTES

1. "Reichsminister Dr. Goebbels auf der Ausstellung 'Entartete Kunst,'" February 27, 1938, in the Das Bundesarchiv, Bild 183-H02648, http://www.bild.bundesarchiv.de/cross-search/search/_1414849849/?search[view]=detail&search[focus]=3 (accessed October 20, 2014).
2. Herschel Browning Chipp, *Theories of Modern Art: A Source Book by Artists and Critics* (Berkeley and Los Angeles, CA: University of California Press, 1968), 487.

Interference Strategies

The theme of 'interference strategies for art' reflects a literal merging of sources, an interplay between factors, and acts as a metaphor for the interaction of art and science, the essence of transdisciplinary study. The revealing of metaphors for interference "that equates different and even 'incommensurable' concepts can, therefore, be a very fruitful source of insight." [1]

The role of the publication, as a vehicle to promote and encourage transdisciplinary research, is to question what fine art image-making is contributing to the current discourse on images. The publication brings together researchers, artists and cultural thinkers to speculate, contest and share their thoughts on the strategies for interference, at the intersection between art, science and culture, that form new dialogues.

In October 1927 the Fifth Solvay International Conference marked a point in time that created a unifying seepage between art and science and opened the gateway to uncertainty and therefore the parallels of artistic and scientific research. This famous conference announced the genesis of quantum theory and, with that, Werner Heisenberg's uncertainty principle. These events are linked historically and inform interesting experimental art practices to reveal the subtle shift that can ensue from a moment in time.

The simple yet highly developed double slit experiment identifies the problem of measurement in the quantum world. If you are measuring the position of a particle you cannot measure its momentum. This is one of the main theories that have been constantly tested and still remains persistent. The double slit experiment, first initiated by Thomas Young, exposes a quintessential quantum phenomenon, which, through Heisenberg theory, demonstrates the quantum universe as a series of probabilities that enabled the Newtonian view of the world to be seriously challenged.

If the measurement intra-action plays a constitutive role in what is measured, then it matters how something is explored. In fact, this is born out empirically in experiments with matter (and energy): when electrons (or light) are measured using one kind of apparatus, they are waves; if they are measured in a complementary way, they are particles. Notice that what we're talking about here is not simply some object reacting differently *to different probings but being* differently. [2]

In the double slit experiment particles that travel through the slits interfere with themselves enabling each particle to create a wave-like interference pattern.

The underlying concepts upon which this publication is based see the potential for art to interfere, affect and obstruct in order to question what is indefinable.

This can only be demonstrated by a closer look at the double slit experiment and the art that is revealed through phenomena of improbability.

INTRODUCTION

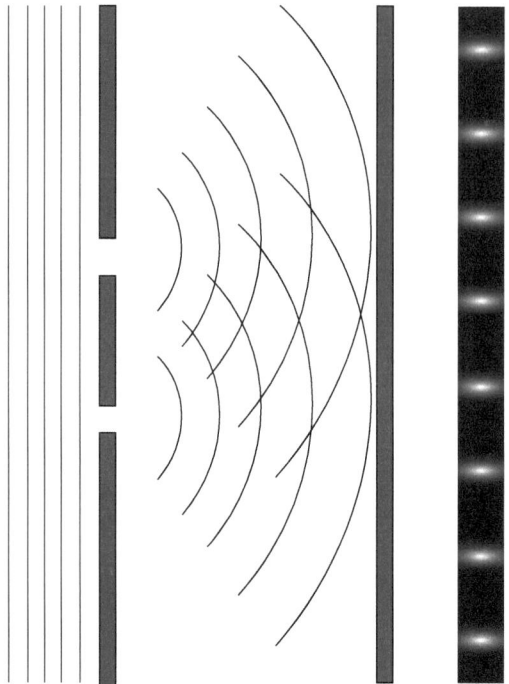

Figure 1. Diagram of the double slit experiment that was first performed by Thomas Young in the early 1800's displays the probabilistic characteristics of quantum mechanical phenomena.

When particles go through the slits they act as waves and create the famous interference pattern. The concept is that one particle going through the slit must behave like a wave and interfere with itself to create the band image on the rear receptor.

Interference Strategies looks at the phenomenon of interference and places art at the very centre of the wave/particle dilemma. Can art still find a way in today's dense world where we are saturated with images from all disciplines, whether it's the creation of 'beautiful visualisations' for science, the torrent of images uploaded to social media services like Instagram and Flickr, or the billions of queries made to vast visual data archives such as Google Images? The contemporary machinic interpretations of the visual and sensorial experience of the world are producing a new spectacle of media pollution, obliging the viewers to ask if machines should be considered the new artists of the 21st century.

The notion of 'Interference' is posed here as an antagonism between production and seduction, as a redirection of affect, or as an untapped potential for repositioning artistic critique. Maybe art doesn't have to work as a wave that displaces or reinforces the standardized protocols of data/messages, but can instead function as a signal that disrupts and challenges perceptions.

'Interference' can stand as a mediating incantation that might create a layer between the constructed image of the 'everyday' given to us by science, technological social networks and the means of its construction. Mediation, as discussed in the first Transdisplinary Imaging conference, is a concept that has become a medium in itself through which we think and act; and in which we swim. Interference, however, confronts the flow, challenges currents and eulogizes the drift.

The questions posed in this volume, include whether art can interfere with the chaotic storms of data visualization and information processing, or is it merely reinforcing the nocuous nature of contemporary media? Can we think of 'interference' as a key tactic for the contemporary image in disrupting and critiquing the continual flood of constructed imagery? Are contemporary forms and strategies of interference the same as historical ones? What kinds of similarities and differences exist?

Application of a process to a medium, or a wave to a particle, for example, the sorting of pixel data, literally interferes with the state of an image, and directly gives new materiality and meaning, allowing interference to be utilised as a conceptual framework for interpretation, and critical reflection.

Interference is not merely combining. Interference is an active process of negotiating between different forces. The artist in this context is a mediator, facilitating the meeting of competitive elements, bringing together and setting up a situation of probabilities.

INTRODUCTION

In response to the questions posed by the conference theme, presentations traversed varied notions of interference in defining image space, the decoding and interpretation of images, the interference between different streams of digital data, and how this knowledge might redefine art and art practice. Within that scope lies the discourse about interference that arises when normal approaches or processes fail, with unanticipated results, the accidental discovery, and its potential in the development of new strategies of investigation.

In "[t]he case of Biophilia: a collective composition of goals and distributed action", [3] Mark Cypher highlights the interference in negotiations between exhibit organisers, and space requirements, and the requirements for artist/artworks, resulting in an outcome that is a combination generated by the competition of two or more interests. As part of the final appearance of *Biophilia*, the artwork itself contained elements of both interests, an interference of competing interests, comprising a system in which the artist and the artwork are components, and the display a negotiated outcome. Each element interferes with itself as it negotiates the many factors that contribute to the presentation of art. In this sense the creation of the final appearance of *Biophilia* is the result of the distributed action of many "actors" in a "network." [4] (To put this in another form all actors are particles and interact with each other to create all possible solutions but when observed, create a single state.)

In summing up concepts of the second Transdisciplinary Imaging conference, particularly in reference to the topic of interference strategies, Edward Colless spoke of some of the aspirations for the topic, entertaining the possibilities of transdisciplinary art as being a contested field, in that many of the conference papers were trying to unravel, contextualise and theorise simultaneously.

The publication aims to demonstrate a combined eclecticism and to extend the discussion by addressing the current state of the image through a multitude of lenses. Through the theme of interference strategies this publication will embrace error and transdisciplinarity as a new vision of how to think, theorize and critique the image, the real and thought itself.

Paul Thomas

REFERENCES AND NOTES

1. David Bohm and F. David Peat, *Science, Order and Creativity* (London: Routledge, 2000), 45.
2. K. Barad, *What is the Measure of Nothingness? Infinity, Virtuality, Justice*, Documenta 13, The Book of Books, 100 Notes, 100 Thoughts, (Ostfildern: Hatje Cantz, 2012), 646.
3. Mark Cypher, "The case of Biophilia: A Collective Composition of Goals and Distributed Action," (paper presented at the Second International Conference on Transdisciplinary Imaging at the Intersection between Art, Science and Culture, Melbourne, June 22-23, 2012).
4. Ibid.

ACKNOWLEDGEMENTS

Special thanks to researcher Jan Andruszkiewicz.

ESSAY

THE ART OF DECODING
n-folded, *n*-visioned, *n*-cultured

by

Mark Guglielmetti

Monash Art Design + Architecture (MADA)
Monash University
mark.guglielmetti@monash.edu

DECODING: THE NATURAL ORDER

Artificial life (A-Life) originates, so the accepted narrative goes, from the domain of science. In this discursive orientation much is underwritten by cybernetics and information theory to generate (evolve) computationally *lifelike* behaviour and the emergence of life, irrespective of material form [3] and to locate "*life-as-we-know-it* within the larger picture of *life-as-it-could-be*." [4] In this undertaking scientists simulate "biological life to evolve patterns, images, programs and more generally to formulate new strategies of control which are more adequate to the liquid space of informational capitalism." [5] The complexity of life is measured not by the metaphorical and material relays through which humans are being redefined as posthuman [6] but by observing "abstract mathematical musings" [7] and complex mathematical patterns as they are *seen* to self-organise and emerge in images.

Notwithstanding this scientific account of artificial life, there are multiple dimensions to examine artificial life. [8] [9] [10] I explore artificial life itself as constituent of the moving image specifically as visualised in three-dimensional computer generated space (3D space). Of particular interest in this examination is the view or

ESSAY

Scientific modelling requires us to suspend disbelief, nowhere is this more palpable than in artificial life, an area of computational research investigating the principles that constitute a living system "without making reference to the materials that constitute it." [1]

This paper investigates artificial life visualisation as both a scientific concern and in relation to media arts. Of interest in this examination is the normative protocol of looking at an artificial life simulation or 'world.' Analogous to looking through a telescope or microscope, the view into the artificial life world is monocular and often fixed; in this regime we look at 'organisms.' This strategy of looking through the scientific lens to observe a 'natural world' enfolds other forms of cultural tactics that require decoding including but not exclusive to Bazin's ontology of the photographic image, Disney nature films and other "apparatus-based universes which robotize the human being and society." [2]

Subsequent to identifying these protocols in artificial life visualisation I describe a number of works which exploit normative computational procedures to align artificial life image making into optical consistency with other forms of contemporary culture and to celebrate the 'ocular madness' found in art forms such as neo-baroque image making and Islamic art.

'window,' from the virtual camera into the artificial life computational model, and how it organises a dense field of expectations. These expectations include how the camera that frames the image is deployed to create the appearance of an unmediated reality into abstracted mathematical models which, when rendered, generate perceptible images of, what is commonly referred to as, the 'world.'

Analogous to looking through a telescope or microscope, the view into the artificial life world is monocular and often fixed in the 'world.' The success of artificial life visualisation is dependent on observing 'lifelike behaviour' [11] within the image and deciphering emergent patterns in, the 'world'; what is perceived in the 'world' or on the screen is what there is to perceive.

The coded generators of this lifelike behaviour are often referred to as "creatures," [12] "cyberbeasts," [13] and "virtual organisms." [14] These creatures, often 'live,' 'fight,' 'breed,' 'trade' and 'die' in the virtual world; that said, rarely do they 'work,' 'shop,' 'shit,' 'fuck' or afford a 'point of view'; sticky messy descriptions that rarely pervade the imaginative and iterative loop of pattern generation. The anthropomorphic machinations of an A-Life 'world' are described through the discursive framework and nomenclature of science and economics, more so than from a personal intimate perspective of life.

This institutionalised orientation is not exclusive to the nomenclature of artificial life as a journalistic enterprise for scientific journals, academic publications and as filter for the artist's press release, but extends to other taxonomies of A-Life such as the interpretive viewing regime of the A-Life world. The normative viewing protocol through which to view an A-Life 'world' is predominantly filtered through the fixed lens of the virtual camera view into the modelled world. In this regime we look 'at' the aforementioned creatures etcetera. This tactic of looking through the instrumentality of science, the arts of reality, is parallel to looking through André Bazin's [15] 'long take' in cinema and documentary filmmaking in which we look 'at' an unmediated view of reality; in other words in looking 'at' an image of artificial life we look 'through' a non-intrinsic regime of seeing.

In the case of the artificial life, observation vis-à-vis the long take stands in reserve as the de facto protocol which functions to record (shoot) an unmediated reality of the A-Life world, perhaps for good strategic reason; when "we abandon the notion of a camera as an adversary to the world ... and instead place the accent on its 'natural' connection to the world, we reach another, more orthodox version of a camera. This approach stresses the necessary, scientific links among objects, light rays, and film emulsion [...] A camera comes the bearer of tokens from the world." [16] A natural order is established in service of scientific method, measurement, classification, documentation and re-presentation arbitrates fact from magic, facts are not man made. In the domain of science "it is not I [the experimenter] who says this; it is the machine." [17] Indeed, the epistemological (scientific) framework through which to legitimately measure the world vis-à-vis the camera (virtual or otherwise), originates through the complex matrix of French politics less than 15 years after Nicéphore Niépce's *View from the Window at Le Gras* (1826) was taken, when M. François Arago persuasively reasons to the government of the French July Monarchy, and confirming to the French public that, "the camera lies no more than does the thermometer, the microscope, and hygrometer, and so on." [18]

The window into artificial life worlds evokes nineteenth-century 'scientific' studies or early twentieth-century photoplays than is suggestive of either Friedberg's [19] "new space of mediated vision [which] is post-Cartesian, postperspectival, postcinematic, and posttelevisual" or the "celebration of ocular madness" [20] in other forms of neo-baroque image making. [21][22]

The advanced expectation from practitioners of artificial life screen-based imaging is the virtual camera itself functions similar to an analogue device, such as the microscope or telescope, in that it impassively enframes the 'world' whilst it simultaneously optimises the credibility or factuality of the 'world' and like an analogue camera it records a temporal image of the 'world'; in other words, the virtual camera functions like Vertov's "microscope and telescope of time." [23]

The camera (virtual or otherwise) does not record an unmediated reality or 'world'; all cameras (virtual or otherwise) are devices that create images. That all images "are mediations between the world and human beings" [24] is an important reminder that an image is not a window into a world – it *is* an image. [25] In this, all image making is rhetorical. Flusser's description of the photographic apparatus is a critical reminder that:

> [the] 'objectivity' of technical images is an illusion. For they are – like all images – not only symbolic but represent even more abstract complexes of symbols than traditional images. They are meta-codes of texts which . . . signify texts, not the world out there. [26]

Flusser's [27] sombre view that the "photographic universe and all apparatus-based universes robotize the human being and society," is a timely cue that the view into an artificial life world, and indeed into the broader spectrum of scientific and data visualisation, is important.

The investigation into the interpretive regimes and the technical apparatus gives only a partial dimension to the relationship between artificial life and the moving image. Other important factors under consideration are the narratives that accompany artificial life works themselves. Scientists often publish in scientific journals fictive accounts of the artificial life system that simply don't accord with the target system, as illustrated in Watson and Lovelock's [28] scientific study of an "imaginary planet [with] a very simple biosphere" in the project *Daisyworld*. After warning the reader that they "are not trying to model the Earth, but rather a fictional world," Watson and Lovelock [29] go on to describe *Daisyworld*: "Owing to a subtle change of climate, clouds appear on daisyworld [sic]. The clouds are light in colour. We will assume that the clouds form only over stands of black daisies because of the rising air generated over these warm spots." [30] To state the obvious, stylised descriptions have properties that the models don't [31] and as Michael Renov convincingly argues, all discursive forms are "at least *fictive,* this by virtue of their tropic character (their recourse to tropes or rhetorical figures)." [32]

The stories that migrate in artificial life are contemporary accounts of 'nature' whose genealogy can be traced to Disney filmmaking, specifically, the nature film (to simulate life as we know it vis-à-vis moral and political refractions) and Disney animation, which, as lead Disney animator Art Babbitt observed, "follows the laws of physics – unless it is funnier otherwise." [33] Artificial life 'world building' is formed in the shadow of Disney nature storytelling: cyberbeasts, virtual organisms and agents are organised, optimised and then observed, like the Disney animal kingdom, to trade, fight, breed and die. Moreover, similar to Disney stories that do "something far more than reveal 'nature's mysteries': they [speak] to us of a living and intelligible world beyond the fence of civilization, a world we [can] enter at will and experience in something like human time." [34] Artificial life is of its essence a dramaturgy of the fitness landscape. [35]

n-FOLDED, *n*-VISIONED, *n*-CULTURED

A high degree of artifice is involved in scientific visualisation in general, more so in artificial life 'worlds.' Take for example the virtual camera that frames the view into the artificial life world. The term virtual camera itself is shorthand to describe an array of algorithmic functions, some of which are mapped to functions that have equivalence in digital cameras. The virtual camera is also host to a large range of algorithms

ESSAY

that simply do not have physical correspondence to the world such as the 'z-buffer.' The z-buffer is a data structure unique to 3D visualisation; it establishes and determines the logical drawing order of objects and elements in 3D space in relation to the virtual camera. As illustrated in Figures 1-3, objects closer to the camera occlude objects or elements far from the virtual camera, correctly reproducing perspective depth perception. Though the z-buffer is programmed into 3D software to create a 'realistic map' of the world it is instructive to remind the reader that 'world' is a social concept [36] and mapmaking is rhetorical. The z-buffer is just another algorithm in a database of algorithms; it too can be re-imagined as a rhetorical device. For example in my project *Laboratories of Thought,* the z-buffer is rewired to my subjective experience of the gallery the Trocadero Artspace in Melbourne, Australia. The drawing logic of three-dimensional space is reordered according to criteria other than spatial. Unlinked from conventional spatial logic the z-buffer is reconfigured along subjective lines, in this case emotional valency; what I like most about the Artspace to what I like least.

The project explores the tensions inherent in employing the mathematical rationalisation of pictorial space as a model through which to filter my emotionally and biologically mediated experience of the physical environment. By encoding the virtual camera to reorder the visual field of the 3D scene to 'what I find interesting' (emotional valency) I unpin the grammar of the image from a spatial field to a grammar of potential; what I find interesting dynamically changes from moment to moment. Mapping the grammar of my emotional valency to the visual organisation of space is of course arbitrary; any data can be used to reorder the spatial field, in fact any data could be rewired to many other virtual artefacts not just the virtual camera.

And this is the point. At stake in artificial life image making is agency. Instead of looking at creatures etc, it is incumbent upon us to examine what it means to look *through* an interpretative agent's 'point of view.' Drawing on a media ecological framework Matt Fuller asks, "What arises when two or more standard processes, with their own regimes, codes, modes of use and deportment, systems of transduction, and so on, become conjoined?" [37] Fuller's question can be restated as, what arises when the conventions, processes and protocols from artificial life are conjoined with those from film, cinema and the moving image? The closest reference point that articulates what this interpretative agent might be is situated in the grammar of the moving image – the filmmaker. This merging of discursive practices frames an examination into an artificial life 'filmmaker', as it (the system) searches for interesting themes, selects interesting shots and adapts to evolve the entire parameter space, including the z-buffer, to generate or evolve a new visual grammar or syntax of the moving image.

Travelogue: A recording of Minute Expressions (*Travelogue*) is a generative work that explores this theme. The central motif of the work draws inspiration from Islamic art and Persian carpet making. The metaphor of the Persian carpet orients both *Travelogue* and artificial life, including themes of 'emergence,' self organisation and "lifelike behavior" [38] as *de rigueur,* into the longer genealogy of the human endeavour. Though much has been made of these themes in artificial life, [39][40] their formation precedes artificial life in that they are well-honed principles in Islamic art and Islamic carpet making. [41][42]

The Persian carpet is a also metaphor to describe the intercultural traffic in both Islamic art [43] and the overarching research into artificial life and generative art. This seems appropriate given the trade in and migration of epistemological, institutional, financial, re-

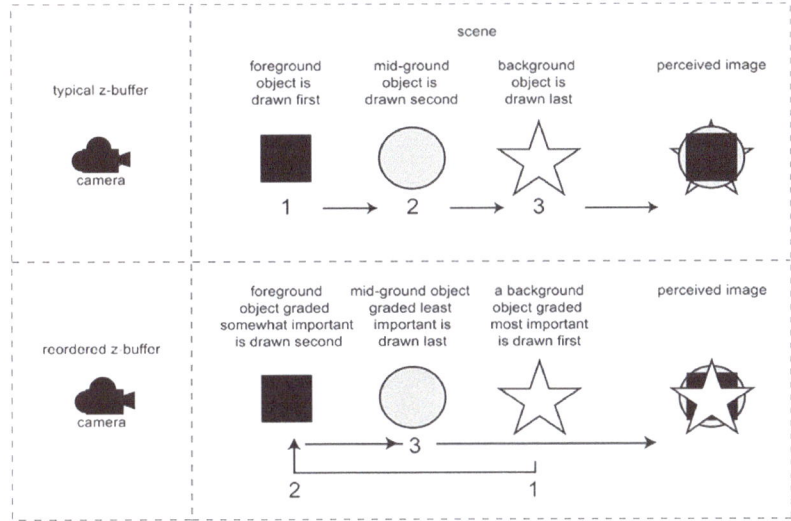

Figure 1. Schematic comparison between a conventional and reordered z-buffer. © Mark Guglielmetti, 2007. Used with permission.

Figure 2. Architectural model of the Trocadero Artspace. © Mark Guglielmetti, 2007. Used with permission.

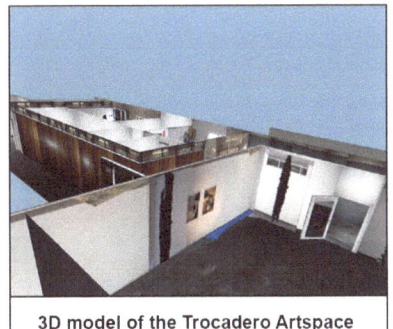
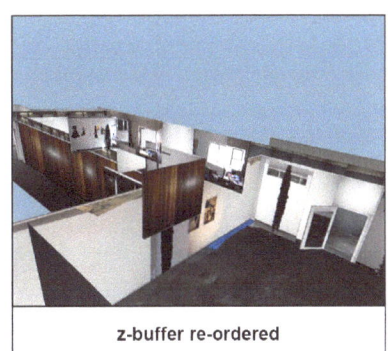

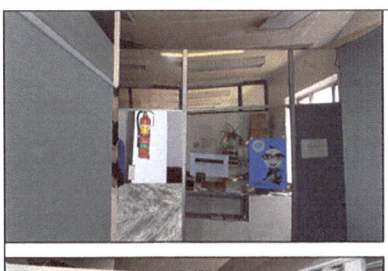
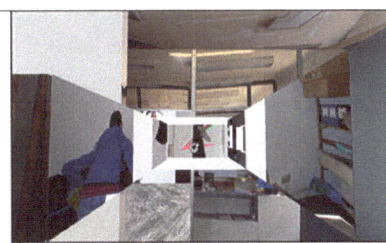
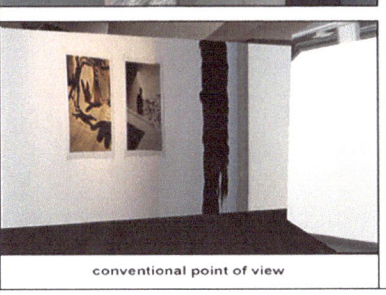
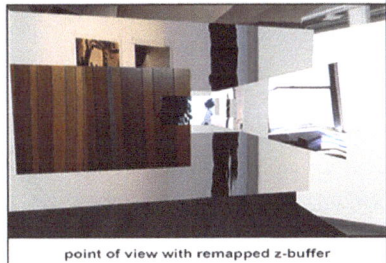

Figure 3. *Laboratories of Thought and Experimentation for Future Forms of Subjectivation*, Mark Guglielmetti, 2007. Software. © Mark Guglielmetti, 2007. Used with permission.

ligious and scientific discourse and artefacts in Islamic culture. In other words, *Travelogue* explores the trade in cultural artefacts, including the migration of encoded grammars and interpretative regimes and, the production of knowing subjects in "an unstill centre of a turning world." [44]

The 'world' in *Travelogue* is seeded or initialised with statistical census data on tourism in Turkey, September 2010. Data from the "monthly number of arriving foreigner visitors" provides the initial resources to populate the work. Other data, such as "$ spent per foreigner" and "number of foreigners of nationality and group of age-gender" populate other variables in the system, which are used to mathematically describe the drawing 'agents' (expressions). During 'runtime', the expressions exchange data with other expressions, but this 'interaction' is not visualised. The exchange of data between expressions provides various mathematical resources to other expressions, which enable the expressions to change scale, colour, location and number; similar functions enacted in other generative systems without personifying the expressions with slippery terms like 'fight,' 'breed' and 'die.'

The work is displayed across multiple screens. One screen displays an orthographic view of the 'world', which references Persian carpet design and provides context to the overall system. This visualisation might be described as a re-imagination of the potential enfolding tourist trade in Turkey but just as well as an expression of the system. See Figure 4.

A second screen displays a view as expressed from the virtual camera *in* the 'world.' The virtual camera draws from a variety of grammars from the moving image, such as zoom and pan but also reorganises other grammars such as the z-buffer. The virtual camera/filmmaker shoots or *n*frames what is 'interesting' to it – whatever that 'interesting' is, of course, immeasurable. See Figure 5. These views into the world render non-perspectival and *non-optical* images of the world, that is, images that do not favour or analogize the camera. See Figure 6.

In this light, the 'virtual camera' is, at best, an impoverished metaphor to describe the expressive potential for an *n* array of visual representations into and of 3D space. A more appropriate idiom for the interrelated algorithms that give rise to the view into 3D space might be "cameraless camera" [45] but this also evades the obvious, there is no camera; software mediates the view into virtual space.

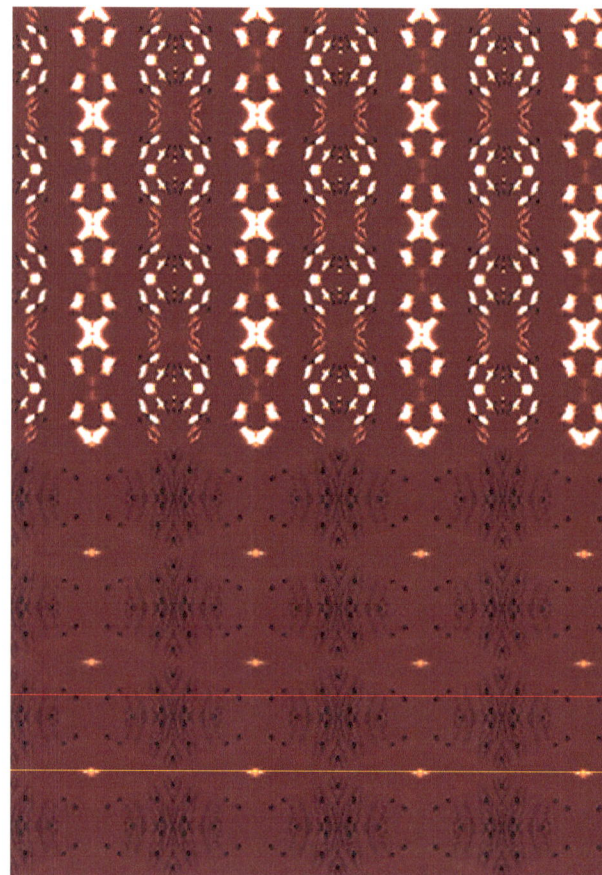

ESSAY

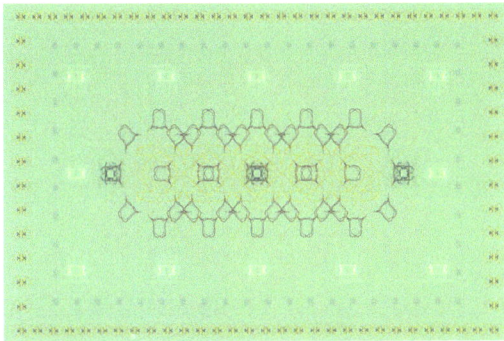

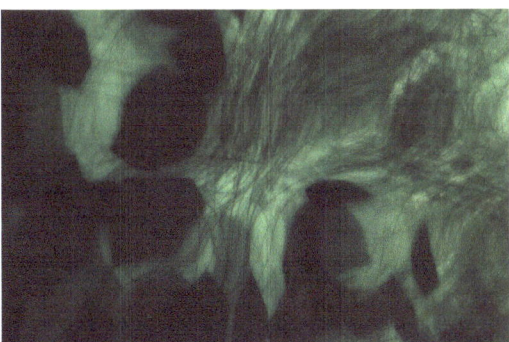

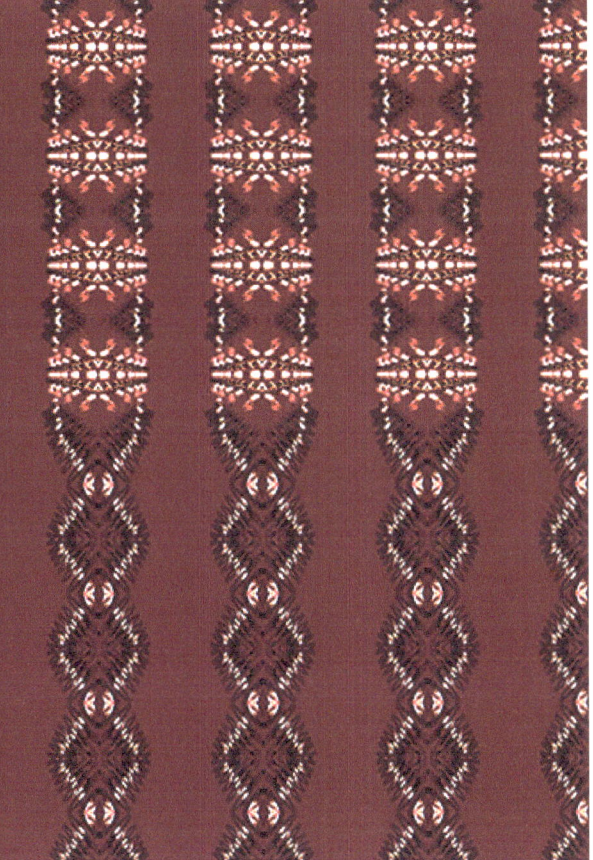

Figure 4, 5, 6. *Travelogue: A Recording of Minute Expressions*, Mark Guglielmetti and Indae Hwang, 2011. Code and software. © Mark Guglielmetti, 2011. Used with permission.

CONCLUSION

Stan Brakhage understood what is at stake perhaps better than most writing:

> *the increased programming potential of the IBM and other electronic machines now capable of inventing imagery from scratch. Considering then the camera eye as almost obsolete, it can at last be viewed objectively and, perhaps, view-pointed with subjective depth as never before. Its life is truly all before it. The future fabricating machine in performance will invent images as patterned after cliché vision as those of the camera, and its results will suffer a similar claim to 'realism', IBM being no more God nor even a 'Thinking machine' than the camera eye all seeing or capable of creative selectivity, both essentially restricted to 'yes-no,' 'stop–go,' 'on-off,' and instrumentally dedicated to communication of the simplest sort. Yet increased human intervention and control renders any process more capable of balance between sub- and-objective expression, and between those two concepts, somewhere, soul.*

In digital media image making, there is an *n* array of potential to reorganise the visual field. From this array, I examine two, apparently disparate, research fields – artificial life and 3D simulation – both of which employ the virtual camera as the interface to 3D virtual worlds or visualisations. If artificial life is to truly generate life-like behaviour and emergence, what could be more lifelike than organising both the visual field and scopic regime/s, whatever they may be. After all, aligning the interpretive regime of artificial life image making into optical consistency with other forms of contemporary visual culture does no more, or less, than align competencies expressed in artificial life after the human endeavour.

REFERENCES AND NOTES

1. C. Adami, *Introduction to Artificial Life* (New York: Springer, 1998), 4.
2. V. Flusser, *Towards a Philosophy of Photography* (London: Reaktion, 2000), 70.
3. C. G. Langton, ed., *Artificial Life: Proceedings of an Interdisciplinary Workshop on the Synthesis and Simulation of Living Systems, held September, 1987, in Los Alamos, New Mexico* (Redwood City, CA: Addison-Wesley, 1989), 5.
4. Ibid., 1.
5. L. Parisi and T. Terranova, "Heat-Death: Emergence And Control In Genetic Engineering And Artificial Life," *CTHEORY*, 2000, http://ctheory.net/home.aspx (accessed March 27, 2011).
6. N. K. Hayles, *How We Became Posthuman: Virtual Bodies in Cybernetics, Literature, and Informatics* (Chicago: University of Chicago Press, 1999), 224.
7. Christopher G. Langton, "Introduction," in *Artificial Life II*, ed. C. G. Langton, C. Taylor, J. D. Farmer, and S. Rasmussen (Redwood City, CA: Addison-Wesley, 1992), 20, quoted in S. Helmreich, *Silicon Second Nature* (Berkeley: University of California Press, 1998), 17.
8. O. Grau, "Remember the Phantasmagoria! Illusion Politics of the Eighteenth Century and Its Multimedial Afterlife," in *MediaArtHistories*, ed. O. Grau (Cambridge, MA: Leonardo, MIT Press, 2007), 137-161.
9. L. U. Marks, *Enfoldment and Infinity: An Islamic Genealogy of New Media Art* (Cambridge, MA: MIT Press, 2010).
10. J. Stapleton, "Black Shoals: A Meditation on Cosmology, Artificial Life and the Aesthetics of Political Economy," the website of Black Shoals Stock Market Planetarium, 2004, http://www.blackshoals.net/Writing.html (accessed September 12, 2007).
11. C. G. Langton, ed., *Artificial Life: Proceedings of an Interdisciplinary Workshop on the Synthesis and Simulation of Living Systems*, 5.
12. L. Mignonneau and C. Sommerer, "Creating Artificial Life for Interactive Art and Entertainment," *Leonardo* 34, no. 4 (2001): 303-307.
13. J. Prophet, "Sublime Ecologies and Artistic Endeavors: Artificial Life and Interactivity in the Online Project TechnoSphere," *Leonardo* 29, no. 5 (1996): 339-344.
14. K. Sims, "Galápagos," Karl Sims' official website, 1997, http://www.karlsims.com/galapagos/index.html (accessed September 12, 2007).
15. A. Bazin, *What is Cinema? Volume 1* (Berkeley: University of California Press, 2005).
16. E. Branigan, *Projecting a Camera: Language-games in Film Theory* (London: Routledge, 2006), 76.
17. S. Shapin and S. Schaffer, *Leviathan and the Air-Pump: Hobbes, Boyle, and the Experimental Life* (Princeton, NJ: Princeton University Press, 1989), 77.
18. B. Winston, "The Documentary Film as Scientific Inscription," in *Theorizing Documentary*, ed. M. Renov (New York: Routledge, 1993), 40.
19. A. Friedberg, *The Virtual Window: from Alberti to Microsoft* (Cambridge, MA: MIT Press, 2006), 7.
20. M. Jay, "Scopic Regimes of Modernity," in *Vision and Visuality*, ed. H. Foster (New York: Bay Press, 1988), 20.
21. S. Cubitt, *The Cinema Effect* (Cambridge, MA: The MIT Press, 2004).
22. A. Ndalianis, *Neo-baroque Aesthetics and Contemporary Entertainment* (Cambridge, MA: The MIT Press, 2004).
23. N. Carroll, *Theorizing the Moving Image* (New York: Cambridge University Press, 1996), 213.
24. V. Flusser, *Towards a Philosophy of Photography* (London: Reaktion, 2000), 9.
25. Ibid., 16.
26. Ibid., 15.
27. Ibid., 70.
28. [A. J. Watson and J. E. Lovelock, "Biological Homeostasis of the Global Environment: The Parable of Daisyworld," *Tellus Series B: Chemical and Physical Meteorology* 35, no. 4 (1983): 284.
29. Ibid.
30. Ibid., 288.

31. R. Frigg and S. Hartmann, "Models in Science," Stanford Encyclopedia of Philosophy, 2009, http://plato.stanford.edu/archives/sum2009/entries/models-science/ (accessed May 17, 2011).
32. M. Renov, *Theorizing Documentary* (New York: Routledge, 1993), 7.
33. Art Babbitt, quoted in D. Chai and A. Garcia, "Physics for Animation Artists," *The Physics Teacher* 49, no. 8 (2011): 480. Source uncited.
34. A. Wilson, *The Culture of Nature: North American Landscape from Disney to the Exxon Valdez* (Cambridge, MA: Blackwell, 1992), 118.
35. I recall Bazin who wrote cinema is of "its essence a dramaturgy of Nature." A. Bazin, *What is Cinema?*, vol. 1, 110.
36. D. Cosgrove, "Mapping the World," in *Maps: Finding Our Place in the World*, eds. J. R. Akerman, R. W. Karrow (Chicago: University of Chicago Press, 2007), 67.
37. M. Fuller, *Media Ecologies: Materialist Energies in Art and Technoculture* (Cambridge, MA: MIT Press, 2005), 98.
38. C. G. Langton, *Artificial Life: the proceedings of an Interdisciplinary Workshop on the Synthesis and Simulation of Living Systems*, 5.
39. Ibid.
40. M. Whitelaw, *Metacreation: Art and Artificial Life* (Cambridge, MA: The MIT Press, 2004), 207-237.
41. C. Alexander, *A Foreshadowing of 21st Century Art: The Color and Geometry of Very Early Turkish Carpets* (New York: Oxford University Press, 1993).
42. L. U. Marks, *Enfoldment and Infinity: An Islamic Genealogy of New Media Art* (Cambridge, MA: The MIT Press, 2010).
43. Ibid., 302.
44. S. Cubitt, "A Brief Case," in *The World Is Everything That Is The Case*, ed. V. Dziekan and P. Thomas, (Melbourne: Ellikon Press, 2011), 10.
45. The idea of cameraless image making in the visual arts has precedent. According to Kris Paulsen, Steve Beck created cameraless video by directly manipulating the basic component of video, the electron. K. Paulsen, "Direct to Video: Steve Beck's Cameraless Television," *ISEA 2011 Proceedings*, http://isea2011.sabanciuniv.edu/paper/direct-video-stephen-becks-cameraless-television (accessed September 12, 2007).

    At the same symposium Meredith Hoy (2011) assessed: "whether there are a set of principles with which [cameraless] computationally based abstractions are concerned, and what kind of 'world' is imagined through this algorithmically generated visual model. Taking into account the history of abstraction in modern art, it considers whether computational abstraction fits into a modernist narrative or whether it envisions a new call to order distinct from that set forth by 20th century modernist movements." M. Hoy, "Virtual Resistance: A Genealogy of Digital Abstraction," *ISEA 2011 Proceedings*, 2011, http://isea2011.sabanciuniv.edu/panel/arabesque-mandala-algorithm-long-history-generative-art (accessed September 12, 2007).
46. S. Brakhage, *Essential Brakhage: Selected Writings on Filmmaking by Stan Brakhage* (New York: McPherson & Company, 2001), 21-22.

ESSAY

The Case of Biophilia

A Collective Composition of Goals and Distributed Action

by

Mark Cypher

Murdoch University, Western Australia
m.cypher@murdoch.edu.au
www.markcypher.com.au

INTRODUCTION

In an application form addressed to the Siggraph 2006 Intersections Gallery, the artist must describe his interactive artwork. The form states:

> The installation Biophilia will enable participants to interact with and generate organic forms based upon the distortion of the user's shadow. Coined in 1984 by sociobiologist Edward O. Wilson, Biophilia refers to the need of living things to connect with others - even those of different species. On one level, Biophilia critiques Wilson's notion that western culture desires a connection with nature, even though that same desire belies a deep unconscious fear of all things natural. With these ideas in mind the installation Biophilia attempts to absorb and synthesize users and their contexts, producing unpredictable patterns of propagation and hybridity.

Although short, this simple paragraph, like many others about the work, belies the complexity of relations that have enabled such a reference to be made.

For the moment though, complexity is not important. The statement must have enough impact to catch the

ESSAY

Rather than follow the machinations of a singular artist in the production and exhibition of an interactive artwork, this paper uses an actor-network approach to collectively hold to account a whole host of actors that literally make a difference in the production of an interactive artwork, Biophilia *(2004-2007). My main argument is that in order for any action to take place both humans and non-humans must on some level collectively work together, or, in actor-network terms translate one another. However, such new relations are predicated and indeed just as dependent on and what these new actors are willing to give up as it is to do with what they can offer. Needless to say that when the negotiations are momentarily over, actors give up individual goals and compel others to collectively form new definitions, new intentions and new goals with each interaction. In other words, the 'work' represents neither the beginning nor the end of a particular event, but is described more as a continually shifting and cumulative series of distributed actions.*

attention and interest of Siggraph and the judges who work on its behalf.

The form together with the inscriptions and reference images, imply a desire for a connection to form, or a movement from disinterest to one of interest.

Several months later, the artist receives an email that accepts the proposal.

Now unbeknown to the artist and the judges, they have just formed the first step in translating the art work *Biophilia,* and the chain of actors that support

it, into a binding sociotechnical relation. Even though the artist is in Australia and Siggraph and its judges are in North America. In the end, the written form and its inscribed references were enough to convince all the actors involved that a relation can be made. The effect will be that the artist's CV will get bigger, Siggraph will also get greater international participation and *Biophilia* will be more attractive to other judges, festivals and curators in the future. In a sense, both actor-networks are now able to achieve effects that would not have been possible on their own.

Several days later the artist receives another email from the Siggraph "Art Show Chair":

> I am concerned about the amount of walk space between your booth and the art walls below it in the plan. [...] We need more space so people can stand back and view the art plus the Fire Marshal does not like us to have close passageways. [3]

Several emails later it is clear that some negotiation over space is required, if the embryonic relation between *Biophilia* and Siggraph is to be sustained.

This description of the trials of strength inherent in the construction and exhibition of an artwork may have started in a rather strange place. But the process demonstrates how actors are co-defined when they begin to form relations. In actor-network terms, the elemental affiliation that enables a network to form is the process called translation. Michel Callon describes translation as:

> 'A translates B'. To say this is to say that A defines B. It does not matter, whether B is human or non-human, a collectivity or an individual. Neither does it say anything about B's status as, an actor. B might be endowed with interests, projects, desires, strategies, reflexes, or afterthoughts. The decision is A's – though this does not mean that A has total freedom. For how A acts depends on past translations. These may influence what follows to the point of determining them.. All the entities and all the relationships between these entities should be described – for together they make up the translator. [4]

The trajectory and relative makeup of a translation can be mapped when we consider the amount of associations and substitutions that go into making a relation stable and thus viable. This process can also be expressed in Figure 1.

So what an actor in translation gains in one area is a result of having lost something in another. It's in this way that all translation requires a series of trans-actions. [6] That is, *Biophilia* will disengage weak or threatening entities whilst incorporating those that are sustaining. It is the nature of these trans-actions,

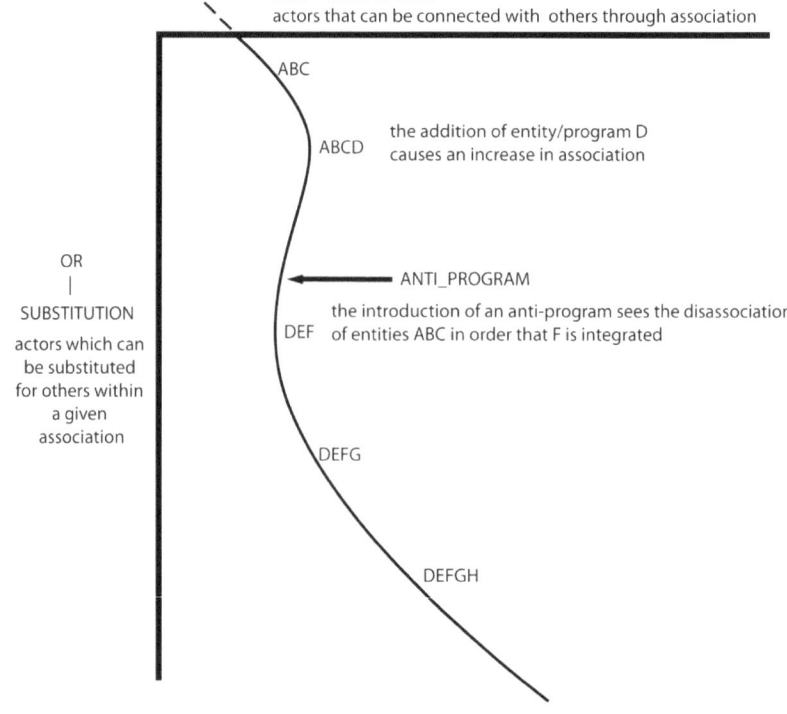

Figure 1. Translation Diagram. [5] Innovation can be traced by both its AND, or, OR positions that successively define the modification of ingredients that compose a translation it. It is impossible to move in any direction without paying a price in the AND or OR direction. © Bruno Latour, 2013. Used with permission.

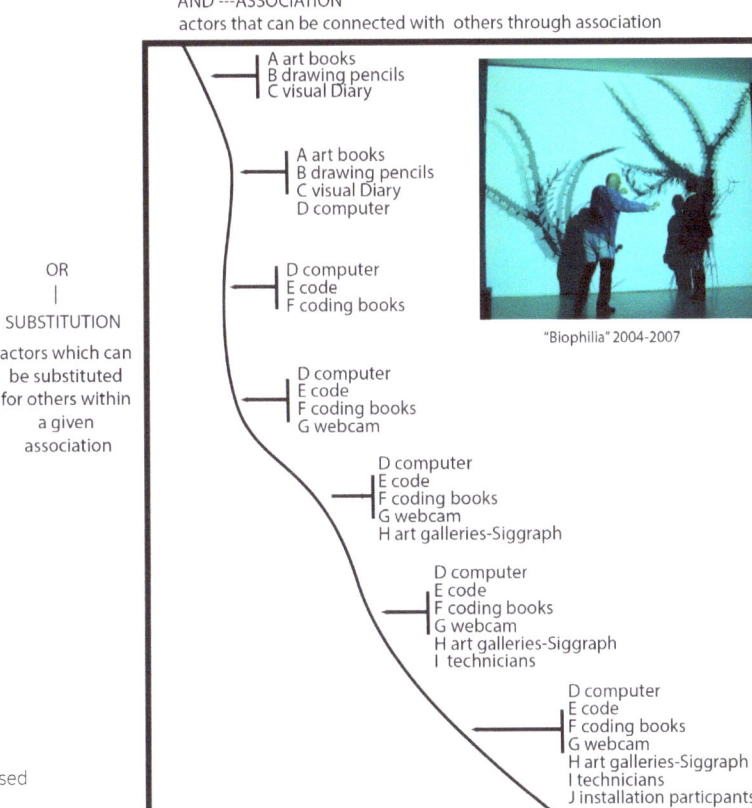

Figure 2. *Mapping the Collective: Biophilia*. © Mark Cypher, 2013. Used with permission.

which defines the strength or weakness of a given translation and will contribute to the explicit shaping of the artwork; apart from the intentions of the artist. [2] Therefore, a collective entity like *Biophilia* cannot be entirely defined by its 'essence' or what we see on the surface in a representation at anyone particular time. Rather, translation as observed in *Biophilia* produces a unique mediatory signature of a specific association of entities at work at any given moment, as is shown in Figure 2.

The notion of translation demonstrates that the problem solving involved in art practice, is a deeply intertwined sociotechnical process. When we see the artist take his position at a desk in front of the computer and begin to work on the problem of Siggraph's lack of space, he will need the desk, the computer and a whole host of other entities to be compelled to solve the problem. But of course in order for this problem-solving process to work it will require that technical components are already socialised for use. Computer vision is socialised, it enables the computer to 'see,' and the computer and camera can 'talk' to each other, just as computer code is compatible with reading. What at first seems like a highly complex objective process with sophisticated technological components is made compatible with social ways of coding and reading. [3] It is in this way that properties are borrowed from the social and inscribed into nonhumans.

At the same time, this process will also extend non-human influence in the social. Whereby, humans will equally absorb nonhuman properties; that is, take the position of sitting and using a mouse, submit to the limits of the technical components, follow structured software patterns or read feedback given, in order to establish a working relation. So much so that what the artist will learn from the production process is the result of contact with nonhumans, which is then re-imported back into the social as conceptual and afforded content through the artwork.

The computer, code and technical components lend their nonhuman properties to what was previously a scattered and unordered bunch of parts and loose intentions. The intersection of nonhuman influence will allow these actors to align and their relations to harden. So much so that the sociotechnical hybrid *Biophilia* will eventually submit to the fire laws of Boston, measured by firewardens, held accountable by the Chair of the art gallery and be granted a social life, worthy of its place in the Siggraph Intersections exhibition. [9]

When we observe the so called 'social' actions of the artist sitting and at work at the computer, trying to solve this problem, it looks as if the human does the 'work.' However, when we take into account the vast amount of translation in the construction of *Biophilia* our observations are undermined. Translation shifts the focus to a vast assembly of actors who are directly related by function, material and ontological inseparability, recombined in a specific time, space, actorial and material sequence, who are also doing the work.

THE PROTOTYPE

Try as he might, the artist is unable to solve the increasing complexity of the code. The computer is not able to 'talk' sufficiently fast enough to the camera, so yet another actor, a technician, is associated to the realization process of the artwork. After meeting with the technician, it is decided that a scale prototype of the artwork will be constructed beforehand. This will accommodate the testing of new goals and new configurations of *Biophilia* and indeed Siggraph's dimensions for its exhibition space.

To say that prototyping happens 'beforehand,' assumes that the most important actions must at some point involve hands. Or that material contact with humans in this time and setting is somehow divorced from the nonhuman flow of activity, procurement of skill and the accumulation of goals, which are essential for any action to take place. But of course many hands and many things outside of this time and place lay embedded in every skill, in every tool. So much so that it should be impossible to clearly define any action, as beholden to any one actor because 'beforehand' should rightly stretch into the long distant millennia. Therefore hands and material are relevant contact points, but they are also just one point of many in the continually shifting and collective trajectories that are part and parcel of all action

Nonetheless, prototyping *Biophilia* in relation to the problem of Siggraph is necessary because it increases the probability that *Biophilia*'s goals will align with that of the gallery. It can only ever be a probability because the actors involved in each situation will be different. Thus the associations the new situation creates will allow or disallow a whole range of unforseen affordances. Although the Art Show Chair and the gallery staff require a certain 'stability,' duly required by professionals, they are not going to get it unless the other half of the relation (the nonhuman kind) is cajoled into line. No matter how obstinate, professional standards also relate to nonhumans. Yet even with all this work done with, and before the artists hand, the prototyping process is tenable and only as strong as the alliances it can maintain and carry forward into space.

John Law describes the construction of space in relation to the actor-network as one in which objects are co-constituted with the surrounding space. This means that "spatial relations are also being enacted at the same time [as translation]... Or, to put it more concisely …, spaces are made with objects." [10] The relation to space, to the actor-network and/or possible actions, seems to fit well with Callon and Latour's early definition of actors as:

Any element which bends space around itself, makes other elements depend upon itself and translates their will into a language of its own. Before the elements dominated by an actor could escape in any direction, but now this is no longer possible. Instead of swarms of possibilities, we find lines of force, obligatory passage points, directions and deductions. [11]

In this way, actors and space are mutually dependent and as such mutually constituted in translation. Prototypes, much like institutions such as galleries, are exemplars of this kind of compelling space. Galleries, installation spaces and indeed prototypes not only regulate physical and material movement but also the cognitive, political and ideological rhythms of the many actors constituted in their frame of reference.

The spatial relations generated by institutions (much like the collectives at work in the construction of *Biophilia*) not only control the networks between inside and outside. They also shape the political, material and practical participation actors have in those spaces. As John Law states, "spatial systems ... are political because they make objects and subjects with particular shapes .... Because they set limits to the conditions of object possibility." [12] Yet this relationship is not a one-way affair. As much as *Biophilia* submits to the limits imposed by the Siggraph gallery, it also pushes Siggraph to negotiate and open the institutional and regulatory boundaries imposed on it. Until both networks become re-aligned each negotiation pushes *Biophilia* and Siggraph to a unique sociotechnical collective that will occupy a distinct spatial topology at a particular point in time. Therefore, *Biophilia* becomes much more than an artwork defined by a singular interaction/representation and more like a nexus of relations that shapes objective, subjective, cognitive, social and institutional associations. [13] In other words, the 'work' represents neither the beginning nor the end of a particular event, but is described more as a continually shifting and cumulative series of distributed actions.

INTERSECTIONS EXHIBITION, SIGGRAPH ART GALLERY, BOSTON, USA

Before the participant arrives, she is already 'prepared' for involvement by various marketing materials and previous 'interactive' experiences. As she steps off the crowded bus, handrails and human attendants guide her to the entrance to Siggraph. On entering the gallery, the space is dark and quiet, and the participant's pass is checked and stamped. The darkened gallery space, gallery attendants and didactic information about each installation ensure that by the time the participants come in contact with the artwork they already know, in part, the role they must play.

At a more intimate level, the point at which the participant enters the installation space of *Biophilia* and begins to interact signifies a change in behaviour. The gallery visitor is now redefined as a 'participant.' The cavernous Boston Convention Centre becomes the Siggraph Intersections Gallery. Siggraph lives up to its promised brand and *Biophilia* becomes truly 'interactive.' The participant literally learns in real time, that they, in association with the artwork are "an interface that becomes more and more describable as each [actor] learns to be affected by more and more elements." [14] Moreover, the participant's objectives to engage the artwork, begins to identify with the physical affordance of *Biophilia*, to the point that the user's intentions are shaped, both in a positive and negative sense of enabling and constraining certain behaviours. [15] In other words, a certain level of influence is distributed throughout the act of engaging with participatory artworks that alters each actor's definition, ontological makeup and associated goals and objectives.

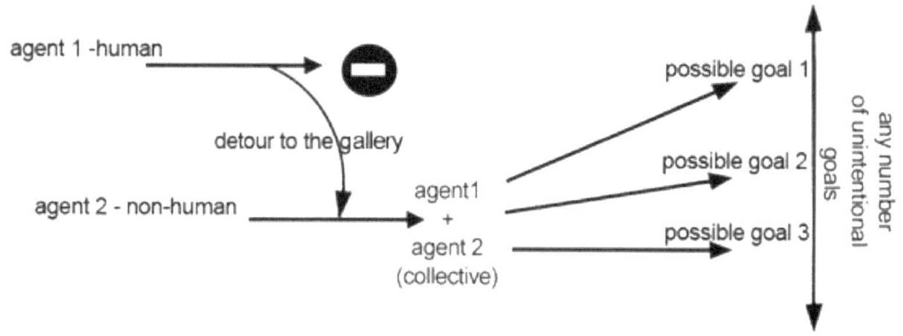

Figure 3. Goal Translation Figure3 adapted from Latour. [16] The explosion in unintentional goals is a result of different combinations of actors interacting. One can never really know what is going to happen, because we can never really know all the elements activated in a given association or context beforehand. © Bruno Latour, 2013. Used with permission.

This is represented in diagrammatic form as goal translation in Figure 3.

Goal translation represents a symmetrical example of how, through interaction, competencies, objectives and possible actions are co-constituted. Both the human participant and the artwork's goals are translated into a collective program of action, in which any number of unintentional consequences could result. In other words, action is shared amongst those in the collective and is in part uncontrollable by any one element, human or otherwise.

This kind of unpredictability is brought to bear by such translations and is used by the artist (whether he recognises it or not) to take advantage of the volatile collective action produced when a multitude of entities come together. It is no wonder then, that Frank Popper conceptualised such phenomena in electronic art works as "neocommunicability [as] an event - full with unaccustomed possibilities..." [17] The uncontrollability of relations in an interactive event is a small articulation of what many artists come into contact with every day. That is, to act means to be perpetually overtaken by the thing you are supposedly building. [18]

In this way goal translation as evidenced in both the construction and interaction with *Biophilia* demonstrates that there is no prime mover of an action and that a new, distributed, and nested series of practices allows all kinds of unintentional actions, ontological variability and exchanges to develop. The implication then is that action can be redefined as follows:

> *[N]ot a property of humans, but of an association of actants [human or nonhuman agents]..[Whereby] provisional "actorial" roles may be attributed to actants only because actants are in the process of exchanging competencies, offering one another new possibilities, new goals, new functions.* [19]

This kind of distributed action not only highlights the implausibility of humans and nonhumans acting alone but that the whole process of gaining some kind of competency is underwritten by exchange. As Latour further explains:

> *Interaction cannot serve as the point of departure, since for humans it is always situated in a framework which is always erased by networks going over in all directions. [...] the attribution of a skill to an actant always follows the realization by that actor of what it can do when others than itself have proceeded to action. Even the everyday usage of 'action' cannot serve here, since it presupposes a point of origin [...] which [is] completely improbable.* [20]

Action and indeed agency is always shared and distributed amongst other entities. The ability to act is therefore mediated by others' actions that have come before it. Such cumulative influence can be illustrated in Figures 4 and 5 below.

ESSAY

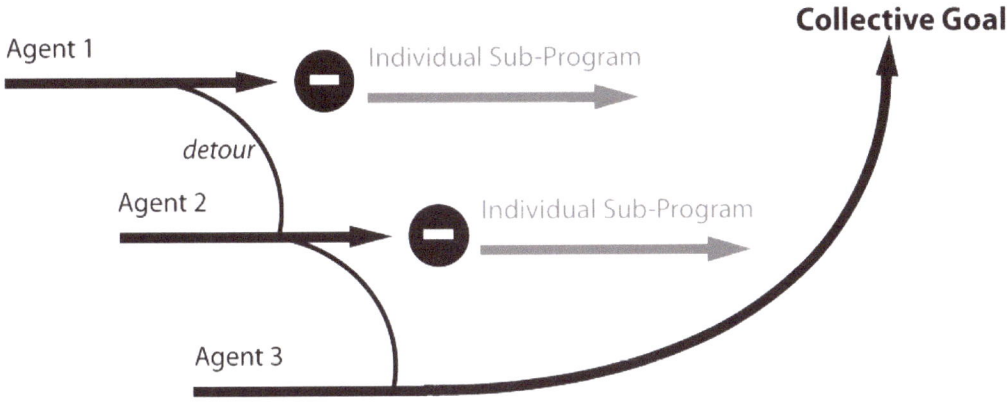

Figure 4. Individual sub-programs of action are bent towards a collective goal. © Bruno Latour, 2013. Used with permission.

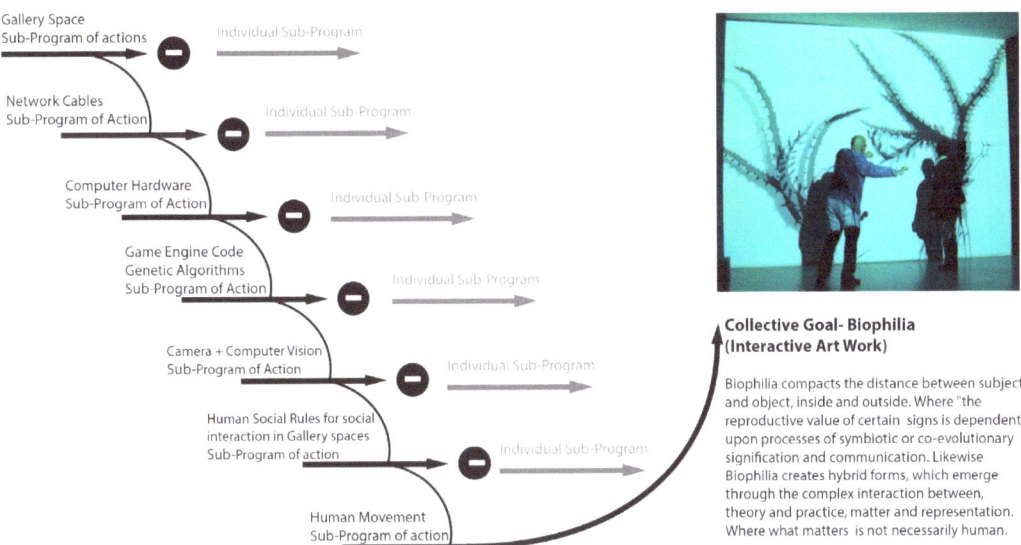

Figure 5. Mapping the cumulative influence of the collective. The composition of new goals is made possible by the colonising of many sub-programs which are then cumulatively bent towards the collective goal for *Biophilia*. © Mark Cypher, 2013. Used with permission.

As Figures 4 and 5 illustrate, there is a long chain of actors that contain their own sub-programs of action. The nature of each subsequent movement not only requires new associations. But it also means that individual sub programs (intentions and motivations) are trans-acted, if not subject to "modes of ordering" [22] implicated in the process of translation and required for a collective goal to be successful.

In this sense translation is important for rethinking production because it usually involves the exchange or trans-action of one actor, to replace another actor to help solve a problem. But as we have seen in Figure 5 these new cumulative problem solving abilities, affordances and skills come at a cost. For example, although the artist spends precious hours rigging the video camera to hang at the optimum height in the installation, the slightest bump throws out the camera's focus. So another set of goals, equipment and technicians is associated and a new reshuffling of actors and associations take place. The order of which is not aligned by mistake, nor wholly by chance, but through the finely tuned or out of tune cumulative translation of goals. Nonetheless a new camera rig collectively eventuates. The cost is time, misplaced intentions, detoured goals, and professional pride. This is not an unimportant detour from the narrative of *Biophilia*'s collective construction. But an integral 'taking into account' of the way relations are predicated and dependent on what actors are willing to give up, ransom or sacrifice, as it is to do with what they can offer.

The means by which collectives like *Biophilia* apply these kinds of enforced behaviours is recognised as a sort of agency. For Lambros Malafouris agency is something that:

> [C]annot be reduced to any of the human–nonhuman components of action. [...] It cannot be too strongly emphasized that neither brains nor things in isolation can do much. [...] Agency is in constant flux, an in-between state that constantly violates and transgresses the physical boundaries of the elements that constitute it. Agency is a temporal and interactively emergent property of activity not an innate and fixed attribute of the human condition. The ultimate cause of action in this chain of micro and macro events is none of the supposed agents, humans or non-humans; it is the flow of activity itself. [23]

By examining *Biophilia* as much more than a discrete artwork in itself we begin to see that the competencies and functions of each actor begin to lose their distinctions in order that the 'work' is made.

In this way, the intentions of the artist are significantly translated and thus altered to the extent that all the actors in the development and exhibition of the artwork shape the conceptual and physical aspects of *Biophilia*. In a sense, the long tail of the sociotechnical translations shape the type of cognitive and functional operations that are possible. As Edwin Hutchins states, "One cannot perform the computations without constructing the setting; thus, in some sense, constructing the setting is part of the computation." [24] In this way, the Siggraph gallery and the installation space are also dependent on similar sociotechnical systems (bricks, mortar, funding bodies, committees, community support) that sustain the types of movements within it. So too are participants' actions, intentions and cognition similarly shaped as an effect of the "modes of ordering" [25] implied by the framing aspect of the gallery and indeed the installation itself. Therefore, for the artwork to emerge the individual goals and functions of each actor must merge into a larger if not distributed action.

CONCLUSION

From an actor-network approach, actual interactions with participatory art works (much like still images of the event) are not a departure point, but one point of many in a chain of associative links. As is seen in the various translations in *Biophilia*, interaction consists of agents that can only act by and through association with others. As these actors associate and thus work together, their initial goals are forcefully exchanged, sacrificed and colonised for the greater good of the collective. Sometimes these goals align with a strong probability that the trajectory of action grows stronger with more associations. Other times they don't. Nevertheless, these unfounded probabilities and lost propositions connote a deeper sense of the multitude of sacrifices required for a strong relation to form. As a result intentions and goals are detoured from their initial trajectory and precipitate new alliances and new actions that would not have been originally possible. It is in this manner that the interactions, and indeed the intentions to act in the production, exhibition and interaction with interactive artworks, is considered collective and distributed. ∎

REFERENCES AND NOTES

1. Mark Cypher, Siggraph Gallery Application form, January, 2006.
2. Sections of this paper are derived from my PhD dissertation. Mark Cypher, Trans-Action: an actor-network Approach to Interactivity in the Visual Arts" (Ph.D. dissertation, University of Western Australia, 2011).
3. Siggraph Art Show Chair, e-mail message to author, March 28, 2006.
4. Michel Callon, "Techno-Economic Networks and Irreversibility," in *Sociology of Monsters: Essays on Power, Technology and Domination*, ed. John Law (London: Routledge, 1991), 143.
5. Bruno Latour, "Where Are the Missing Masses? The Sociology of a Few Mundane Artifacts," in *Shaping Technology / Building Society: Studies in Sociotechnical Change*, eds. Bijker Wiebe and Law John (Cambridge, MA: MIT Press, 1994), 172.
6. Mark Cypher, "Trans-action: an Actor-network Approach to Interactivity in the Visual Arts."
7. John Law, "On the Social Explanation of Technical Change: The Case of the Portugese Maritime Expansion," *Technology and Culture* 28, no. 2 (1987): 237.
8. Bruno Latour, "Where Are the Missing Masses? The Sociology of a Few Mundane Artifacts," 796.
9. Ibid., 799.
10. John Law, "Objects and Spaces," *Theory, Culture & Society* 19, no. 5-6 (2002): 96.
11. Michel Callon and Bruno Latour, "Unscrewing the Big Leviathan: How Actors Macro-Structure Reality and How Sociologists Help Them to Do So," in *Advances in Social Theory and Methodology: Toward an Integration of Micro and Macro Sociologies*, ed. K Knorr and A Cicourel (London: Routledge and Kegan Paul, 1981), 96.
12. John Law, "Objects and Spaces," 102.
13. Albena Yaneva, "Chalk Steps on the Museum Floor the `Pulses' of Objects in an Art Installation," *Journal of Material Culture* 8, no. 2 (2003):176.
14. Bruno Latour, "How to Talk About the Body? The Normative Dimension of Science Studies," *Body and Society* 10, no. 2-3 (2004): 206.
15. Lambros Malafouris, "At the Potter's Wheel: An Argument for Material Agency," in *Material Agency Towards a Non-Anthropocentric Approach*, ed. Carl Knappett and Lambros Malafouris (New York: Springer, 2008), 33.
16. Bruno Latour, *Pandora's Hope: Essays on the Reality of Science Studies* (Cambridge, MA: Harvard University Press, 1999), 179.
17. J. Nechvatal, "Origins of Virtualism: An Interview with Frank Popper," *CAA Art Journal* 62, no. 1 (2004): 62-77.
18. Bruno Latour, "On Interobjectivity," Bruno Latour's website, http://www.bruno-latour.fr/articles/article/063.html (accessed January 15, 2014).
19. Bruno Latour, *Pandora's Hope: Essays on the Reality of Science Studies*, 182.
20. Bruno Latour, "On Interobjectivity."
21. Bruno Latour, *Pandora's Hope: Essays on the Reality of Science Studies*, 181.
22. John Law, "Actor Network Theory and Material Semiotics," in *The New Blackwell Companion to Social Theory*, ed. B. S. Turner (Malden, MA: Wiley-Blackwell 2009).
23. L. Malafouris, "The Cognitive Basis of Material Engagement: Where Brain, Body and Culture Conflate," in *Rethinking Materiality: The Engagement of Mind with the Material World*, eds. E. DeMarrais, C. Gosden, and C. Renfrew (Cambridge: McDonald Institute, 2004), 34.
24. Edwin Hutchins, *Cognition in the Wild* (Cambridge, MA: The MIT Press, 1995).159.
25. John Law, "Actor Network Theory and Material Semiotics."

ESSAY

Contaminated Immersion and Thomas Demand
THE DAILIES

by

David Eastwood

UNSW Art & Design
University of New South Wales, Australia
d.eastwood@unsw.edu.au
www.davideastwood.com.au

IMMERSION AND INTERFERENCE

Oliver Grau has stated that immersion "is characterized by diminishing critical distance to what is shown and increasing emotional involvement in what is happening." In that sense, any artwork might be thought of as offering a potentially immersive experience, inviting a level of engagement best described as a kind of absorption, engrossment or immersion. Does a large-scale installation or virtual reality environment offer greater immersion than the experience of being transfixed by a small painting on a wall? Arguably, immersion is a condition contingent upon the viewer responding to the artwork, rather than an inherent quality within the artwork alone.

Writing about the pictorial tradition of still life, Hanneke Grootenboer draws upon the notion of conflict, as identified by Victor Stoichita. [2] This 'conflict' exists as a schism (or *cut*, as Stoichita refers to it), between the foreground and background in paintings such as Joos van Cleve's *Holy Family* (1513). The objects on the shelf in the lower portion of the composition are distinct from the space of the Madonna and Child with Saint Joseph. Although the still life objects are relegated to a minor position within the

ESSAY

If, as Oliver Grau has stated, immersion "is characterized by diminishing critical distance to what is shown and increasing emotional involvement in what is happening," any artwork might be thought of as potentially immersive. Arguably, immersion is a condition contingent upon the viewer responding to the artwork, rather than an inherent quality within the artwork alone. Considered in relation to some art historical contexts, the relationship between immersive experience and interference will be discussed in order to contextualize Thomas Demand's Kaldor Public Art Project, The Dailies. *Demand's project both relates to and departs from some of the key aspects of what is conventionally thought of as immersive art. It is useful to consider this in order to engage with the implications of immersion in art, and reflect on the possibility of strategic interferences operating within what might be described as contaminated immersion.*

image, they complicate the pictorial space because of their ambiguous location between the viewer and the scene beyond. Grootenboer argues that the notion of the conflict between foreground and background continued to have ramifications throughout the development of seventeenth century Dutch still life painting. [3] Pieter Claesz's *Little Breakfast* (1636) can be seen in this context, as Grootenboer demonstrates. [4] Both Pieter Claesz and Willem Claesz Heda were the primary exponents of the breakfast still life, an art form that occupied a relatively brief period of Dutch painting during the 1630s and 1640s. Such works are distinct from the more abundant banquet pieces of the seventeenth century Dutch era. Grootenboer writes, "Not afraid of empty spaces, Claesz and Heda allow a void to appear in a genre where *horror vacui* once ruled.

There is no compensation for this emptiness." [5] Focusing her attention on the nondescript background, Grootenboer interprets the void in such a work "as a commentary on the complexity of spatial representation." [6] The void here could be said to operate on the level of interference. Where one would conventionally find the articulation of more objects, a narrative scene or an architectural context, the artist has chosen to paint a soft enveloping haze. The schism between foreground and background is articulated in the absence of the background. While this painting belongs to a tradition of illusionistic representation, it also signals a turning away from the 'view.'

Describing the impact of the window view implied by linear perspective, Joseph Nechvatal has pointed out "there has been a de-emphasis in the peripheral and the ambient as vision has become restrained by the habits of linear perspective; pre-established habits now encoded in the methods and expectations of photography, video and film. Thus vision has increasingly taken on the attributes of a focused, singular, narrow vision which is staring straight ahead." [7] While Nechvatal identifies strategies of immersion that utilize digital virtual reality environments to expand the image and lead the viewer toward a more comprehensive spatial awareness, I would challenge the notion that such an awareness is entirely the domain of the computer and identify a work such as Claesz's *Little Breakfast* as very much concerned with the peripheral and ambient.

In the Hugh Lane Municipal Gallery in Dublin, we are able to literally peer through a window into a painting space. Here, we find the studio of Francis Bacon, posthumously reconstructed after having been relocated from its original site in London, where the artist lived and worked from 1961 until his death in 1992. The entire contents of the London studio, including the dust on the floor, were catalogued by archaeologists and moved into the museum in Dublin with painstaking attention to detail. Bacon accumulated detritus to the point of filling his studio to impractical proportions. Here perhaps is an expression of the *horror vacui* referred to by Grootenboer. But there is a notable absence: the easel is empty and the majority of canvases in the studio have been turned to face the wall. Scanning the floor, one can see a pile of small paintings, destroyed with slashes that leave gaping voids in the canvas. Although Bacon's paintings themselves are not visible, his visual sources are evident among the many photographs and various other fragments, and his palette is in evidence in expansive proportions across the door, walls, and surrounding objects. This is the peripheral and ambient space of Francis Bacon's paintings; the indexical signs of his art, perhaps even its aura, without the art itself. Hermetically sealed behind glass, Bacon's studio is not physically accessible, but the viewer is granted multiple vantage points strategically placed at the doorway, two windows, and through two small peep-holes in the wall opposite the doorway. As a scopic apparatus for art, the peephole may be considered a rudimentary antecedent of head mounted displays developed for virtual reality technology.

Immersive art is typically thought of in terms of an all-encompassing organization of the visual field, so that a viewer is surrounded by an image, as though he or she has stepped inside a pictorial space. Immersion frequently invokes polysensory experience, i.e., it is typically more than visual and can engage, for example, aural, spatial, kinaesthetic, tactile, and olfactory awareness. Char Davies is an often-cited artist in this field whose two key works *Osmose* (1995) and *Ephémère* (1998) are exemplars of immersive technology. Davies contends that immersive virtual space can "redirect attention from our usual distractions and assumptions to the sensations of our own condition as briefly embodied sentient beings immersed in the flow of life through space and time." [8] A key strategy behind immersion seems to lie in the purging of interferences, by which I mean any distraction that might call one's attention away from the sovereignty of the work of art over its environment. These interferences occupy the space between the art and the audience, or the peripheral space around the art. An immersive environment might be described as one that removes or diminishes the presence of that which is extraneous to the artwork (e.g. surrounding architecture, furniture, other people, etc.). The head-mounted display for immersive virtual environments is an effective means to deal with this, even obscuring the participant's own body. In the aforementioned works by Char Davies, a participant is able to navigate through digitally constructed space in real time through the control of breathing and balance.

However, the experience of immersion is always contingent upon a participant's responsiveness and susceptibility. According to Jay David Bolter and Richard Grusin, an immersive medium is one "whose purpose is to disappear. This disappearing act, however, is made difficult by the apparatus that virtual reality requires." [9] Francis Dyson points out "there are *multitudes* of technical and circumstantial impediments to forgetting the presence of the apparatus." [10] Referencing Char Davies' work in particular, Dyson quotes Richard Coyne's remarks regarding "the heavy headset, the low image resolution, the noises in the museum, the time constraint, and so on." [11] If one regards interference as an inevitable component of immersion, immersive methodologies might logically incorporate strategic interference, allowing for the peripheral, incidental environment to encroach upon the immersive experience. Writing about virtual reality, Bolter and Grusin refer to the technology's "many ruptures: slow frame rates, jagged graphics, bright colors, bland lighting, and system crashes." [12] In the terminology employed by Bolter and Grusin, such ruptures interfere with the 'transparent immediacy' of a medium, instead contributing to a condition of 'hypermediacy,' multiplying the signs of mediation and making them more apparent. [13] Strategic incorporation of such ruptures or interferences that disrupt the ideal of a pure immersive experience might be best understood as contaminated immersion.

While digital technology has been implemented to simulate the sensation of entering the image, such a strategy is not unprecedented. As Oliver Grau has demonstrated, [14] there is a long history of immersive art practices that can be traced back to classical antiquity, and the nineteenth century panorama is worth considering in this respect. The term panorama is a combination of words of Greek origin: *pan*, meaning 'all', and *horama*, meaning 'view'. In a publication to commemorate the centenary of the Mesdag Panorama in Den Haag (constructed in 1881 by Hendrik Willem Mesdag), Paul A. Zoetmulder wrote, "the secret of the panorama lies in the elimination of the possibility to compare the work of art with the reality outside, by taking away 'all' boundaries which remind the spectator that he is observing a separate object within his total visual field." [15] In practice, however, the image of the panorama does not constitute the totality of the visible space, and strategies were employed to address the transition between the viewer and the image. One such strategy is the placement of extraneous objects in front of the panorama as props to aid the illusion, expanding the image into the three-dimensional space of the interior that the panorama encircles. The objects in this zone were known by the French term 'attrapes', and Zoetmulder attributes this innovation to the French panorama painter Jean-Charles Langlois, also known as 'The Colonel.' Zoetmulder writes, "Gradually this technique was further refined to the extent that the tri-dimensional attrapes faded perfectly into the bi-dimensional canvas, thus creating a very realistic effect." [16]

Many of the panoramas popular with audiences in the 19th century are no longer in existence, however, firsthand experience of one of the few surviving 19th century panoramas, the Mesdag Panorama, leads to questions regarding the supposedly perfect integration of *attrapes* into the illusion. Indeed, it is possible to discern a rupture between the intermediary terrain where the *attrapes* are situated and the illusionistic space of the painting. Viewing the panorama at its perimeter, an angle not normally visible to the spectator, this rupture is revealed as an actual chasm. In fact, a gap big enough to fall through separates the foreground terrain and the painted panorama beyond it. Mesdag's panoramic painting is disrupted, or contaminated, by the surrounding environment, calling one's attention to the space that separates the viewer from the image as much as contributing to a sense of immersion.

ESSAY

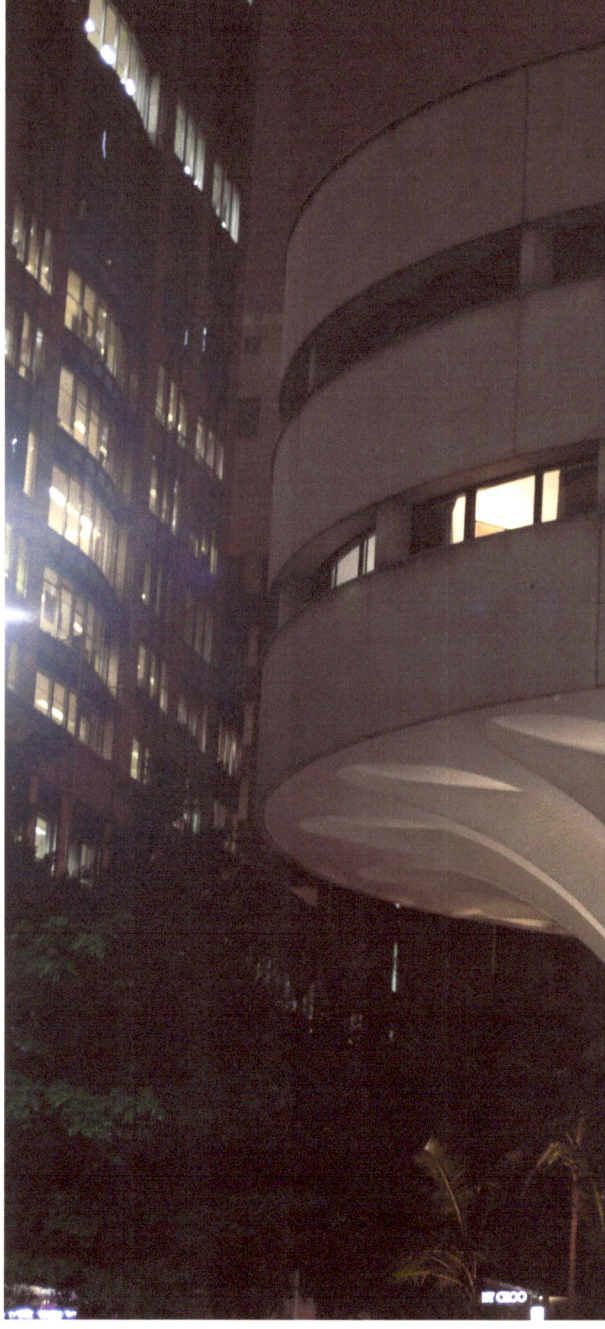

Figure 1. Kaldor Public Art Project 25: Thomas Demand's *The Dailies*, 2012. View of the Commercial Travellers' Association, Sydney in Martin Place, at night. Photograph by Paul Green. © Kaldor Public Art Projects, 2012. Used with permission.

At the *New Imaging* conference held at Artspace in Sydney in 2010, Stephen Little recounted his experience of being intrigued by the wall space between two paintings, in which holes indicated that a painting had possibly been removed from the exhibition. The experience correlates with Little's strategies to critique painting through "a refusal of traditional means." [17] He remarked that the blank space "had offered a more fulfilling and informative encounter with painting than any of the works on show." [18] While this may be interpreted as an indictment of the paintings in that particular exhibition, it also evidences the potential significance of the environment extraneous to the art on display. If the wall-space between two paintings can be valuable contemplative terrain in competition with the adjacent art, it is apparent that no space is entirely neutral, just as no space is inherently immersive.

THE DAILIES

Thomas Demand's exhibition *The Dailies* could be said to activate the space between, calling attention to the peripheral and ambient. The project occupied the Commercial Travellers' Association club at Sydney's MLC Centre, [Figure 1] a building designed by Harry Seidler and specifically selected by Demand to house the installation. As the 25th Kaldor Public Art Project (March 23 – April 22, 2012), *The Dailies* is one of a series of Kaldor-sponsored major projects by international artists in public spaces primarily located in Australia, beginning with Christo and Jeanne-Claude's wrapped coast in 1969 and including the work of Gilbert & George, Jeff Koons and Bill Viola.

Installed throughout hotel rooms on the fourth floor of the building, the surrounding environment of *the Dailies* was integral to the reception of Demand's photographs, and taken as a whole, the project may be considered an immersive installation. The idiosyncratic design of the hotel was at the forefront of the viewer's experience of the exhibition. The artist did not try to dominate the space; rather, the installation was more like a series of understated interventions designed to assimilate with the environment.

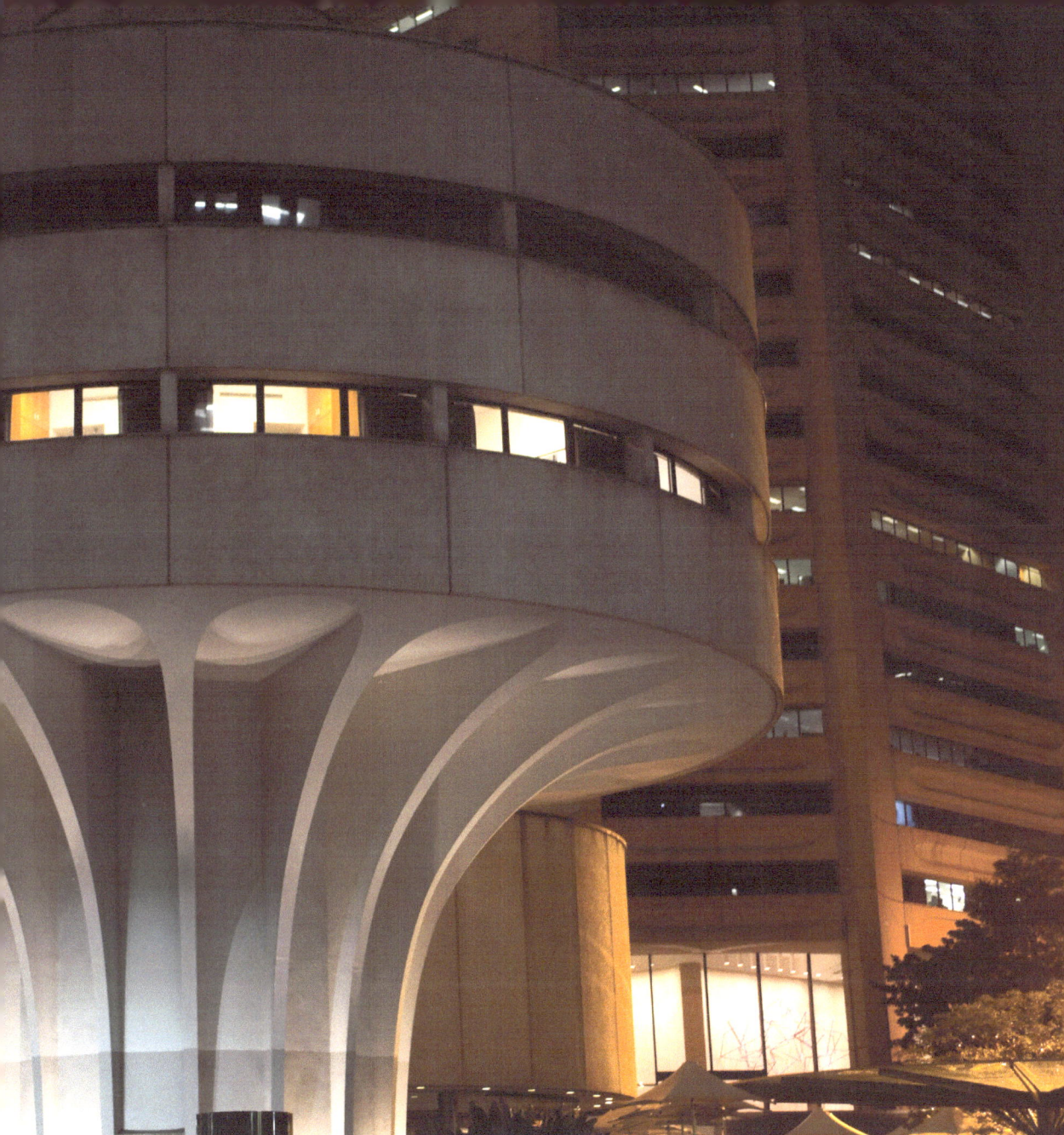

Demand enlisted collaborators to contribute to his installation. Having noticed the Prada store in Martin Place from the window of one of the CTA hotel rooms, Demand invited Miuccia Prada to manufacture a fragrance for the exhibition. Every room was installed with a scent dispenser that emitted an aroma made from a synthesis of green leaves. The scent was subtle and difficult to discern. Also for the exhibition, the novelist Louis Begley wrote a short story, *Gregor in Sydney*, entailing a series of experiences in the CTA hotel narrated by a fictional business traveler. Fragments of the story were disguised as menu cards and inconspicuously placed in each room.

The venue of the exhibition significantly informed the reception of the work. The central shaft of the tower houses the elevator and rises from the underground bar and function rooms up to the floors above on levels four and five. Level four consists of 16 single hotel rooms, 15 of which were used for the installation

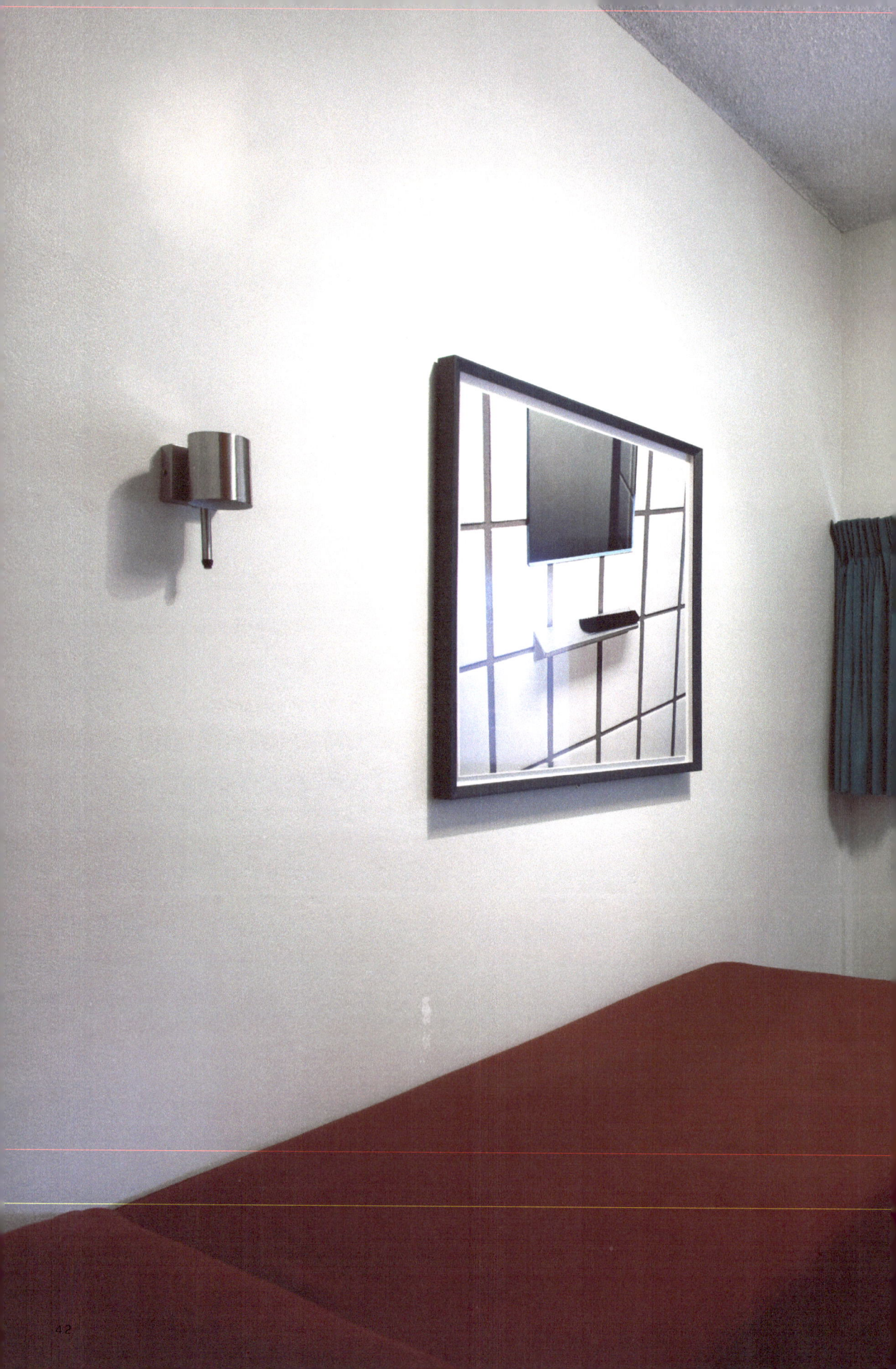

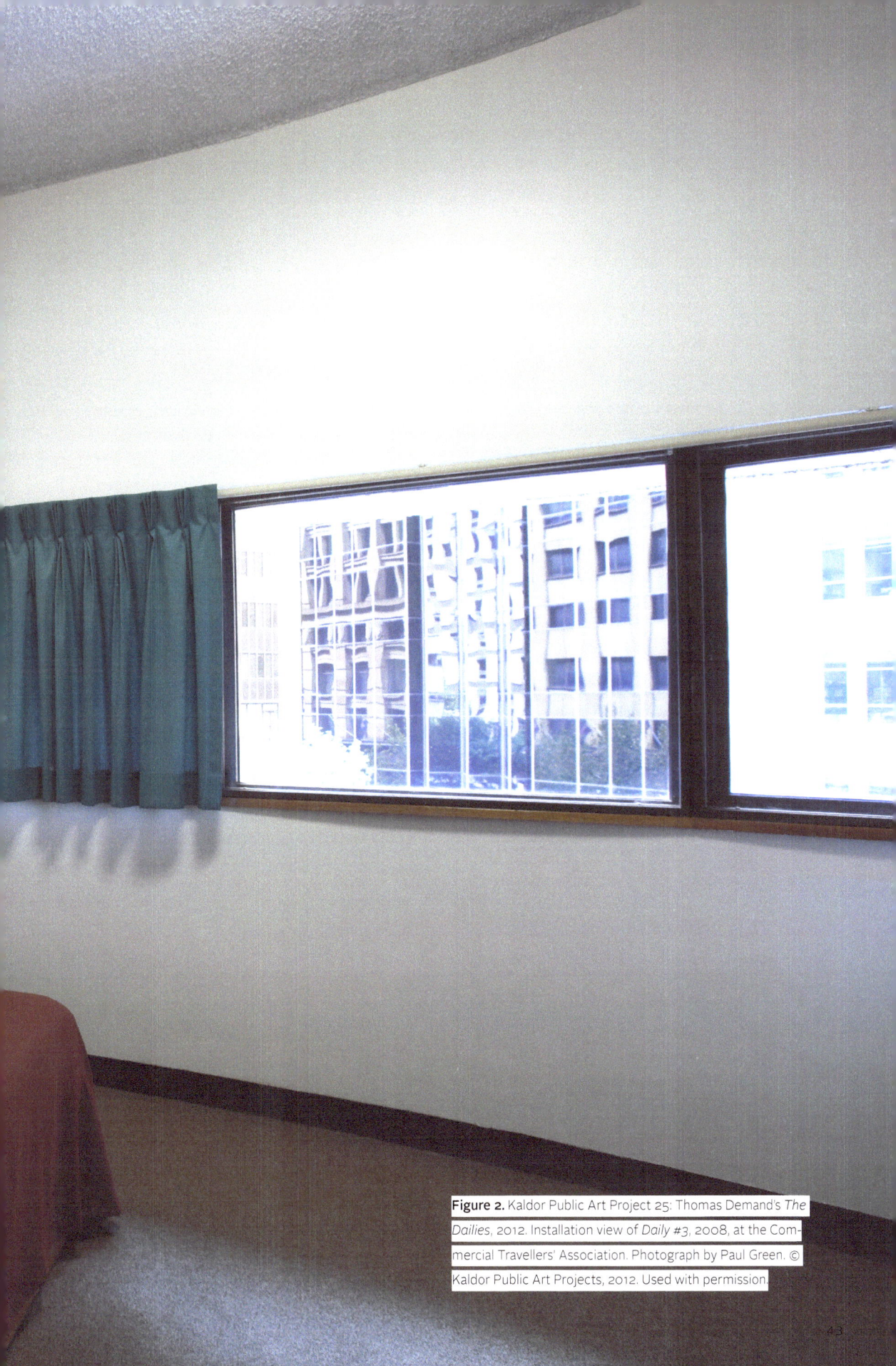

Figure 2. Kaldor Public Art Project 25: Thomas Demand's *The Dailies*, 2012. Installation view of *Daily #3*, 2008, at the Commercial Travellers' Association. Photograph by Paul Green. © Kaldor Public Art Projects, 2012. Used with permission.

of *The Dailies*. Visiting the exhibition on a typical day in March or April 2012, one exited the lift on level four and entered a circular corridor punctuated by a series of closed hotel room doors. A volunteer was there to welcome visitors and encourage exploration of the environment. Selecting a door and entering, a visitor would find a wedge-shaped room just large enough to accommodate a single bed, a desk, a wardrobe and a mini-bar fridge. At the wider end of the room one could look through the curved window in the outer wall of the building to a view of buildings and streets in the vicinity. [See figure 2.] On the wall above each single bed was a framed photograph by Thomas Demand.

ENTERING THE IMAGE

Demand is known for his process of photographing life-size paper models constructed in his studio. A characteristic feature of his practice is the use of the Diasec-mounted photographic process, in which photographs are face-mounted onto acrylic glass, producing images of high gloss and brilliant color. Speaking in conversation with Judy Annear at the Art Gallery of New South Wales in 2011, Demand commented on the rationale behind the format of his work: "It's kind of a way of making the photographic print invisible… I wanted people looking at the thing I made, not the thing somebody else printed for me… I want to have them like windows, basically… you look through a window… you look into my studio. And that's why they don't have a frame, they don't have any edges." [19] Demand's description of the experience of looking at his photographic prints aligns closely with Bolter and Grusin's notion of a medium effacing itself to establish an immersive experience: "the logic of immediacy dictates that the medium itself should disappear and leave us in the presence of the thing represented." [20] On a significantly reduced scale and printed using an early, superseded color photographic technique known as dye transfer rather than the Diasec mount process, *The Dailies* project is notable for its departure from the format typically associated with Demand's work. Unusually, the photographs were presented in a dark frame in keeping with their context as hotel room décor. The presentation of these works in such a context was a conscious departure from the transparent immediacy sought in earlier modes of presentation. Instead, Demand's photographs can be understood as fragments within a complex set of associations that include the Prada scent, the Begley story, the window views and Seidler's architectural interiors.

Insulated from the noise of the city streets visible through the hotel room windows, the interior of the CTA hotel is faithful to its 1970s origins, as though caught in a time warp. According to Demand, upon entering the building, "somehow you're just completely removed from reality there." [21] Walking through the installation elicited the kind of odd sensation one might imagine feeling if it were possible to walk into one of Demand's photographs. Just such an experience is available to the artist himself when he is in the studio with a life-size paper model. Demand has described walking through his constructions:

> *The funny thing is, once you've finished a place and you've got it right in front of you, large as life, you can go through it like a computer simulation. You don't actually exist yourself. This sense of timelessness and virginity, a feeling that everything is new and unused, communicates itself to the viewer moving around in this kind of space.* [22]

It is as though Demand were describing an experience of immersive virtual reality. In conversation with Alexander Kluge, Demand stated of his models:

> *When I walk around them I feel a strange sense of destabilization. Once such a space is finished you are very cautious in it, because you know that you would destroy everything if you took a wrong step. Yet it's the idea of the space that you remember, even if you can't yourself experience the memory of it. That's the strange thing – you transpose yourself to a time and place in which you could never be. Yet you can of course be there in your imagination. You are standing in the midst of the thing that arose in your imagination and then it's all gone and the photo takes over.* [23]

It could be argued that visitors to *The Dailies* encountered a strange, otherworldly experience similar to Demand's description of walking through his own models.

Navigating one's way through the hotel and observing the photographs on the wall, it is almost as though the immersive ideal of an image that one can enter has been realized.

PARERGA

Demand's models are typically based on found photographic images from the media and are often charged with historical or political content. The artist undertakes careful research to find out as much as he can about his source photographs. He has commented, "I try to find the photographer, the publisher, how it came to the photo-agency. And I often discover even more interesting photos in the process." [24] The significant historical events or newsworthy incidents behind many of the images to which Demand is drawn give credence to Robert Storr's description of Demand's practice as "reviving 'history painting' by other means." [25] It is rare for Demand to seek subjects that have had no prior incarnation as images circulated in public. An image "sufficiently devoid of significance," as he described *Sink*, a work from 1997, is considered by the artist himself to be "a precious counterpoint to my other works." [26] The fact that the artist once more turned to quotidian subject matter for *The Dailies* may be considered another such counterpoint within his oeuvre.

The Dailies, a project the artist had worked on since 2008, initiated from a series of photographs taken with his own phone camera, capturing images of ordinary things the artist observed on his travels: a power outlet detached from a wall in an Ethiopian airport [Figure 3], a paper cup stuck in a chain link fence, an ash tray full of butts, a screwed up piece of paper in the gutter. These photographs became the source for a series of paper reconstructions built in his studio, which were then photographed. The images could be classified as rhopography, defined by Norman Bryson as "the depiction of those things which lack

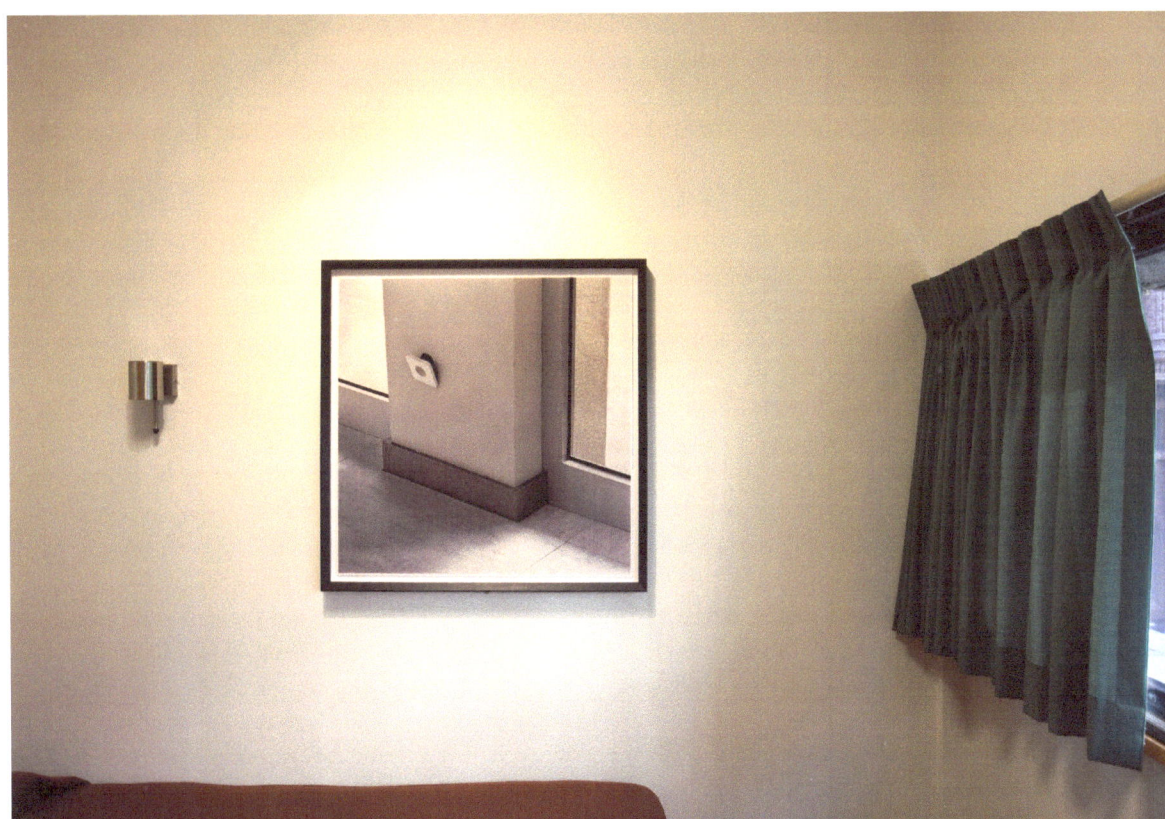

Figure 3. Kaldor Public Art Project 25: Thomas Demand's *The Dailies*, 2012. Installation view of *Daily #1*, 2008, at the Commercial Travellers' Association. Photograph by Paul Green. © Kaldor Public Art Projects, 2012. Used with permission.

importance, the unassuming material base of life that 'importance' overlooks." [27] In relation to the historical emergence of still life as a genre, Grootenboer refers to still life objects as 'parerga'; in other words, subsidiary or peripheral. As she points out, still life objects traditionally "appear at the border of representation, at its margins, on its frame or verso." [28]

Peripherality played a key role in *The Dailies*. The installation directed one's attention toward the extraneous and tangential. To experience the exhibition was to experience a series of digressions. In the context of the installation in the hotel, one cannot consider Demand's fifteen photographs in isolation. Clearly, Demand intended to trigger a range of experiences within the installation, not only by commissioning the Prada scent and Louis Begley's short story, but also by mounting the exhibition in Harry Seidler's distinct architectural space and selectively modifying the décor. Beyond the intentionality of Demand's highly considered installation in the CTA building, remain the unexpected conditions that rupture any possibility of a hermetically immersive experience. Instead, a complex set of associations between the photographs and the environment were to be detected. Amelia Douglas has discussed the role of detective work in relation to strategies within Thomas Demand's work that:

> *push the viewer into detective mode. Reading Demand's images requires involvement. We are never quite looking at what we are looking at. This uncertainty generates a covert thrill that, of course, stems first from acknowledgement of the illusion and the cleverness of the architectural artifice, but also from an enjoyment of role playing. The blankness of the images engenders narrative speculation.* [29]

In *The Dailies*, this blankness remained present, but extended beyond the photographs themselves. The surrounding space of the hotel's décor seemed to echo Demand's familiar aesthetic. New red-brown bedspreads were manufactured to ensure consistency from room to room. Likewise, the walls were freshly painted a particular shade of off-white. The exterior windows were cleaned to improve and highlight the view of the city outside, and new light globes installed to enhance the lighting. These modifications to the décor contributed to a pronounced sense of sterility throughout. Like the crisp planes of clean paper in his photographs, the clean walls and new bedspreads were devoid of indexical signs of the kind of history and events that one might imagine in a hotel room. Indeed, the single beds further underscored an abiding sense of asceticism and isolation. Such observations generated the impression that Demand's fabricated worlds had extended beyond the photographs themselves and had somehow spread into the space of the viewer.

Beyond the immediate space of the hotel interior were further associations to be made with Demand's photographic images. The view outside the hotel windows could often be found to have a visual resonance with an aspect of *The Dailies*. For instance, Demand's photograph depicting a ceiling with missing panels related to the trace of removed signage from a nearby building façade. The connections between the photographs and the surrounding space were there to be found by astute observers. Demand has spoken about his Kaldor Project as leading the viewer to discover "constellations" [30] which expand the image beyond the frame and blur distinctions between art and non-art, emphasizing the viewer's agency to locate hidden or unanticipated connections in the surrounding environment. Moving through the series of uniformly designed rooms around the circular building elicited a sense of disorientation. Once inside a room, there was little about the interior to distinguish one from another aside from Demand's photographs. To

ESSAY

aid one's bearings, the visitor would be better served to be attentive to the series of views through the windows, which cumulatively amounted to a 360-degree view. In this respect, the design of the CTA building's design has obvious parallels with the enveloping space of the 19th century panorama, as does the panopticon, Jeremy Bentham's prison design. [31] From the vantage point of the fourth floor of the CTA building, one is well positioned to surveil the pedestrians below.

It is noteworthy that so many features of Demand's Kaldor Project appeared to comprise peripheral details, or parerga. Shifting the format of his photographic process, particularly in terms of presentation, Demand moves away from the immediacy that characterizes his Diasec-mounted prints. This shift marks a deflection away from the photograph's immersive potential, directing the viewer towards a more hypermediated condition in which the viewer is made all the more conscious of the photograph as a framed print on a wall, a single item among a multitude of diversions within the environment of the CTA hotel.

CONCLUSION

The subjects in Demand's photographs reveal themselves as ersatz objects, like the *attrapes* of the panorama, designed to misdirect and confound. Upon scrutiny, the paper-thin veneers that constitute Demand's tableaux reveal themselves as lacking in substance and weight; they are all artifice and pure contrivance. Regarding the space surrounding the photographs in the CTA hotel rooms, everything became contingent. *The Dailies* simultaneously courted immersion and interference, to disorienting effect. Expanding the image beyond the confines of the frame, Demand's installation blurred distinctions between art and 'non-art,' emphasizing the agency of the audience to locate hidden or unanticipated connections in the surrounding environment. Upon entering the fourth floor of the hotel from the lift, the viewer encountered the cumulative experience of moving from room to room, finding oneself in the contradictory situation of an immersive space that incorporated diversions as an integral component of the installation. The exhibition presented multiple layers of experience in which it was unclear where the work began and ended. It was a hypermediated environment that required connections to be located across a fragmented terrain. Bolter and Grusin state, "the logic of hypermediacy acknowledges multiple acts of representation and makes them visible." [32] Demand's hypermediation is apparent through the remediation of source photographs into paper sculptures and back into photography. In the Sydney presentation of *The Dailies*, hypermediacy extended into the environment of the CTA hotel. Enlisting Seidler's architecture, subtly manipulating its décor, introducing a manufactured scent and a fictional short story, Demand asks us to notice that which lies outside the photograph. The size and color of the frames around the photographs closely matched the window frames, as though to draw a close comparison. Demand directed attention toward an all-inclusive experience related to Bolter and Grusin's description of hypermediacy as offering "a heterogeneous space, in which representation is conceived of not as a window on to the world, but as 'windowed' itself—with windows that open on to other representations or other media. The logic of hypermediacy multiplies the signs of mediation and in this way tries to reproduce the rich sensorium of human experience." [33]

Roland Barthes wrote about an element that will "break (or punctuate)" a setting... "it is this element which rises from a scene, shoots out of it like an arrow, and pierces me. A Latin word exists to designate this wound, this prick, this mark made by a pointed instrument." [34] Barthes' word for this is *punctum*, which he likens to a "sting, speck, cut, little hole—and also a cast of the dice." [35] Barthes indicates that the *punctum* is an element of chance, outside of the photographer's control: "the detail which interests me is not, or at least is not strictly, intentional, and probably must not be so; it occurs in the field of the photographed thing like a supplement that is at once inevitable and delightful." [36] The highly controlled scenes constructed and photographed by Demand might be better understood as falling into Barthes' other category, that of the *studium*. "To recognize the *studium* is inevitably to encounter the photographer's intentions." [37] Michael Fried has highlighted the role of intentionality in relation to Barthes' distinction between the *studium* and *punctum*, commenting, "the detail that strikes him as a *punctum* could not do so had it been intended as such by the photographer." [38] Demand's highly controlled tableaux in *The Dailies* are opened up to the more contingent condition of the *punctum* through the context of the installation. It is this contingency that contaminates immersion and highlights the potential for the role of interference, operating as a cut, or rupture, as in the schism of the breakfast still life or the chasm of the Mesdag Panorama. ■

REFERENCES AND NOTES

1. Oliver Grau, *Virtual Art: From Illusion to Immersion* (Cambridge, MA: MIT Press, 2003), 13.
2. Victor Stoichita, *The Self-Aware Image: An Insight into Early Modern Meta-Painting*, trans. Anne-Marie Glasheen (Cambridge: Cambridge University Press, 1997), quoted in Hanneke Grootenboer, *The Rhetoric of Perspective: Realism and Illusion in Seventeenth-Century Dutch Still-Life Painting*, (Chicago, IL: The University of Chicago Press, 2005), 64-65.
3. Hanneke Grootenboer, *The Rhetoric of Perspective*, 65.
4. Ibid., 64.
5. Ibid., 72.
6. Ibid., 73.
7. Joseph Nechvatal, *Immersive Ideals / Critical Distances: A Study of the Affinity Between Artistic Ideologies Based in Virtual Reality and Previous Immersive Idioms* (Ph.D. diss., Centre for Advanced Inquiry in the Interactive Arts, University of Wales College, 1999), 395-396, http://www.eyewithwings.net/nechvatal/iicd.pdf (accessed June 25, 2012).
8. Char Davies, "Virtual Space," in *Space: In Science, Art and Society*, ed. François Penz, Gregory Radick and Robert Howell (Cambridge: Cambridge University Press, 2004), 69-104, http://www.immersence.com/publications/char/2004-CD-Space.html (accessed June 25, 2012).
9. Jay David Bolter and Richard Grusin, *Remediation: Understanding New Media* (Cambridge, MA: MIT Press, 1999), 21-22.
10. Francis Dyson, "Immersion," chap. 5 in *Sounding New Media: Immersion and Embodiment in the Arts and Culture* (Berkeley: University of California Press, 2009), http://www.immersence.com/publications/2009/2009-FDyson.html (accessed June 25, 2012).
11. Richard Coyne, *Technoromanticism: Digital Narrative, Holism, and the Romance of the Real* (Cambridge, MA: MIT Press, 1999), 159, quoted in Francis Dyson, *Sounding New Media*.
12. Jay David Bolter and Richard Grusin, *Remediation: Understanding New Media*, 22.

13. Ibid., 34.
14. Oliver Grau, *Virtual Art*.
15. Paul A. Zoetmulder, *The Panorama Phenomenon: Mesdag Panorama 1881-1981* (Den Haag: Foundation for the Preservation of the Centenarian Mesdag Panorama, 1981), 18, http://www.n3krozoft.com/dead/08.8.html (accessed June 25, 2012).
16. Ibid., 19.
17. Su Baker, Melanie Oliver, and Paul Thomas, eds., *Column 7: New Imaging: Transdisciplinary Strategies for Art Beyond the New Media* (Sydney: Artspace Visual Arts Centre Ltd, 2011), 89.
18. Stephen Little, "Painting in Transit," in *Column 7: New Imaging: Transdisciplinary Strategies for Art Beyond the New Media*, 28.
19. "Photographic Artist Thomas Demand," YouTube video, 1:16:37, Thomas Demand in conversation with Judy Annear at the Art Gallery of New South Wales on February 23, 2011, posted by "Art Gallery of NSW," August 18, 2011, http://www.youtube.com/watch?v=hKd1FlXkicU.
20. Jay David Bolter and Richard Grusin, *Remediation: Understanding New Media*, 5-6.
21. "Thomas Demand – The Dailies," YouTube video, 8:25, T. Demand interviewed by Matthew Hanson, video by Nick Garner, Rococo Productions, 2012, posted by "DasPlatforms," April 29, 2012, https://www.youtube.com/watch?v=TBrCT8Zmp2I#t=437.
22. Michael Fried, *Why Photography Matters as Art as Never Before* (New Haven and London: Yale University Press, 2008), 268.
23. "A Conversation Between Alexander Kluge and Thomas Demand," in *Thomas Demand*, exhibition catalogue (London: Serpentine Gallery, 2006), 56.
24. Thomas Demand, quoted in Michael Fried, *Why Photography Matters as Art as Never Before*, 264; also quoted in Susan van Wyk, "Close Encounters with Recent History: The Photography of Thomas Demand," in *Thomas Demand*, exhibition catalogue (Melbourne: National Gallery of Victoria, second edition, 2012), 63.
25. Robert Storr, "Paper Thin and Thick as Thieves," in *Yellowcake*, by Germano Celant and Thomas Demand (Milan: Progretto Prada Arte, 2007), 41.
26. Ibid., 274.
27. Norman Bryson, *Looking at the Overlooked: Four Essays on Still Life Painting* (London: Reaktion Books, 1995), 16.
28. Hanneke Grootenboer, *The Rhetoric of Perspective*, 64.
29. Amelia Douglas, "The Paper Trail: History and Excess in the Photography of Thomas Demand," *antiTHESIS* 15 (2005): 191.
30. Thomas Demand in conversation with Sylvia Lavin at the Art Gallery of New South Wales, Sydney, Australia, March 23, 2012.
31. Stephen Oettermann has pointed out the parallels between the origins of the panopticon and the panorama: "In 1787 - the same year Robert Barker began his first attempts to paint a panorama - the British jurist and utilitarian philosopher Jeremy Bentham (1748-1832) began campaigning for his most ambitious project: a new type of prison, which he appropriately called a 'panopticon' or 'inspection house.'" Bentham's prison design enabled guards ample visual access to prison cells but restricted physical access. "Cell tract was separated from watchtower, prisoners from guards, by an unbridgeable gap." Stephan Oettermann, *The Panorama: History of a Mass Medium*, trans. Deborah Lucas Schneider (New York: Zone Books, 1997), 40.
32. Jay David Bolter and Richard Grusin, *Remediation: Understanding New Media*, 33-34.
33. Ibid., 34.
34. Roland Barthes, *Camera Lucida: Reflections on Photography*, trans. Richard Howard (London: Vintage Books, 2000), 26.
35. Ibid., 27.
36. Ibid., 40.
37. Ibid., 27.
38. Michael Fried, *Why Photography Matters as Art as Never Before*, 100.

Gesture in Search of a Purpose
A PREHISTORY OF MOBILITY

by

Darren Tofts & Lisa Gye

Swinburne University of Technology
Melbourne, Australia
dtofts@swin.edu.au
lgye@swin.edu.au

NEW MEDIA ART AS NEW MEDIA CREATIVITY?

The image seems innocuous enough: Ireland's Ronnie Delany stands over a fallen John Landy at the dramatic conclusion of the 1500 metre final in Melbourne in 1956. An iconic expression of the Olympic spirit, the image captures the wrenching disappointment as the gutted favourite is consoled by an unlikely victor. With Roland Barthes in mind, the image's studium is straightforward: sport photojournalism witnessing a moment of completion, the realisation of the promise of a winner and a loser. The detail that punctuates and disrupts this generic effect, its punctum, is literally a distraction from the central detail, as you need to stray into the crowd observing the scene for it to find you, for it to exert its effect. [2] The punctum here is a sensation of the uncanny, an anachronistic impossibility. It is uncanny because it seems to represent the image of a man apparently talking on a mobile phone at a time when television had only just been introduced into Australia, and selectively at that. It is also anachronistic since international direct dialling was still two decades away.

This image is part of a Melbourne Olympic Games memorabilia display at the eponymous Olympic Hotel

ESSAY

This paper explores the uncanny anticipation of mobile telephony in the history of the visual image. Drawing on our remix project, The Secret Gestural Prehistory of Mobile Devices, *it critically engages with contemporary media culture's obsession with the occupation of the hands as an unwitting gesture in search of a purpose. This gesture is a bodily pantomime imagining an indispensable, intimate apparel that has modified the body's relation to itself and remote others through mobile media. These images are suggestive of bodily rhythms that synchronize the hand, the ear, the eye and the mouth that have not always made sense. In this they foreshadow the potential media that will, in time, resolve this postural ergonomics into a meaningful function: the immediate and continuous communion with unseen and absent others. The visual archive can become the unconscious of contemporary media when its images are re-coded through the writing of implicit and anachronistic narratives. The combination of image and text, in the form of captions, denotes and detonates at one and the same time, creating a double vision that, once seen, can never be unseen.*

in Preston, a northern suburb of Melbourne. The hotel was built in 1956 specifically for the occasion of the Olympic Games, along with much of the cheap, social housing around it. The notion of a specific occasion that is historically marked, ordained and commemorated in the physicality of a building is fitting in relation to the phantom image we encountered there on that day in 2010. In itself the image, while a curiosity, doesn't amount to much. It has the same sense of weird, otherworldly novelty of Italian exploitation film *Mondo Cane* (1962), or the interstellar traces of astronauts glimpsed in Inca rock carvings and the flight paths for extra-terrestrials on the Nazca plane in Peru featured in Erich von Däniken's book *Chariots of the Gods?* (1968). And as well the more bucolic, though still purportedly otherworldly manifestation of crop circles in a Wiltshire barley field or images of Christ or the Madonna in vegemite toast or a Big Mac from Mexico City.

In the genre of critical remix, however, the found object is certainly not enough, no matter how compellingly 'other' it is. An act of counter-denotation is required to alter the morphology of the image, to translate it into something else, something it was never intended to be, nor could have ever been, but can nonetheless become. It can become perhaps another version of itself, though not a fractal replication of self-similarity, but rather variation within a finite set. When the image is altered by an act of *detonation* it can become a different iteration of itself. Under such circumstances it is always already an image of someone using a mobile phone. Like anagrams, which generate lexical variation within a finite set, linguistic denotation must also, and at the same time, be a detonation, an explosive reprogramming of the image's semiotic DNA (fittingly one term is an anagram of the other). This is what we set out to do with the *Secret Gestural Prehistory of Mobile Devices*. If the initial image was found by accident, we wanted to reproduce this happenstance by actively seeking out other images like the one found at the Olympic Hotel. This meant trawling through back issues of *National Geographic* and *Time/Life* books, old newspapers and encyclopaedias. As other images were found we set about re-coding them through the practice of one of the simplest genres of writing, the caption, which would accompany each image.

MORPHOLOGY

How then to repeatedly alter the semiotic DNA of an image? What does it mean to recode and interfere with its pictorial contract with a viewer and to irresistibly alter it? We had to supplant the image's noeme and explore its accidental, whimsical or wilful misprision in order to transform the unlikely into the only possible meaning. This challenge meant nothing short of short-circuiting the semiotic contract of the image as a supplement of the real. After inferring in the caption a signified that is implied rather than described, the image becomes irreversibly something else. Within critical remix, the metaphysics of the real yield to that of the irreal, the fabulatory insinuation of a real in excess of the real, and the prescient announcement of a real yet to come. Such images, as Jorge Luis Borges reminds us of books, need only "be possible" to exist.[3] What we want to describe here is a morphology of this shift in a selection of indicative images from *The Secret Gestural Prehistory of Mobile Devices*. As we described in the *Secret Gestural Prehistory* blog, the visual archive foreshadows the

psychopathology of unconscious gesture in search of a purpose... (the) unconscious of contemporary media culture's obsession with the occupation of the hands. It is a familiar, too familiar gestural ergonomics, a bodily pantomime imagining an indispensable, intimate apparel that has modified the body's relation to itself and remote others. At times this seems ordinary, in the form of a glancing touch of the ear, a casual glimpse of one's own hand. Yet it can be uncomfortably distorted, a contortion of ear and shoulder reminiscent of the arthritic malaise known as St. Vitus' Dance. Or an obsessive flailing of the hands while talking to oneself, as in certain pathological forms of mania and hysteria. These images are suggestive of gestural rhythms that synchronize the hand, the ear, the eye and the mouth. In this they foreshadow the potential media that will, in time, resolve these postural gestures into a meaningful function: the immediate and continuous communion with unseen and absent others.[4]

LITERAL

With many images in the archive the degree of semiotic work that captions are required to do can be minimal. In the face of a scenario of mobile ergonomics that governs the project and precedes the re-writing of any image, all that is often required is the detonation of a kind of logic bomb that sets off a semantic chain reaction or interference of the image's semiosis. Some have a convergent and suggestive immediacy that brings to mind gestures that have become part of the technologically modified body. These are suggestive of the pleasant aesthetics of unexpected coincidence. The 1976 photograph of two women in a Manhattan jewellers, for instance, is an indicative image of the techno-mediated body. [5] The older woman in the background uncomfortably cradles an analogue handset between her left shoulder and ear that in a weird way is more contemporary for us perhaps than that of the woman in the foreground, whose gesture resembles a pre-mobile ergonomics. Her countenance speaks of the easy composure of "anywhere, anytime" associated with mobile telephony. As well it is the performance of an ironic and reflexive "I'm talking on the phone" pantomime.

This image is the heraldic *mise en abyme* of the entire project. It is an image, in miniature, of the expansive journey of postural distortion suggesting the becoming-media as intimate apparel associated with the vectors of mobility. This was something of the response we had when the *Atlantic Monthly* ran a feature on the project in 2010. [6]

In the casual image of a jogger in Central Park in New York in 1976 is the intuitive, becoming third nature of the seamless punctuation of immediacy by mediation. [7] It demonstrates the doing of something, in this instance, jogging, that not so long ago would require a more elaborate and labour intensive rupture of the event to make a phone call. That is, it would have necessitated a definite pause in the act of jogging, the pursuit of a telephone booth, a conversation, then the resumption of jogging. This sequence of discrete events is captured as a singularity in this image, as something that happens simultaneously, as suggested in the caption that accompanies the image: "54 at 10. cul8r."

Here the two actions are co-existent: the seemliness of different things is seamless, as in a suturing or stitching together of separate and even discordant elements. Paul and Linda McCartney visit Bill Wyman backstage at a 1978 Rolling Stones concert in New York. The mediated countenance of both Linda and Paul distracts the eye and the ear respectively, suggesting something, perhaps, of the quality of their company (the caption for this image reads "Bill basks in self-congratulation, knowing that at least two people bought, or at least have seen *Stone Alone*. Its influence exceeds his expectations as Paul McCartney brings a new inflection to 'the look'"). [8] The idea of the 'look' was developed early on in the history of the project, to capture anachronistic, pre-mobile gestures that would not emerge till the end of the century but seem to have been anticipated in Swinging London, as other images from this period suggest. And even more broadly the happening vibe of the 'Sixties' generally. Take the image Students, University of Sydney, 1969. [9]

The literal caption that accompanies this image, "Intimations of the tweet economy," describes what is familiar to us via the "look." But it also captures the social displacement associated with mobility. The student is there but not there, present *and* absent. Here is a totemic icon of the familiar punctuation of the social by a tacitly accepted removal from the present. But as in the previous image of Wyman and the McCartneys, both acts are enacted at the same time. It is an instance of what we understand today as multi-tasking. But more specifically, in terms of the co-presence of speech and writing, talking and texting, it is an instance of a co-present orality and literacy.

Another example similar to this is Melbourne University Student 1967. This image unwittingly adds a nuance to the idea of the academic Trivium, adding banality to logic and rhetoric. Amid an assembly of other students whose gaze is fixed elsewhere, the young man in question is also somewhere else ("The urgency of this anti-Vietnam war 'sit-in' fails to hold the attention of at least one student. His interlocutor was apparently 'doing nothing' at the time"). [10]

Here we see at work the notion of performative utterance of anything, no matter how trivial, simply for the fact of its possibility wherever, whenever. And often when it happens it punctuates, disrupts a scene of discourse that is prior to it. As here, this may be in the middle or a lecture, a meeting or, in this instance a demonstration. Cheek by jowl with many other people who can't escape the ambience of his response (and usually at high volume), the young man's focus on the speech of an absent other unavoidably becomes public information. It's no accident, of course, that Sadie Plant's notion of "enforced eavesdropping" was coined in relation to a Motorola-commissioned study of the sociality of mobile phone use in 2001. [11] The cultural critic Mark Dery wrote an eviscerating 2010 essay on the same topic called "The Age of Always Connect," in which he described the pathogens of over-sharing, listening without consent to private conversations and the implicit death of shame that comes with them as the psychopathology of our mobile times. The essay is a cautionary tale about the allegorical aspects of mobility that are explored in the *Secret Gestural Prehistory* images. It speaks of the double-headed hydra of mediated solipsism, the silent fixation on screens that makes "solitude portable," and the unwanted broadcasting of privacy, such as "the stranger with the headset, chattering blithely about her irritable bowel as she elbows past you at the supermarket meat counter." [12]

The ergonomics of certain physical contortions and gestures to do with cradling a phone to the ear while carrying two bags of shopping and opening a car door is now so imprinted on the psyche that when we look at historical images such as these it seems unwittingly to be the only possible explanation, even in the event of its impossibility. For instance a group of students in Tel Aviv in 1968 sit talking in the sun. The caption, "Yet another early instance of cervical spine dysplasia," may require some glossing. But the epiphany certainly comes when the image becomes an emblem of the text. [13]

The contortions of telesthesia range across class, anonymity as well as celebrity. Two shots of John Lennon captured during the *White Album* sessions in 1968 reveal a locution of the body to do with a new medium that is akin to the becoming prehensile of the thumb in primates on the way to lighting fires.

Or putting out fires, as in the case of a group of protestors in Saskatchewan in 1979. The caption underlines the point: "Citizens of mixed heritage (metis) denied the status of 'treaty Indians' blockade the entrance to a national park in Regina, Saskatchewan. Reinforcements will soon be on their way." This caption re-codes the visual casualness of what was probably a scratch of the ear into an unlikely call for assistance. [14]

The anonymous image of a sheep farmer in the Wimmera in the 1940s similarly engages quite self-consciously with a mobile narrative: "Checking the latest bale prices from Dalgety. The loyal heeler awaits the resumption of his master's voice." [15]

And further, take the image of a group of trend-setting teenagers in Australia in 1974. [16]

Attending a concert of the rock band the Coloured Balls at the Melbourne Showgrounds, this young woman proves once again that while Australia in the 1970s was still considered 'the Antipodes,' in the age of mobile telephony being "antipodal" is a relative concept.

RELATIONAL

The Secret Gestural Prehistory of Mobile Devices is ostensibly a writing project. In wanting to re-write an image's semiotic DNA, it tactically juxtaposes images with captions to generate a composite meaning that suggests an alternative to what we are looking at. The suggestiveness of the relations between text and image is crucial, since it enables a dramatic, rather than didactic engagement between viewer and image. The moment of realisation, of seeing something that might not have been immediately apparent (let alone intended), is akin to the generative force of a Joycean epiphany. James Joyce translated the religious significance of the epiphany into a secular understanding of the sudden manifestation, after Aristotle, of the essential *"quidditas"* or "whatness" of a thing; an unexpected radiance in an image that was not implied or intended. This was very much the motivation behind the caption for the image of an unnamed archaeologist in 1908: "One can only wonder if the classicist Eric Havelock drew inspiration from this image while writing his *Preface to Plato* (1963)."

The image of a distracted French archaeologist is a fitting emblem of the "silent revolution" of people reading that Havelock described when mapping the historical shift from orality to literacy. The caption, then, not only frames the image, but re-defines it.

As in the image of Andy Warhol and Mick Jagger from the early 70s, in which Warhol sits determinedly with both hands covering his ears: "At first appearance this image suggests that Andy has clearly had enough of Mick's relentless talk about himself. A closer reading reveals Mick's displeasure that his friend prefers the company of others not even in the room."

The relational aesthetics at work in this photographic imagery are imminent, not immanent. They emerge from the juxtaposition of a written narrative, scenario or situation that is suggested, a heuristic that guides a specific reading of the image. What we were surprised to find, though, was how potent this dramatic relational aesthetic was in relation to the rich and varied history of visual art, a pictorial form not often given to the casualness of isolated moments. The history of photography, and specifically vernacular candid images or snap shots, seemed an appropriate and even logical site for acts of re-writing. However paintings from different historical periods and cultural traditions also revealed unexpected anachronisms. Such invitations to transform historical, pre-photographic images suggest that the unconscious becoming of mobile ergonomics has always been part of the Western imagination at least (as of this writing we have not yet explored Eastern or other pictorial traditions). One may not be surprised, then, to encounter an image of technological innovation during the Renaissance, a time of dramatic experimentation in the aesthetics and optics of pictorial space. A detail from Sandro Botticelli's "Three Miracles of St. Zenobius," from 1500-1505, is such an image. The rather droll caption, "The fourth, unforeseen miracle in this image would only become apparent several centuries later," is deliberately dramatic, in the Aristotelian sense, in that it prompts the viewer to seek out and discover a fugitive, previously unknown image of the miraculous rather than simply read about it.

Even the imagination of the late Middle Ages seems to have been preoccupied with the unconscious lure of a modernity to come. In Hieronymus Bosch's 1475 "The Cure of Folly," the allegorical image of folly that is central to the image, when detonated by the caption, re-wires the image in such a way that once it is seen in this light is difficult to see in any other way: "Medieval allegory bespeaks a folly to come, in the form of grandiloquent banality. Researchers at the University of California (Davis) recently identified a previously unknown Latin inscription in this image, discovered from X-Ray analysis of the book teetering on the nun's head (historically taken to be an image of folly). The text, 'Non ultum. Quis es vos usque?'" roughly translates as 'Not much. What are you up to?'" [23]

NARRATIVE

The centrality of a modernist meta-narrative associated with "the look" became a recurrent theme as the project evolved. This was irresistibly suggested by a Eugene Atget portrait of a vernacular street scene in 1900: "Eugene Atget unwittingly captures an image of an unforeseen expression of literary modernism in the streets of *belle epoque* Paris." [24] Again, this is where the caption, as a micro-narrative, re-writes the image in the diegetic process of its telling. A 1967 image of the Velvet Underground in situ at the Factory in New York City focuses attention away from John Cale, who seems to be the focal point of the shot, on to Paul Morrissey who sits in the background: "At the Factory with Andy's latest find, The Velvet Underground, collaborator Paul Morrissey has tuned in and turned on. With a discreet turn of the head John Cale senses what is happening and is keen to succumb to the new habit." [25]

In an image of Andy Warhol and Jonas Mekas from 1965, the banality that Warhol made famous in his signature utterance of "gee" seems to be the downplayed, under-whelmed vibe of the image's portent of a banality to come, the bland ordinariness of things that are said on the phone; especially when encountered in public, such as on buses and trains. [26] And of course we all learned to love the alien during the 70s. Ziggy Stardust not only played guitar, was well hung and snow white tanned, but as David Bowie intoned, he also blew our minds. [27] Images such as staged studio portraits of Ziggy (and there are many others like it) seem to preclude the need for a caption even though they invite one. The relational situation of the image under the rubric of something called *The Secret Gestural Prehistory of Mobile Devices* is sufficient to make it bristle with an impossible electricity, the echo of a past-future tense. The strategy of the double-take, the invitation or reflex to look again, was also a key to the tone of the captions. In an image of John Lennon in Hamburg in 1962, for instance, it is not immediately clear what his gaze is fixed upon. The caption helps to guide our attention and bring it into focus: "Rare image of John Lennon distracted during a performance at the Kaiserkeller Club." [28]

Other images irresistibly invite a more mischievous approach to the relational intimacy of an obscure or hidden narrative to be discovered. The poetic at work in this re-writing and re-coding is a literate as much as visual technique of observation, to borrow from Jonathan Crary's study of optics and ways of seeing in the nineteenth century. Rather like the optical phenomenon of a "retinal afterimage" central to the act of viewing, textual captions or narratives inscribe a kind of palimpsest over the image. [29] The superimposition of a telephonic connotation in the image over its pre-telephonic denotation is not only in the eyes of the observer, but is a blurring of semantic sense in the act of observation. It is a variation on the persistence of vision associated with proto-animation techniques such as the thaumatrope, where separate images of a bird and a cage can be superimposed as a bird in a cage through movement. In such examples micro-narratives draw the viewer into a scenario that is culturally specific and relies upon regional, ethnic or topical knowledge appropriate to the image in question, such as the image of an unidentified man at a picnic in Madeira in 1959. If the punctum doesn't find you, the caption prompts you to be more responsive to its possible call: "The *Echium candicans syn fastuosum*, not to mention Malvasia, Terrantez and Verdelho may well be known throughout the world. Here we see the innocuous, vernacular potential for a new Pride of Madeira." [30] In this instance there is an uncanny plausibility associated with the fictional anachronism that is generated by the specificity of visual detail: mobility and speech at a distance, along with fortified wine and the *Echium candicans* are among the treasures of the eponymous Portuguese island.

Similarly, the image of a group of young Italian lace makers in 1959 is irreversibly short-circuited by a rather oblique refraction in what is being seen: "Dating back to 1530, *Lo Giuoco del Lotto d'Italia* (more commonly known as Bingo or "Housey Housey") was the first known instance in Western culture in which participants observed the call to 'eyes down.' These young Italian women respond to the irresistible call of another." [31]

This project and others like it [32] discipline their visual objects and textual narratives into loose coalitions that only hold together as long as they are held together. In this case, the textual denotation that reprograms the image, as well as the detonation that explodes its connotative capacity is temporary and will only last as long as it is remembered by the viewer. In this sense it fits with Edward Colless' discussion of transdisciplinarity. Colless argues that the "trans-" suggests "drift and errancy, as disciplines cross each other with the eventful possibility of collision or collusion but without the eventuality of their consensus." [33] In *The Secret Gestural Prehistory of Mobile Devices* this drift and errancy is a kind of Situationist *derive*. It precipitates not only the possibility of consensus, of seeing what is implied, but also of another kind of sense. Telesthesia, or sensing at a distance is one name for this. Another is mobile telephony.

In the spirit of critical remix, the genre in which this project is situated, it is appropriate to conclude by speaking through someone else, to quote someone already quoted. We need to speak, as Mark Amerika would have it, in an act of remixological ventriloquism. [34] This "transit of disciplinarity" is itself unsettled by an "etymological alternation between being a passage 'across' states (a transfer that doesn't lose its sovereignty or citizenship) and an extensive vector 'beyond' states." [35] In other words, for a long time we have been hangin' on the telephone. ■

ESSAY

REFERENCES AND NOTES

1. See the image entitled "Olympic Games, Melbourne, 1956," *The Secret Gestural Prehistory of Mobile Devices* (blog), by Darren Tofts and Lisa Gye, www.secretprehistory.net/?p=272 (accessed April 10, 2012).
2. Roland Barthes, *Camera Lucida: Reflections on Photography*, trans. Richard Howard (London: Fontana, 1984), 26-27.
3. Jorge Luis Borges, "The Library of Babel," in *Labyrinths: Selected Writings & Other Stories*, eds. Donald A. Yates & James E. Irby (New York: New Directions, 1964), 57.
4. Darren Tofts and Lisa Gye, *The Secret Gestural History of Mobile Devices* (blog), 2010, http://www.secretprehistory.net/ (accessed April 10, 2012).
5. See "Jewellers, 47th Street, Manhattan, 1976," *The Secret Gestural Prehistory of Mobile Devices* (blog), www.secretprehistory.net/?p=272 (accessed April 10, 2012).
6. Alexis Madrigal and Nicholas Jackson, "Cell Phone Users through History," *Atlantic Monthly*, November 10, 2010, http://www.theatlantic.com/technology/archive/2010/11/cell-phone-users-through-history/66363/ (accessed April 10, 2012).
7. See "Unidentified Jogger, Central Park, New York City, 1976," *The Secret Gestural Prehistory of Mobile Devices* (blog), www.secretprehistory.net/?p=272 (accessed April 10, 2012).
8. See "Bill Wyman, Linda and Paul McCartney, Backstage, New York, 1978," *The Secret Gestural Prehistory of Mobile Devices* (blog), www.secretprehistory.net/?p=272 (accessed April 10, 2012).
9. See "Students, University of Sydney, 1969," *The Secret Gestural Prehistory of Mobile Devices* (blog), www.secretprehistory.net/?p=272 (accessed April 10, 2012).
10. See "Anti-Prohibition Rally, Chicago, 1932," *The Secret Gestural Prehistory of Mobile Devices* (blog), www.secretprehistory.net/?p=272 (accessed April 10, 2012).
11. Sadie Plant, *One the Mobile: The Effects of Mobile Telephones on Social and Individual Life* (n. p. : Motorola, 2001), http://books.google.com.au/books/about/On_the_mobile.html?id=DWcEAQAAIAAJ (accessed April 10, 2012).
12. Mark Dery, "Always Connect," Mark Dery's website, 2010, http://markdery.com/?p=118 (accessed April 14, 2012).
13. See "Students, Tel Aviv, 1969," *The Secret Gestural Prehistory of Mobile Devices* (blog), www.secretprehistory.net/?p=272 (accessed April 10, 2012).
14. See "Protestors, Saskatchewan, 1979," *The Secret Gestural Prehistory of Mobile Devices* (blog), www.secretprehistory.net/?p=272 (accessed April 10, 2012).
15. See "Sheep Farmer, Wimmera, 1940s," *The Secret Gestural Prehistory of Mobile Devices* (blog), www.secretprehistory.net/?p=272 (accessed April 10, 2012).
16. See "Sharpies, Melbourne Showgrounds, 1974," *The Secret Gestural Prehistory of Mobile Devices* (blog), www.secretprehistory.net/?p=272 (accessed April 10, 2012).
17. Wark, McKenzie, "Suck On This, Planet of Noise! (Version 1.2)," in *Cultural Studies: Pluralism and Theory*, ed. David Bennett (Melbourne: University of Melbourne Press, 1993), 157.
18. James Joyce, *A Portrait of the Artist as a Young Man* (Harmondsworth: Penguin 1969), 213.
19. Eric Havelock, *Preface to Plato* (Oxford: Basil Blackwell, 1963), 41.
20. See "Unnamed Archaeologist, Laugerie, France, 1908," *The Secret Gestural Prehistory of Mobile Devices* (blog), www.secretprehistory.net/?p=272 (accessed April 10, 2012).

21. See "Andy Warhol and Mick Jagger, New York, early 1970s," *The Secret Gestural Prehistory of Mobile Devices* (blog), www.secretprehistory.net/?p=272 (accessed April 10, 2012).
22. See "Alessandro Botticelli, 'Three Miracles of St. Zenobius,' c.1500-1505 [detail]," *The Secret Gestural Prehistory of Mobile Devices* (blog), www.secretprehistory.net/?p=272 (accessed April 10, 2012).
23. See "Hieronymous Bosch, 'The Cure of Folly,' c.1475 [detail]," *The Secret Gestural Prehistory of Mobile Devices* (blog), www.secretprehistory.net/?p=272 (accessed April 10, 2012).
24. See "Unidentified Woman, Paris, 1900," *The Secret Gestural Prehistory of Mobile Devices* (blog), www.secretprehistory.net/?p=272 (accessed April 10, 2012).
25. See "Paul Morrissey, New York, 1967," *The Secret Gestural Prehistory of Mobile Devices* (blog), www.secretprehistory.net/?p=272 (accessed April 10, 2012).
26. See "Andy Warhol and Jonas Mekas, New York, 1965," *The Secret Gestural Prehistory of Mobile Devices* (blog), www.secretprehistory.net/?p=272 (accessed April 10, 2012).
27. See "David Bowie, London, 1972," *The Secret Gestural Prehistory of Mobile Devices* (blog), www.secretprehistory.net/?p=272 (accessed April 10, 2012).
28. See "John Lennon, Hamburg, 1962," *The Secret Gestural Prehistory of Mobile Devices* (blog), www.secretprehistory.net/?p=272 (accessed April 10, 2012).
29. Jonathan Crary, *Techniques of the Observer: On Vision and Modernity in the Nineteenth Century* (Cambridge, MA: MIT Press, 1992), 97.
30. See "Unidentified Man at Picnic, Madeira, 1959," *The Secret Gestural Prehistory of Mobile Devices* (blog), www.secretprehistory.net/?p=272 (accessed April 10, 2012).
31. See "Italian Lacemakers, Positano, 1959," *The Secret Gestural Prehistory of Mobile Devices* (blog), www.secretprehistory.net/?p=272 (accessed April 10, 2012).
32. See *Classical-gas* (blog), by Darren Tofts and Lisa Gye, www.classigal-gas.com (accessed April 10, 2012).
33. Edward Colless, "Transdisciplinary Aesthetics: An Occultation and Occultism," the website of Transdisciplinary Art Research, 2011, http://blogs.unsw.edu.au/tiic/leaf/leafrewire/darren-tofts-being-indisciplined/leafisea/edward-colless-transdisciplinary-aesthetics-an-occultation-and-occultism/ (accessed April 13, 2012) .
34. Darren Tofts, "Outsourcing the Origins of the 'I,'" in "Shape of the 'I,'" *English Language Notes* 50, no. 1 (2012): 231-236.
35. Edward Colless, "Transdisciplinary Aesthetics: An Occultation and Occultism."

Headless and Unborn, or the Baphomet Restored

Interfering with Bataille and Masson's Image of the *Acephale*

by

Leon Marvell

School of Communication and Creative Arts
Deakin University
leon@deakin.edu.au

A MONSTROUS EMBLEM

At a certain period in European intellectual history, a comparatively large number of artists and intellectuals – arguably the most important thinkers and artists of the times – were all involved to a greater or lesser degree in the envisioning of a new myth that might lead European civilization out of the gathering darkness of fascism, a myth they hoped would provoke the total and radical transformation of society and culture.

Two principle groups were involved: the Surrealists, constellated around the ideas and political interventions of André Breton, the foremost ideologue of the Surrealist movement, and a group of 'dissident' surrealists that included Georges Bataille, Roger Caillois and Michel Leiris, key figures in the radical boys club, the *Collège de Sociologie*, which coalesced in 1936. Hovering between these two camps were a number of artists and intellectuals who appeared to loath to choose between the two encampments, or who periodically aligned themselves first with one, then the other. Overriding these vacillating allegiances and the petty clash of personalities was the unifying dream of finding a new myth through which society could

This paper investigates Bataille and Masson's drawing of the Acephale, the escutcheon of Bataille's esoteric cabal and the journal (*Acéphale*) that espoused his vision of a violently sacralised society. Masson's drawing of the acephalic monster is the emblem of Bataille's negative Absolute, and is therefore the *final image*, a talisman to wipe out all other images. I unearth a hitherto unsuspected connexion between the Acephale and a magical text, one of the *Papyri Graecae Magicae*. Noting that the Acephale is an 'emblem', I point towards the tradition of the emblematic books, a tradition that began with Horapollo's *Hieroglyphica*. I then propose that Caillois's 'objective ideograms' and the idea of mantic decaptitation was in part responsible for the production of Masson's image. Capitalising on these imaginal connexions, I conclude by re-imagining the image of the Baphomet, and in particular Eliphas Levi's famous drawing of the 'Goat of Mendes.' I suggest that the Baphomet is the secret twin of the Acephale, and that it is Levi's aim to make his Baphomet the ultimate hieroglyphic emblem, the supreme condensation of the mysteries of the occult tradition. Thus the Baphomet is the necessary occult complement to the headless monster of Bataille and Masson.

be transformed. This dream was at first principally fomented within two vectors of cultural intervention: the journal *Minotaure* and the political activities of a group of *engagés* known as *Contre-Attaque*.

Minotaure saw its first issue in 1933. The editorial philosophy of *Minotaure* was summed up by the publisher and editor in this way: "Starting from the fact that it is impossible in our era to isolate the plastic arts from poetry and science, the review proposes to associate these three domains." Thus "the plastic arts, poetry, music, architecture, ethnology, mythology, spectacle, psychology, psychiatry and psychoanalysis" were all to be included within its pages in an effort to showcase "the most audacious intellectual activity of the day." In effect this was the reinvention of an experiment that Georges Bataille had began several years before with the publication of *Documents*, a journal that had sought provocation through a violent juxtaposition of ideas and images, the pages exploiting a paratactical arrangement of essays (on gnostic gems, ethnography, jazz, the big toe, and Buster Keaton, for example) and images from contemporary visual artists, photographs of slaughterhouses and pictures of African and Oceanic art. *Documents* appeared the year that *La Révolution surréaliste* ceased publication, Bataille no doubt hoping that it would symbolically represent a final, devastating salvo in Bataille's ongoing critique of Surrealism and of André Breton in particular.

Boiled down in the alembic of retrospection, we can see that what was primarily at stake in this drawn out intellectual contretemps between two heavy hitters was the nature and relevance of images, of representation itself. Breton was committed to the championing of the importance of images from the very first *Manifeste du Surréalisme* of 1924. Conversely, Bataille, by the early 1930s, seemed to be not so sure that images, art and literature had any relevance at all anymore. The rise of Fascism with its emphasis on spectacularity and the illusory fascination of imagery [1] – what we might call today the rhetoric of the image – had led to a crisis of faith in representation itself.

Most of the usual suspects that had been associated with *Documents* had subsequently become associated with *Minotaure*. Soon *Minotaure* was effectively being edited by André Breton and his close friend Pierre Mabille, a surgeon, writer, scholar of alchemy and Haitian voodoo. *Minotaure* was a kind of high-rent 'neutral ground' where dissident Surrealists, existing Surrealists, ex-Dadaists and members of the (soon to be formed) *Collège* – primarily Bataille, Leiris, Patrick Waldberg and Caillois – all contributed. The title of the journal indexed one of the key mythologems around which many of the writers and artists constellated

their ideas in the divining of a new myth. In foreshadowing the lineaments of this future myth, they looked to the past, and the minotaur seething in the heart of its crepuscular labyrinth was one of the key players.

Contre-Attaque was a small group of revolutionary intellectuals who had provisionally banded together to present a double front: to aggressively denounce the ever-expanding threat of fascism, and to agitate for what they regarded as a concomitant radical transformation of society and culture. In April of 1936 Georges Bataille resigned from the group. This break with *Contre-Attaque* is doubly significant in that previous to this severing, Bataille's participation in the group represented a *rapprochement* between himself and André Breton, but it also signaled his violent frustration with the manner in which intellectuals had pursued their aims in the recent past. Bataille's solution to this perceived impasse was to create a secret society formed of like-minded *enragés*, all of whom were seemingly dedicated to following the hoof-prints of the minotaur *au fond du temple sacré*.

Directly following his break with *Contre-Attack*, Bataille traveled to the Spanish coastal town of Tossa de Mar to visit the on again/off again Surrealist artist André Masson, a friend and associate of both Bataille and Breton. It was good timing for a soul in tumult: the Spanish Civil War was just breaking out.

Holed up in Masson's kitchen, listening to a recording of *Don Juan*, Bataille witnessed Masson quickly produce a drawing that would become the escutcheon of Bataille's esoteric cabal and the exoteric journal (*Acéphale*) that would come to espouse his vision of a new, violently sacralised society. André Masson's drawing is the emblem of Bataille's radical break with *Contre-Attaque* and the pretensions of both *Minotaure* and the public face of the *Collège de Sociologie*. It is his 'rite du passage,' his initiation into another world.

The figure of the acephalic "monster" (as Bataille called it) is described by Masson in this manner:

> I saw him immediately as headless...but what to do with this cumbersome and doubting head? – Irresistibly it finds itself displaced in the sex, which it masks with a 'deaths head'... Automatically one hand (the left!) flourishes a dagger, while the other kneads a blazing heart (a heart that does not belong to the Crucified, but to our master Dionysus)... The pectorals starred according to whim...(W)hat to make of the stomach? That empty container will be the receptacle for the Labyrinth that elsewhere had become our rallying sign. This drawing, made on the spot, under the eyes of Georges Bataille, had the good luck to please him. Absolutely. [2]

Absolutely – not provisionally, not temporarily, not just for today, but forever, outside of space and time. I don't believe I am making too much of Masson's concluding statement here. It is inarguable that a great part of Bataille's mission in life was to define an Absolute that was the very inversion of the Absolute as previously, endlessly discussed in the West. Masson's drawing of the acephalic monster is the emblem of this negative Absolute, and of Bataille's quest. In his introductory essay in the first issue of the journal *Acéphale* Bataille is uncompromising in his rejection of the Absolute as conceived of in the past. What he is calling for is an *absolute rupture*:

> It is time to abandon the world of the civilized and its light. It is too late to countenance being reasonable and educated – which only leads to a life without appeal. Secretly or not, it is necessary to become totally Other or cease to be. [3]

The last sentence is perhaps a snide reference to Breton's *Nadja* and its famous concluding line: "La beauté sera convulsive ou ne sera pas," and thus Bataille levels his scimitar squarely at Breton and what Bataille considered Breton's barely sublimated yearning for the light. This light is that of the *intellectus*, the light which streams through the Western philosophical imaginary ever since Plato's philosopher first struggled out of the cave to apprehend the true sun. The light of the sun, the light of the world that had existed up until the appearance of the acephalic monster, is the manifestation in the phenomenal world of the light of the Absolute beyond it: civilization and its light are one. The Acephale signals an end to all that. An end to all the useless light, and an end to all images illuminated by the light.

The Acephale thus becomes a substitute god, a substitute for the Absolute. No more the light of god, no more the light of the image. Masson's emblematic Acephale is therefore the final image, the talisman that will wipe out all other images.

Furthermore the Acephale does not *represent* this totally Other world without light, it *invokes* it. The acephalic monster of Masson and Bataille is a talismanic, incantatory machine. Bataille's introduction in the first issue of the journal *Acéphale* is entitled *La Conjuration Sacrée*. There are several possible translations of this: Sacred Conspiracy, Sacred Confederacy, or Sacred Conjuration. All these meanings are possible and all, I would suggest, are *necessarily* present. It is the last possible meaning, sacred conjuration, that I want to run with here.

> The acephalic man mythologically expresses sovereignity committed to the destruction and death of God, and in this the identification with the headless man merges and melds with the identification with the superhuman, which is entirely 'the death of God.' [4]

I will make no comment on the obvious Nietzschean aspirations here, it is the *identification* that Bataille emphasizes which I want to dilate upon now. Bataille's day job was as an archivist/paleographer/numismatist at the *Bibliothèque nationale de France*, and as such he had access to a large and prestigious collection of rare books and manuscripts. I suggest that among these recondite texts Bataille had discovered a particular text in the collection of Greco-Egyptian magical texts collectively known as the *Papyri Graecae Magicae*.

The *Papyri Graecae Magicae* were collected in the 19th century by an enterprising and avaricious diplomat in Alexandria, shipped to Europe and subsequently sold to various libraries, including the British Museum and the *Bibliothèque nationale de France*. It has been hypothesised that these papyri were originally the collection of one man, a magician, "who was also a scholar, probably philosophically inclined, as well as a bibliophile and archivist concerned about the preservation of the material." [5]

A man, in other words, remarkably similar to Georges Bataille. His well-known interest in Gnosticism may have inclined him to search out similar material, and inevitably he would have come across the magical texts of the Greco-Egyptian magician.

If this seems far-fetched, one only has to remember that in the early 1930s in Paris, many of the foremost intellectuals and artists of the time – at least, those of the particular persuasions and allegiances of which I am writing – were regularly attending [6] the soirees of occultist Maria de Naglowska, the self-styled "satanic woman" and hierarchess of the Order of the Golden Arrow.

André Breton, Man Ray and his friend the American adventurer William Seabrook regularly attended her evenings of occult weirdness, and certainly Bataille would not have been outdone in this. It is quite possible that Naglowska's demonstrations of magical rituals and her ideas on ritual practice were a direct inspiration behind Bataille's formation of his secret society of the Acephale. It is certainly true that Bataille seemed to be emulating Naglowska when he attempted to drag his fellow *Acéphalists* into the depths of the forest...for ritual sacrifice. [7]

Amongst the *Papyri Graecae Magicae* there is one text that stands out from the standard magical spells that provide solutions for petty objectives, the spells for keeping a lover for example, or for getting bugs out of the house. This text is *Papyri Graecae Magicae* V. 96 – 172, named by its English translator as the "Stele of Jeu the Hieroglyphist."

The ritual begins in this way:

> *I summon you, the Headless One, who created earth and heaven, who created night and day, / you, who created light and darkness; you are Oso-ronnophris whom none has ever seen...you have distinguished the just and the unjust; you have made female and male; / you have revealed seeds and fruits; you have made men love each other and hate each other.* [8]

The being that is summoned is explicitly named *Acephalos* (Ἀκέφαλος), the Headless One, in this ritual. [9] What makes this ritual even more unusual, unusual in terms of the entire Greco-Egyptian magical corpus in fact, is that after the standard banishing of demons from the ritual chamber, the magician invokes the "Holy Headless One" *into* himself, thus *becoming* the one who "makes the lightning flash and the thunder roll...the one whose mouth burns completely...the one who begets and destroys." [10]

Masson's emblem of the Acephale holds a flaming heart in its right hand, and the Headless daemon in the *Stele of Jeu the Hieroglyphist* says that its name is a "heart encircled with a serpent, come forth and follow." In his text Sacred Conspiracy/Confederacy/Conjuration Bataille writes:

> ...he holds a steel weapon in his left hand, flames like those of a Sacred Heart in his right. He is not a man. He is not a God either. He is not me but he is more than me: his stomach is the labyrinth in which he has lost himself, loses me with him, and in which I discover myself as him, in other words as a monster. [11]

A magician who has invoked a Headless daemon into himself is of course no longer a man and not a god, but something that is neither one nor the other. He is himself but more than himself. He is, in other words, an Acephalic monster, as Bataille avers in the above passage.

If all this seems circumstantial, I totally agree – yet this hitherto unsuspected connexion is certainly not unlikely, and moreover possesses a high degree of *imaginal logic*, if I may use the term. Allow me to proceed a little further in my interference with Masson and Bataille's Acephale.

I have consistently called this image an "emblem." I have done this in order to point towards a tradition in which I believe the Acephale is the final arrival. This is the tradition of the emblematic books, a tradition that was kick-started when the text of Horapollo's *Hieroglyphica* was purchased by Cosimo d'Medici from a Byzantine monk in 1422. The translation of this text (which was originally written, incidentally, in the same period as the texts of the *Papyri Graecae Magicae*) caused as much an intellectual furor as Ficino's later translations of the *Corpus Hermeticum* and Plato's dialogues. The *Hieroglyphica* purported to explain ancient Egyptian hieroglyphs as emblematic figures containing layers of embedded meanings. The translation of the *Hieroglyphica* set in motion an entire industry that led to the production of hundreds of emblematic books, and possession of these collections was considered *de riguer* by the learned in the 16th and 17th centuries. In the hands of a few dedicated publishers (such as Theodor de Bry, who published books by Robert Fludd and Michael Maier, both notable Hermeticists) the hieroglyphic and graphic tradition of the emblem developed into an efflorescence of Hermetic publishing, which would have a defining influence on alchemy:

> *Allegorical images accompanied by a few cryptic lines of prose or verse, emblems presented to the learned a kind of pictorial riddle containing a solution of a moral nature. But emblems which could easily conceal more than one meaning constituted ideal vehicles for the secret transmission of esoteric information, and as such...were adopted by the alchemists.* [12]

Allegorical representation in the form of *personification* – an ingenious method of encapsulating an abstract idea in the form of a human figure – has probably the longest tradition in the history of Western culture. Emblematic personification was a method in which a host of interconnected, often difficult ideas were subsumed into the one, easily comprehensible image. Examples that are still with us today would include the personification of Justice as a blindfolded woman carrying a sword and a set of scales, and the medieval figure of Fortuna, a woman turning a giant wheel, the symbolism of which perhaps only survives through a certain television game show.

Considering that hermetic emblems were "allegorical images accompanied by a few cryptic lines of prose or verse," the cover of the first issue of *Acéphale* is a perfect example of such an emblem – an hieratic figure beneath which we can see a few cryptic lines: *The Sacred Confederacy*, or *Nietzsche Against the Fascists*. Indeed, I would insist that the form and function of this cover serves the very same purpose as the emblem in the hermetic and alchemical books, images the purpose of which is to accomplish much more than mere representation.

Masson and Bataille's figure of the Acéphale is also an emblem with a special purpose: it is a magical machine that begins the apocalyptic annihilation of images altogether.

As exactly the same figure was reproduced on the cover of the journal *Acéphale* in each successive issue (there were only three issues), and as only a single line of text on the cover changed with each successive issue (*The Sacred Confederacy*, or *Nietzsche Against the Fascists*, for example) – thus serving the function of an allegorical figure with a "few cryptic lines of prose" – one can say that this emblem was envisioned as belonging to that unchanging Other world of the sacral, standing outside of the pornography of images with which we are daily bombarded, and thus serving as the herald of the sacred darkness that would subsume all representations. A more recent agent provocateur, Jean Baudrillard, in describing a similar vision of violent iconoclasm, notes:

> Obscenity begins when there is no more spectacle, no more stage, no more theatre, no more illusion, when everything becomes immediately transparent, visible, exposed in the raw and inexorable light of information and communication. We no longer partake of the drama of alienation, but are in the ecstasy of communication. And this ecstasy is obscene. [13]

If one additionally recalls Fredric Jameson's despair at the "pornography" of images which miscegenate around us at an astounding daily rate, then the figure of the *Acéphale* must be regarded as a daemonic buzzbomb sent to devastate the endless plain of representation.

THE BAPHOMET RESTORED

> *One kinde of Locust…stands…in a large erectnesse… by Zoographers called mantis.*
> – Sir T. Browne, *Pseudodoxia Epidemica*, 1646.

These thoughts about Bataille and Masson's hieratic emblem can take a further speculative *détournement*. Following the momentum of my reasoning,[14] it should be acknowledged that the headless monster of Bataille and Masson no doubt finds at least some of its provenance in the writings and ideas of Bataille's colleague, Roger Caillois.

As is well known, Caillois' essay *Mimicry and Legendary Psychasthenia*, originally published in *Minotaur* in 1935, has had a surprising influence on 20th century thought, not the least being that it was partly responsible for Jacques Lacan's development of the idea of the 'mirror stage.' This more famous essay was a development of an earlier essay devoted to a discussion of the praying mantis as the supreme representative of what Caillois called 'objective ideograms,' published the year before. For Caillois, the predatory sexual activities of the mantis were evidence of the 'over-determination' of the universe: that interconnected causal chains of affective influence stretched from even the mineral and insectoid worlds into the psyche of humankind.

> [I]t is utterly unthinkable that causal series could be totally distinct. This also contradicts experience,

which constantly demonstrate their numerous intersections and sometimes supplies overwhelming, crushing expressions of their unfathomable solidarity. Although their meaning is hidden and ambiguous, such expressions never fail to reach their destination. In short, these are objective ideograms, which concretely realize the lyrical and passional virtualities of the mind in the outside world. [15]

The phrase "passional virtualities" is a clue as to the origin of Caillois' strange meditation on the interconnectedness of all things, and of the anthropomorphic resonances produced through the study of the mantis. Caillois had recently read Toussenel's *L'Esprit des bêtes, zoologie passionelle*, first published in 1853. Toussenel was a follower of Charles Fourier, the utopian socialist who proposed ingenious ways to reform industrial society based on 'attractive labour' – that is, industry based on the erotic predilections of individual workers. Clearly, this work on 'passional zoology' was not your average 19th century biological textbook.

Influenced by Toussenel's ideas, Caillois sought to demonstrate the "existence of a certain kind of lyrical objectivity," a continuity of affect, which could be para-scientifically illustrated by, and condensed into, a single figure – in this case, the praying mantis in its various forms.

Caillois' attempts to demonstrate the "systematic over-determination of the universe" and his exhaustive description of the mantis, the objective ideogramme of the "continuity between nature and the mind," would without doubt have been a latent presence in the minds of both Bataille and Masson. I suggest that the defining attribute of the *Acéphale* group's emblem, namely, that it is headless, is an effect produced by Caillois' essay – one might even say an *over-determination* produced by Caillois' mantis. The sexual cannibalism of the female mantis is discussed at length by Caillois. The fact that the female mantis chews the head off the male while engaged in coitus is something that, as Caillois avers, one can never really forget.

It is obviously impossible to 'prove' that the idea of mantic decaptitation was in part responsible for the production of Masson's emblem, but if one provisionally entertains Caillois' proposal of the continuity between nature and psyche, and of the consequent complexification of casual chains, then I do not consider this an untenable proposition. It has, at the very least, an *imaginal logic*, as I have suggested earlier. For my purposes this imaginal logic can be pursued further with one more step.

In his essay Caillois mentions various folk names for the mantis such as "Pray-to-God" and "Pray-to-the-Devil." At one point he mentions that the predatory sexuality of the mantis could be "correlated with the medieval concepts of the *incubi* and *succubi*." [16] In a further note he suggests that the mantis ideogram can be observed operating in Bodin's *De la Demonomanie des sorciers* of 1580 and "other demonographers of the period." Yet oddly enough, despite Caillois' synoptic studies of the mantis both entomological and etymological, he neglects to mention probably the most interesting etymological curiosity associated with the insect.

The word 'mantis' comes from an ancient Greek word that has the meaning of 'seer' or 'prophet, diviner' (μαντικός). It's Proto-Indo-European root form is the origin of our *mania*, a person inspired by a 'divine frenzy,' one who is ὑπὸ τοῦ θεοῦ μαίνεται, "possessed by a god," as Herodotus says in his *Histories* (Book 4, 79). Caillois could easily have made this observation when he mentions Bodin's *Demonomanie*, as the 'demonomania' in the title clearly shows this ancient connexion. Yet he does not, so this is where I come in.

I have noted the idea of demonological possession in relation to Bataille's conception of the *Acéphale* and the ancient magical text, the *Stele of Jeu the Hieroglyphist* earlier in this essay. Capitalising on the etymological/imaginal connexions between the mantis and demonomania, I will now invoke my final image.

In 1307 King Philip the Fair ordered that his once-trusted Crusaders, the Knights Templar, all be arrested and interrogated about their activities in the Holy Land and elsewhere. The Templars were tortured, tried and condemned, and many of their number summarily executed. Following the trials, Philip arrogated the considerable wealth of the Templars to his own fortunes. Considering that the confessions of the knights were all extracted under torture, Philip's epithet must now be regarded as perversely ironic (of course, the epithet 'fair' [*le beau*] was in reference to his appearance, not his character. Yet it is still true that even in his own time, he was regarded as a particularly *unfair* monarch.)

Among the list of wrong doings of which the Knights Templar were accused was the charge of idolatry. Specifically they were charged with worshiping an idol in the form of a decapitated head. This bearded head was called *Baphomet*, and it was supposedly kept secreted somewhere within the Knights' temple in Paris. There has been considerable debate as to the nature of this head. Was it a sculptured head? A mummified head? Or perhaps it was a reliquary containing a human skull, like that of the hand of St. John the Baptist that now resides in the *Topkapı Sarayı* in Istanbul?

And what did the name *Baphomet* mean? It has been assumed that this was a corruption of *Mahomet* (Mohammed), but no one is really sure. What is certain is that these infamous trials of the Templars, and this mysterious head, the Baphomet, inspired two outré cultural activities both of which have inspired this last section of my essay. The first is that the often contradictory descriptions of the Baphomet led to the creation of a special kind of gargoyle in France, also called Baphomet: a bearded, horned, winged androgynous demon, which can even now be found on the portals of several cathedrals in France. In Italy a figure called *bafometto* can be found in a grotto in Padua, the *Grotta dei Cavalieri Templari*. [17]

The second outré activity that was inspired by the Templars and their Baphomet was the creation, many centuries later, of esoteric societies that imagined themselves as heirs to the mysteries and secret rites of the Templars.

These two eccentric streams are the background to the production of probably the best known reimagining of the image of the Baphomet: Eliphas Levi's (Alphonse Louis Constant) drawing of the 'Goat of Mendes' in his *Dogma et Rituel de la Haute Magie*, published in 1854. Possessing the attributes of the baphometic gargoyles, and symbolising the secrets and rites of the European occult tradition, Levi's description and defense of this figure aims to rescue it from associations with the demonic and, indeed, the satanic.

Levi states that the Baphomet, "a chimera, a malformed sphinx, a synthesis of deformities" symbolises the 'astral fire,' the 'Great Magical Agent,' the 'odic force' and the "devil of M. Eudes de Mirville," this latter a reference to the now forgotten author of *Pneumatologie: Des esprits et de leurs manifestations fluidiques,* published a few years before Levi's magnum opus. Levi asserts that "the frontispiece to this *Ritual* reproduces the exact figure of the terrible emperor of night, with all his attributes and all his characters," this benighted emperor being none other than the "Baphomet of the Templars, the bearded idol of the alchemist, the obscene deity of Mendes, the goat of the Sabbath." He furthermore announces, "let us state boldly and precisely that all inferior initiates of the occult science and profaners of the Great Arcanum, not only did in the past but do now, and will ever, adore what is signified by this alarming symbol."

The Grand Masters of the Order of the Templars worshipped the Baphomet, and caused it to be worshipped by their initiates; yes, there existed in the past and there may be still in the present, assemblies which are presided over by this figure.. for them it is that of the god Pan, the god of our modern schools of philosophy, the god of the Alexandrian theurgic school and of our own mystical Neo-platonists..the god of Spinoza and Plato, the god of the primitive Gnostic schools; the Christ also of the dissident priesthood. [18]

Clearly it is Levi's aim to make of his Baphomet the *ultimate* hieroglyphic emblem, the supreme condensation of all the great mysteries of the occult tradition. The gesture of Levi's Baphomet, one arm pointing aloft, the other to the earth, is (evidently) the "the sign of occultism." Levi says that one of the arms is feminine and the other masculine to represent the mystical androgyne, and that these attributes have been "combined with those of our goat, since they are one and the same symbol." Here we have the *coincidentia oppositorum*, the resolution of antimonies, beloved of mystics and occultists alike.

Levi's attempt to make of the Baphomet the ultimate emblem of all occult secrets, rather than a decapitated head that was an object of worship by the Templars, has received support from a contemporary scholar of Templar lore, Bernard Marillier, in his *Essai sur la Symbolique Templière*. [19] Marillier asserts that the Baphomet was a symbol of the "rite of the severed head," which is the "source of all the myths that relate to the primordial Tradition." [20]

Marillier adumbrates a list of related stories from world mythology that serve to support his theory: the head of the Medusa severed by Perseus, the heads which the Celts took from their slain enemies, various incidents of decapitation in the Grail cycle of stories, etc. All these point, he says, to a 'mythico-initiatic' tradition to which the Knights Templar were heirs.

The rite of decapitation is linked to a double initiation: by cutting off the head of an enemy – the initiate as conqueror – the neophyte receives both the mana *contained in the head and spiritual power, and abandons his envelope of flesh for the Spirit.* [21]

According to Marillier the Baphomet was not an idol at all, rather it was the hieratic emblem of "an initiation rite of the heroic-solar type":

For the rite of symbolic decapitation, the Templars.. captured the spirit and spiritual power, aligned themselves with the divine, and prepared to defeat both their visible and invisible enemies, the most formidable of which reside in the very depths of their being. [22]

Furthermore,

The neophyte, by reciting formulas and participating in dramatized scenes, identifies with the deity, *allowing him to make his spiritual rebirth in intimate communion with the divine.* (My italics.) [23]

In Marillier's interpretation of the Baphomet, the 'divine frenzy' – the mantic sublimation – is the summit of the 'mythico-initiatic' tradition which the Templars had brought from the East, and of which the Baphomet was the mysterious, ultimate emblem. Regarded in this manner, the Baphomet appears as the secret twin of, and the necessary occult complement to, the headless monster of Bataille and Masson.

ESSAY

The foregoing considerations of an emblematic head and a headless emblem, of esoteric traditions and an occult synthesis of deformities, leads me inevitably to contemplate the creation of a new hieroglyph, to produce, in effect, the alchemical resolution of this strange iconography – *solve et coagula*, as Levi's idol impels. I propose therefore a synthesis of the obscurities presented by an analysis of these figures, to unite the *Acéphale* and the Baphomet in a form of *chymical marriage*: the Baphomet Restored.

I offer, then, my own hieratic emblem, my own 'synthesis of deformities': Levi's 'Goat of Mendes' seated upon a half sphere. Its left hand is now transformed into the hooked arm of the praying mantis, and points to a black moon below. Its right arm is similarly transformed into the supplicative gesture of the insect, and points to a silver moon surrounded by dark clouds above. The black wings behind the creature are now clearly the appendages of a monstrous insect, its chitinous wing covers clearly visible behind the luminous wings themselves. Its body is still androgynous: a phallus in the form of the mercurial caduceus, a woman's breasts high on its chest. But its head! Now it is far more frightening: we see the glaring, inquisitive, multi-faceted eyes of the praying mantis; quivering antennae in place of goat horns, chattering mandibles instead of a goat's snout.

The torch of illumination still burns between its antennae, and the emblem is now transfigured into its final form. ∎

REFERENCES AND NOTES

1. By which I mean a sorcerous *fascinans* – to be entranced and captured by an illusory appearance.
2. Robert Lebel and Isabelle Waldberg, eds., *Encyclopeadia Acephalica* (London: Atlas Press, 1995), 12.
3. My translation of: *Il est temps d'abandonner le monde des civilisés et sa lumière. Il est trop tard pour tenir à être raisonnable et instruit – ce qui a mené à une vie sans attrait. Secrètement ou non, il est nécessaire de devenir tout autres ou de cesser d'être.*
4. Georges Bataille, in *Encyclopeadia Acephalica*, 14.
5. Hans Dieter Betz, ed., *The Greek Magical Papyri in Translation* (Chicago: University of Chicago Press, 1996), xlii.
6. See the *Introduction* to Maria de Naglowska, *The Light of Sex: Initiation, Magic and Sacrament*, trans. Donald Traxler (Rochester, VT: Inner Traditions International, 2011).
7. Refer to Robert Lebel and Isabelle Waldberg, eds., *Encyclopeadia Acephalica*, 14-15.
8. Hans Dieter Betz, ed., *The Greek Magical Papyri in Translation*, 103.
9. McGregor Mathers, hierophant of the late 19th century Hermetic Order of the Golden Dawn, translated the daemon of this text – inexplicably – as the 'bornless' one, a reference found in the title of this essay.
10. Hans Dieter Betz, ed., *The Greek Magical Papyri in Translation*, 103.

11. Georges Bataille in *Encyclopeadia Acephalica*, 14.
12. Stanislas Klossowski de Rola, *The Golden Game, Alchemical Engravings of the Seventeenth Century* (London: Thames and Hudson, 1988), 13.
13. Jean Baudrillard, *The Ecstasy of Communication* (Los Angeles: Semiotext(e), 1988), 22.
14. The phrase is Caillois'. I have stolen it for reasons that I hope will soon become clear.
15. Roger Caillois, "The Praying Mantis," in *The Edge of Surrealism: A Roger Caillois Reader* (Durham & London: Duke University Press, 2003), 80.
16. Ibid., 75.
17. In point of fact the transcripts of the confessions of the Templars do not confirm that they referred to their mysterious idol by the name of Baphomet, rather one of the Templars, Gaucerant de Montpezat, refers to a 'tête baphométique' (a baphometic head), the meaning of which adjective has eluded scholars ever since.
18. Eliphas Levi, *Transcendental Magic*, trans. A. E. Waite (London: Rider & Company, 1968), 307.
19. Bernard Marillier, *Essai sur la Symbolique Templière* (Editions Prades, n.d.). excerpts accessed at http://www.templiers.net/symbolique/index.php?page=le-baphomet-bernard-marillier (accessed August 21, 2013).
20. The 'Tradition' in this case being the 'perennial tradition' espoused by such 20th century esotericists as René Guénon, Frithjof Schuon and Seyyed Hossein Nasr for example.
21. Bernard Marillier, *Essai sur la Symbolique Templière*. "Le rite de la décollation est lié à une double initiation : en sectionnant le chef d'un ennemi – initiateur, le vainqueur – néophyte captait à la fois le mana contenu dans la tête et sa puissance spirituelle, et abandonnait son enveloppe de chair à l'Esprit."
22. Ibid. "Par le rite de la décapitation symbolique, les Templiers…captaient l'esprit et la puissance spirituelle, se mettaient en phase avec le divin, et se préparaient à vaincre à la fois leurs ennemis visibles et invisibles, ceux qui gîtent au tréfonds de l'être, les plus redoutables."
23. Ibid. "Le néophyte, par la récitation de formules et le jeu de scènes dramatisées, s'identifiait à la divinité, lui permettant d'opérer sa renaissance spirituelle en intime communion avec le divin."

IMAGES (R)-EVOLUTION

Media Arts Complex Imagery Challenging Humanities and Our Institutions of Cultural Memory

by

Oliver Grau

oliver.grau@donau-uni.ac.at

1. LOSING CONTEMPORARY ART

Compared to traditional art forms – such as painting or sculpture – Media Art has a multifarious potential of expression and visualization; although underrepresented on the art market which is driven by economic interests, it therefore became "the art of our time"; thematizing complex challenges for our life and societies, like genetic engineering [1] and the rise of post-human bodies, [2] like ecological crises, [3] like the image and media [4] revolution and with it the explosion of human knowledge, [5] the rapid growing mega-cities, the change towards virtual financial economies [6] and the processes of globalization [7] and surveillance to name just a few. Visually powerful, interactive media art, often supported by databases or the world wide web, is offering more and more degrees of freedom in creative expression and evidently is much better equipped to directly address the challenges of our complex times within the very medium that shapes them. Although it has been around for decades and even quantitatively dominated many art schools, digital media art has not fully arrived in the core collecting institutions of our societies. Due to the lack of institutional support and rapid changes in storage and presentation media, works that origi-

Considering its technological and thematical contexts, digital art conveys different – even more complex – potentials of expression than traditional art forms (such as sculptures, paintings, etc.), what makes digital art a paradigmatic expression of its time? This article emphasizes the variety of (complex) topics that are expressed within digital art, ranging from globalization, ecological and economic crises (virtual economy), media and image revolution to questions of the body and its societal norms. Due to the imminent problems of archiving, the digital arts are threatened by its loss – a problem that is reinforced by the insufficient practices of cultural institutions to display, collect and research digital art. Post-industrial societies require digital arts based on contemporary media dispositive to reflect upon current and future challenges, just like art history was always informed by its contemporary media technologies. By establishing concerted international strategies and new scientific tools it is the aim of this essay to provide a framework to enable media art histories and image science as well as the digital humanities to engage more fully with current digital developments in order to enable the humanities to meet with its (current) responsibilities. By discussing examples from a variety of projects from the natural sciences and the humanities, this article tries to demonstrate the strategic importance of these collective projects, especially in their growing importance for the humanities.

nated approximately ten years ago can often not be shown anymore. It is no exaggeration to state that we are facing the 'total loss of an art form' created in the early times of our post-industrial digital societies.

Over the last fifty years digital media art has evolved into a vivid contemporary factor. Although there are well attended festivals worldwide, [8] funded collaborative projects, discussion forums, publications [9] and database documentation projects, [10] digital media art is still rarely collected by museums, barely supported within the mainframe of art history and with relatively low accessibility for public and scholars.

It is ironic that this loss takes place in a time, when the world of images around us changes faster than ever before. Images are advancing into new domains: new private platforms like YouTube, Flickr with its billion uploads or Facebook that has now over 1 billion members and is now the largest image archive in the world. Television became a zappy field of thousands of channels, now also in 3D, and 3D experiences a renaissance in cinema as well. Large projection screens are invading our cities, buildings' surfaces meld ever more often with moving images, so that the old dream of talking architecture gets a new arsenal of options. [11] Cell phones transmit movies in real time, VJing represents an entirely new amalgamation of music and moving images [12] and *Google StreetView* and *Google Earth* step up the concepts of panoramic image spaces including satellite views, for example of our Center for Image Science in Göttweig.

The historical development of the image between innovation, reflection and iconoclasm reaches a new level of global complexity in the 21st century. Digital images have become ubiquitous and key tools within the global reorganization of work, but these transformations have hit a society that is to a large extent unprepared. [13] All of these visualizations and virtualizations require an unknown and undisclosed amount of material. Google, for example, runs more than one million Servers in a dozen countries, even on the ocean, and processes twenty-four PetaBytes of user generated data per day while the four to six million people, who died in the race for so called "conflict minerals," [14] did not even receive a monument for the unknown victim.

2. MEDIA ARTS MULTIFARIOUS POTENTIAL OF EXPRESSION

Gerhard Dirmoser has created a diagram to give an overview of the tremendous development that media art went through during thirty years of Ars Electronica. Hundreds of names of artists, of artworks, art trends, theories of media art in keywords, are presented in an enormous circle. Thirty-two slices are offered as a subdivision into themes, like representation, emotion and synesthesia, atmosphere, games, art as spatial experience; here we find glimpses of a history of media art. [15]

Thousands of artworks make use of and express the multifarious potential of media art. In the installations *Osmose* (1995) and *Éphémère* (1998) Charlotte Davies transports us into a visually powerful 3D-simulation of a lush mineral-vegetable sphere, which we can explored via a bodily interface consisting of a vest that monitors breathing; both works are classics of digital media art that generated more than one hundred scientific and art-historical articles but were ignored by museum collections. [16]

Open-ended questions about the complicated ethical issues involved in the manipulation of DNA are raised by Eduardo KAc's installation *Genesis*. [17]

With UNMAKEABLELOVE Jeffrey Shaw and Sarah Kenderdine created in their cybernetic theatre *Re-Actor* a real time augmented world of thirty humans inspired by Samuel Beckett's *The Lost Ones*. In a dark space or even a prison camp formed by a hexagon of six rear-projected silver screens, the artwork functions in the most powerful reappearance and aesthetic interpretation of the phantasmagoria. [18] For years also William Kentridge, one of the most well-known artists of our time, has been working on the subject of a history of vision. Even historic image media, like the mirror anamorphosis, made its way into his contemporary media art. In 2007 he created a hybrid that had not existed before in the media history of seeing. He used

ESSAY

his eight min. short *What Will Come (Has Already Come)* and linked a hand-drawn animation film with the anamorphosis, which appears connected now for the first time with moving images. He is one of the artists helping us to put the latest image revolution into a historical perspective.

Victoria Vesna's *Bodies@ Incorporated* allows visitors to construct their own avatars. Using a variety of Web tools, the users can make a 3D representation of their body. References are made throughout the site to identity politics and other concepts used to separate and identify bodies. [19] Also largely ignored by museums was golden Nica awarded *Murmuring Fields* by Fleischmann & Strauss. The interacting users maneuver through a virtual space of media philosophy, where they can hear statements by Flusser, Virilio, Minsky, and Weizenbaum. *Murmuring Fields* is a new type of a Denkraum – a sphere of thought, [20] – and an early prefiguration of web-based knowledge exchange.

Today we know that the virtualization and increasing complexity of financial products is partly responsible for the global financial crisis that cost us trillions of Euros and Dollars. But already more than a decade ago, the studio Asymptote proposed a 3D info-scape for the NYSE to manage financial data within a real-time virtual environment, providing a better, more transparent image and thereby a better idea of transactions – before we get driven into the next mega-crash. [21] The NYSE, however, did not want further development of a visualization of their "financial products" – and since the Lehman Brothers' bankruptcy in 2008 we know why.

Ingo Günthers' obsessive cartographic work *Worldprocessor* – an artwork that implicitly conveys the explosion, ubiquity as well as the availability of data by the introduction and consolidation of digital media On illuminated globes – appears as a clairvoyant prefiguration of the attempts of the growing visualization industries to make our complex time understood. Since the late 1980s until now, Günthers destroyed in his making process more than ten thousand globes, following the attempt to create a more realistic image of economy, power, and all kinds of meaningful parameters. [22]

Since Edward Snowden's release of documents we know that Facebook also is systematically used for NSA Surveillance, but many artists, like Seiko Mikami in her robotic installation *Desire of Codes*, 2011, dealt with this big issue of our time already before the worldwide espionage became known. Paolo Cirio's and Alessandro Ludivico's *Face to Facebook* was a media hack performance through a social experiment: stealing one million Facebook profiles, filtering them with face-recognition software and then posting them on a custom-made dating website, sorted by their facial expression characteristics. Cirio's and Ludovicos' mission was to give all these virtual identities a new shared place to expose themselves freely, breaking Facebook's constraints and social rules. [23] During the performance the artists counted one thousand media coverage around the world, eleven lawsuit threats, five death threats and three letters from the lawyer of Facebook. In Johanna and Florian Dombois' work *Fidelio, 21st Century*, named after Beethoven's *Fidelio*, for the first time a classical opera was directed as an interactive virtual 3D experience. Protagonists embody music, follow the dramaturgic direction and react to the interventions of the visitors. [24]

All these examples demonstrate that media art can deal with the questions and challenges of our time in ways that traditional art media simply can't. In the best humanistic traditions, digital media art takes on the big contemporary questions, dangers and proposed transformations but is not adequately collected, documented and preserved by our public museums. A techno-cultural society that does not understand its challenges, which is not equally open for the art of its time, is in trouble.

We know that media artists today are shaping highly disparate areas, such as time based installation art, telepresence art, genetic and bio art, robotics, Net Art, and space art; experimenting with nanotechnology, artificial or A-life art; creating virtual agents and avatars, mixed realities, and database-supported art. As we know, the relation / guarantee 'artist-original,' which was still apparent in the age of craftsmanship, became in the post-industrial era fairly complicated through mechanization and multiplication. Today, software of digital artwork often exists in a multiplied state by definition. What intensifies this process of multiplication are the complicated iterations developed through the interactive interventions of the users in the framework of a piece enabled by the varied degrees of freedom offered by the author/artist; the artwork becomes a multiplication of the multiplied expressions of the artwork itself.

The more open the construction of the artwork's system, the more the creative dimension of the work moves towards the normally passive beholder, who is transformed into a player and can select from a multitude of information and aesthetic expressions. He/she can recombine, reinforce or weaken, can interpret, and in part can even create. On the other side, the previously perhaps critically distanced relationship towards the object – the precondition of the aesthetic experience and scientific insight in general, as described by Cassirer, [25] Adorno [26] or Serres [27] – changes now towards a field of participative aesthetic experience.

3. INTEGRATING MEDIA ART INTO ITS MEDIA & IMAGE HISTORIES

It is essential to create an understanding of the fact that the present image revolution, which uses new technologies and has also developed a large number of so far unknown visual expressions, cannot be conceptualized without our image history. [28] Art history and media studies help understand the function of today's image worlds in their importance for building and forming societies. By telling the history of illusion and immersion, the history of artificial life or the tradition of telepresence, art history offers sub-histories of the present image revolution. Art history might be considered a reservoir in which contemporary processes are embedded, an anthropologic narration, on the one hand, and the political battleground where the clash of images is analyzed, on the other. [29] Furthermore, art-historical methods may strengthen our political-aesthetic analysis of the present through image analyses. Last but not least, the development and significance of new media should be illuminated, since the first utopian expressions of a new medium often take place in artworks.

Older definitions, by Gottfried Böhm, Klaus Sachs-Hombach, or W. J. T. Mitchell, of what an image is became problematical in the context of the digital age. I shall therefore begin by quoting a carefully crafted definition by Thomas Hensel:

> *IMAGES are not reducible to a particular technology (like graphic prints or neutron autoradiography), not to certain devices or tools (paint brushes or telescope), not to symbolic forms (perspective), not to genres in the broadest sense (still life or summation image), not to an institution (museum or lab), not to a social function (construction or diagnostics), not to practices/media (painting or Morse Code), materials (canvas or photographic paper) or certain symbolism (Christian iconography or alphanumeric code) – but they are virulent in all of them.* [30]

ESSAY

In the current social media based image world it has become even more difficult to provide a definition. Images today, along with the cultures from whence they originated, are on the move; myriads of images flow with extreme mobility in fractions of a second around the globe as messages of transnational and transcultural communication. Images from formerly separate contexts are occupied, interpreted, amalgamated, and given new meanings. What we are seeing at the moment is a shift in our image cultures, which are connected to international media, in the direction of a single image culture that increasingly operates transculturally. Formerly passive recipients – who reflected on discrete works of art in a distanced yet intellectually active manner – have now become interactive users with considerable degrees of freedom. What is more, they have become active mediators and facilitators of image worlds as well as producers of the same in that they increasingly collect, modify, distribute and position images selectively and strategically. New visual information arises not least through dialogue in which one or more networks are involved.

The *mise en scène* of the images, singly or in clusters, their metamorphoses and their dissemination, are significantly determined by the users of social networks. Vibrant sub-cultures develop with a speed of image turnover that was hitherto unimaginable. Often something completely new arises – from the contradictions, tensions, and differences – which is manifested visually. This process is nothing new for theories of interculturalism: the fruitful fusion of Roman and Greek culture, for example, or of Christian and Islamic culture in medieval Spain, demonstrated this process over long periods of time.

In addition to global icons, seemingly banal but actually highly complex, there are also myriads of image-clouds arranged in clusters, which overlay the globe like a second visual sphere. This is where different ways of seeing the world encounter each other and are negotiated actively; this is where the rudiments of a new culture form. Nevertheless, if one wants to understand an image then the image, at least in part, has to be considered in context. Contexts are becoming more and more complicated due to the many different visual media: also there is now apparently no limit to the acceleration of visual exchange processes, which, because of their multifaceted branching and connections, cannot be captured or analyzed by the instruments employed by the humanities in the nineteenth and twentieth centuries.

If ever the theory of a homogeneous or pure culture, elevated ideologically and repeatedly misused, had any validity, this idea is now virtually obsolete. On the other hand, a theory of culture that is playful and favors egalitarian exchange may be desirable, but it is rather naïve when one considers the power of commercial international players to create global icons, the inroads of political control over the networks, language barriers, inadequate knowledge about digital cultural techniques, and the power of certain media concerns that are coming together to form economic cartels.

Building bridges for media art means also to further the establishment of new curricula, and we developed the first international Master of Arts in MediaArtHistories for working professionals (with faculty members like Erkki Huhtamo, Lev Manovich, Christiane Paul and Sean Cubitt) which deals also with the practice and expertise in curation, collecting, preserving and archiving of media arts. Students come from five continents and there is a Facebook forum with more than four thousand members. [31]

Already in the 1990s it became clear, that media art research was spread over many disciplines and the need became urgent to give it some common ground.

Subsequently we organized the Media Art Histories Conference over the last ten years coordinating more than two thousand papers and applications on MediaArtHistory.org. [32] Held at Banff's New Media Centre in cooperation with *Leonardo*, *Refresh* represented a wide array of nineteen disciplines involved in the rapidly emerging field of media art histories [33] and through the success of *re:place* 2007 in Berlin's House of World Cultures, Melbourne 2009 and Liverpool 2011, the conference series was established. Riga 2013 was the last step. [34] The field of media art histories examines the subhistories and implications of present day image revolution in media art: paradigms like artificial life/automata [35] or telepresence, [36] the history of panoramic perception and its knowledge with the related history of immersion [37] or the history of phantasmagoric imagery, [38] an historical continuum of the image machines developed after the French revolution, which are reflected in the aesthetic approaches of contemporary artists like Zoe Beloff, Jeffrey Shaw, Rosângela Rennó, Gary Hill or Tony Oursler.

Our Archive of Digital Art counts many media artworks, which are, for example, part of the history of immersion, a recently recognized phenomenon that can be traced through almost the entire history of art. History has shown that there is cross-fertilization between large-scale spaces of illusion which fully integrate the human body (360°frescoes, the panorama, Stereopticon, Cinerama, IMAX cinemas, and CAVEs) and small-scale images positioned immediately in front of the eyes (peepshows of the seventeenth century, stereoscopes, stereoscopic television, Sensorama, or HMDs). [39] The media art landscape of recent years is even increasingly being seized by a phenomenon, which has yet to receive significant research, the use of historic media configurations. Renowned artists like Douglas Gordon, William Kentridge, Olafur Eliasson, Mischa Kuball, Maurice Benayoun, Rafael Lozano-Hammer and others create optical experiments, panoramas, phantasmagoria, perspective theaters, dioramas, camerae obscurae, anamorphoses, magic lanterns, etc. And this sounds like redefining images in their historical dimension, as we know approaches of comparison are based on the insight that images act diachronic, within a historical evolution and not function simply without any reference. [40] Reinterpreting old optical media these artists contextualize and help to reflect on our digital image revolution. [41]

4. NEW SCIENTIFIC TOOLS FOR OUR FIELD

Thinking about new tools for media art history in the twenty-first century we remember Warburg's Mnemosyne Atlas tracking image citations of individual poses and forms across media. We might even say that he redefined art history, as medial bridge-building, arguing that art history could fulfill its responsibility only by including most forms of images. Let us remember too, that film studies was started by art historians: the enormous Film Library at New York's MoMA was founded on an initiative by Barr and Panofsky, nicknamed the "Vatican of Film." [42] The same spirit for new infrastructures and networks for media art of the last decades is needed today. Although taking a different approach, the history of image databases should also mention André Malreaux with his *museé imaginare*. [43] And now we are witnessing the birth of the virtual museum, a key project for the digital humanities.

Looking for a moment beyond the humanities, in the natural sciences during the last decade, large collective projects have addressed new research goals. In astronomy, the *Virtual Observatory* compiles several centuries of celestial observations; [44] global warming is understood through projects like the *Millenium Ecosystem Assessment*, [45] at a detail never before calculable, and the *Human Genome Project* [46] has become legendary.

ESSAY

Comparable to natural sciences, digital media and networked research catapult the humanities within reach of new and essential research in the documentation and preservation of media art, or as a realistic utopia where an entire history of visual media and their human reception might be amalgamated as collections of sources.

In 1999 at Humboldt University the first online media art documentation was originated, known as the Database of Virtual Art (Archive of Digital Art, ADA). [47] This pioneering database documents renowned media artists, researchers and institutions over the last decades of digital installation art, as a collective open source project. Since today's digital artworks are processal, ephemeral, interactive, multimedial, and fundamentally context dependent they require modification, which we call an "expanded concept of documentation." [48] As probably the most complex media art resource available online with several thousand documents and related technical data, the database is a platform for information and communication. The ADA, which is the only university-based archive, represents a selection of five hundred of approximately five thousand evaluated artists. The policy determining whether an artist is qualified to become a member includes two criteria: "the number of exhibitions, publications – at least five; high importance we ascribe also to artistic inventions like innovative interfaces, displays or software." Artists can be nominated by the members of the board. [49]

Media art documentation becomes a resource that facilitates research on the artists and their work for students and academics, who, it is hoped – now in a new Facebook-like communication structure – will contribute to expanding and updating the information. [50] In this way, documentation changes from a one-way archiving of key data, to a proactive process of knowledge transfer.

Together with an important graphic print collection, the Göttweig Monastery Collection – representing thirty thousand prints emphasizing Renaissance and Baroque works and a library of one hundred and fifty thousand volumes going back to the ninth century, such as the Sankt Gallen Codex – ADA strives to achieve the goal of a deeper media art historical cross pollination. Reaching to the present day, the print collection has grown to be the largest private collection of historical graphic art in Austria. [51] Just as the Media Art Histories conference series bridges a gap, the combination of the two and other databases hopes to enable further historic references and impulses. The collection also contains proofs of the history of optical image media, intercultural concepts, caricatures, landscapes in panoramic illustrations. [52] For the future this may provide resources for a broader analysis of media art.

The Göttweig collection is being made public through three strategies: [53]

The "Scientific Facsimile"; high resolution allows researchers the chance to find details in digital prints, which are difficult to discover in the "original" prints.

The concept of Virtual Exhibitions (now adopted by main museums) offers the public online exhibitions since 2006 like "Venetian Views," or "Theory of Architecture." Virtual exhibitions are divided into sub themes and enriched with different picture formats, literature and meta data.

Fortunately, we have the unique situation to have the media art archive next to a historic art collection. The Collection will be further networked with archives of contemporary media art via keywording.

Keywording can be a bridge building tool. The hierarchical thesaurus of ADA constitutes an approach to systemize the field of digital art. In *Out of the Getty Arts & Architecture Thesaurus* and the subject catalogue of the Warburg Library in London, keywords were selected which have relevance also in media art. On the other side, out of the most commonly used terms from media festivals like *Ars Electronica* or *Transmediale*, new keywords were empirically selected. Important innovations such as "interface" or "genetic art" have been considered as well as keywords, that play a role in traditional arts such as "body", "landscape" or "Illusion" and thus have a bridge-building function. It was important to limit the number to approximately three hundred and fifty words so that members of the database could keyword their works without an overly complex index. The categories led to natural overlapping, so that the hybrid artworks could be captured through clustering.

5. FOR INTERNATIONAL AND SUSTAINABLE MEDIA ART RESEARCH

Let me finish with remarks on the challenging and serious situation of media art research today. With ADA involved in the field of tool development, from its inception, we have witnessed the crisis of documentation during the last years. Since the foundation of the Database of Virtual Art (1999 – ongoing) a number of online archives have arisen. Langlois Foundation in Montreal (1999-2008), Netzspannung at the Fraunhofer Institute (2001-2004), MedienKunstNetz at ZKM (2004-2006) and the Boltzmann Institute for Media Art Research in Linz (2005-2009) were all major projects of the field that were terminated. Their funding expired or they lost key researchers like V2 in Rotterdam (2001-present). In this way the original scientific archives lose their significance for research and preservation and in the meantime partly disappear from the web. So we face the ironic situation that we lose not only the media art itself, but also its scientific

documentation, so that future generations will not be able to get an idea of this art of our time. Even the *Europeana*, a large but underfunded project for Europe-wide networks of digital collection documentation is rendered meaningless if the foundation – the archives themselves – are not continued. To put it another way, until now, no sustainable strategy exits.

If we examine media art research over the last fifteen years, it becomes clear that we need a concentration of high-quality scholarly documentation as well as a huge expansion of strength and initiative. Recommendations area as follows:

1) In the field of documentation – systematic preservation campaigns do not exist so far [54] – it is essential to unite the most important lessons learned and strategies developed by initiatives either existing or abandoned under the single roof of an international institution, that can guarantee persistent existence, such as the Library of Congress or an equivalent international institution. It would need to be supported with adequate expertise from the network of important archives and initiatives, organized in a corona around the long-lasting institution.

2) The establishment of an appropriate research institution bringing together the best heads of the field would be necessary. In Germany interdisciplinary questions incorporating research on digital cultures from computer games to avantgarde art are too extensive for a single university. Thus, the Max Planck Institute structure was created.

3) For current digital humanities, the funding structures must be internationalized in ways similar to those enabling modern astronomy, genomics or climatology. In order to create enough momentum and the necessary sustainability, sponsors like NSF, DFG, Getty, EU etc. need to ensure international

long-term sustainable structures. Only when we develop systematic and concerted strategies of collecting, preservation and research will we be able to fulfill the task that digital culture demands in the twenty-first century. In astronomy, funding agencies developed and modernized their systems towards sustainability. The virtual observatory infrastructure is funded on an ongoing basis and there is international coordination between more than a dozen countries that produce astronomical data.

A significant commitment has to be made for media art research. Let's recall the enormous and sustaining infrastructure that was developed for traditional artistic media, painting, sculpture, architecture, even film, photography and their corresponding archives over the course of the 20th century. What is needed is an appropriate structure to preserve at least the usual one to six per cent of present media art production, and the best works. If we compare the worldwide available budget to preserve and explore traditional art forms with the one for digital culture then we understand how inadequate the support for our present digital culture is; it is almost statistically immeasurable. The faster this essential modification to our cultural heritage record can be carried out, the smaller the gap in the cultural memory; shedding light on the dark years, which started about 1960 and continue now. As recently expressed in our international declaration, signed so far by more than four hundred colleagues and leading artists from forty-five countries, there is urgent need to internationalize research and establish an international, sustainable platform of interoperable archives. [55]

Hearing that there are experts of contemporary art (old media art, sculpture, painting etc) that try to exclude the art of our time with the widest need is sad – and ironically, as we learned from Shanken, Cubitt and Thomas, the exponents of an exclusion of media art justify this by its connection with technology. This confession truly is a disaster, not so much for the interests of those people but for the tax-paying public, who deserve the right to be enabled to think about our time through media art. This ignorance is not something we should just tolerate. It means that although our societies' political, financial, and cultural infrastructures are increasingly driven by modern technologies, the art market and a number of biennales and state-financed contemporary art museums deny the public, which pays their bills, the needed aesthetic and intellectual confrontation with current art. The attempt to separate art from its time is not new, it is also comparable with earlier movements of world escapism, like the forms of nineteenth-century historicism. Our modern societies need to be enabled to reflect on their time and future and media art plays a seminal role in that process.

Media Art, as we understand, needs as many bridges as possible: conferences, new scientific tools like databases and text repositories, new strategies for documentation and visual analysis of complex data, new curricula for the next generation of teachers and collectors. Maybe in a near future we can create collective tools, as represented in Christa Sommerer and Laurent Mignonneau's work *The Living Web*, which generates a spatial sphere from search engines for web images in a CAVE. Their work represents a new instrument for visual analysis, with the option of comparing up to one thousand images in a scientific discussion. Captivating new visualization tools could provide access to the BREATH of digital cultural production: Coupled with the DEPTH of historical optical media, new unpredictable understandings of today's image revolution can be enabled. ■

ESSAY

REFERENCES AND NOTES

1. See Suzanne Anker and Dorothy Nelkin, *The Molecular Gaze: Art in the Genetic Age* (New York: Cold Spring Harbor Laboratory Press, 2004); Jens Hauser, ed., *Sk-interfaces: Exploding Borders – Creating Membranes in Art, Technology and Society* (Liverpool: Liverpool University Press, 2008); Eduardo Kac, ed., *Signs of Life: Bio Art and Beyond* (Cambridge, MA: The MIT Press, 2009); Ingeborg Reichle, *Kunst aus dem Labor: Zum Verhältnis von Kunst und Wissenschaft im Zeitalter der Technoscience* (Wien: Springer, 2005), a.o.

2. See Lynn Hershman-Leeson, "The Raw Data Diet, All-Consuming Bodies, and the Shape of Things to Come," in *Database Aesthetics: Art in the Age of Information Overflow*, ed. Victoria Vesna (Minneapolis, MN: University of Minnesota Press, 2007), 249-252.

3. The topic of the Transmediale Berlin in 2009: "Deep North; Ars Electronica festival in 2009: "human nature."

4. See Oliver Grau, ed., *Imagery in the 21st Century* (Cambridge, MA: MIT Press, 2011); W. J. T. Mitchell, *Cloning Terror: The War of Images, 9/11 to the Present* (Chicago: The University of Chicago Press, 2011). a.o.

5. See Lev Manovich, "Info-Aesthetics," Academia.edu, 2004, https://www.academia.edu/542793/Info-aesthetics (accessed February 4, 2014).

6. See the forthcoming dissertation of Daniela Plewe, Paris, Sorbonne, 2011: www.transactional-arts.com/summary.html (accessed February 4, 2014).

7. Ars Electronica´s festival theme in 2002: "Unplugged: Art as the Scene of Global Conflicts," a.o.

8. For example: Ars Electronica, Austria; Transmediale, Germany; Intersociety of Electronic Arts (ISEA) Conference; Dutch Electronic Art Festival; European Media Art Festival, Germany; FILE, Brasil; Microwave Festival Hong Kong; Korean Media Art Festival; Siggraph, a.o.

9. Beatriz da Costa and Kavita Philipp, eds., *Tactical Biopolitics: Art, Activism, and Technoscience* (Cambridge, MA: MIT Press, 2010); Stephen Wilson, *Art + Science Now: How Scientific Research and Technological Innovation Are Becoming Key to 21st Century Aesthetics* (London: Thames & Hudson, 2010); Hazel Gardiner and Charly Gere, eds., *Art Practice in a Digital Culture* (Farnham: Ashgate, 2010); Frank Popper, *From Technological to Virtual Art* (Cambridge, MA: MIT Press, 2007); Edward Shanken, *Art and Electronic Media* (London: Phaidon, 2009); Christa Sommerer and Laurent Mignonneau, eds., *Interface Cultures: Artistic Aspects of Interaction* (Bielefeld: Transcript, 2008); Victoria Vesna, *Database Aesthetics: Art in the Age of Information Overflow* (Minneapolis: University of Minnesota Press, 2007); Steve Dixon, *Digital Performance: A History of New Media in Theatre, Dance, Performance Art, and Installation* (Cambridge, MA: MIT Press, 2007); Oliver Grau, *Virtual Art* (Cambridge, MA: MIT Press, 2003), a.o.

10. For example: Database of Virtual Art / Archive of Digital Art (ADA), virtualart.at; Netzspannung.org, http://netzspannung.org/archive/; V2_Archive, http://framework.v2.nl; Docam, www.docam.ca; Daniel Langlois Fondation, www.fondation-langlois.org; Variable Media Initiative, http://variablemedia.net; Ludwig Boltzmann Institute, Media.Art.Research, http://media.lbg.ac.at; a.o.

11. See Gerd Zimmermann, ed., "Medium Architektur, 9. Internationales Bauhaus-Kolloquium, Weimar," special issue, *Thesis, Wissenschaftliche Zeitschrift der Bauhaus-Universität Weimar* 3 (2003).

12. SOUND:FRAME's website, www.soundframe.at (accessed December 16, 2013).

13. See Oliver Grau, ed., *Imagery in the 21st Century*.

14. See "Congressional Testimony of Les Roberts, Director of Health Policy at the International Rescue Committee," 107th Congress, 2nd session, May 7, 2001, 2. By 2009, over 6 million died directly due to the conflict minerals trade: U.S. House of Representatives Bill H. R. 4128, 111th Congress, 1st Session, November 19, 2009.

15. Gerhard Dirmoser, "Art-in-context (Die Kunst der Ausstellung)," Servus.at, www.servus.at/kontext/ausstellungskunst/Folie1.GIF (accessed December 16, 2013). See also Folies 2 to 4.

16. Char Davies and John Harrison, "Osmose: Towards Broadening the Aesthetics of Virtual Reality," in *Computer Graphics (ACM)* 30, no. 4 (1996): 25-28. Char Davies, "Landscape, Earth, Body, Being, Space and Time in the Immersive Virtual Environments Osmose and Ephemére," in *Women, Art, and Technology*, ed. Judy Malloy, 322-337 (Cambridge, MA: MIT Press, 2003).

17. See Eduardo Kac, *Life, Light & Language/ La vie, la lumière & le langage* (Enghien-les-Bains: Centre des Arts, 2011); Eduardo Kac and Avital Ronell, *Life Extreme: An Illustrated Guide to New Life* (Paris: Dis Voir, 2007); Eduardo Kac, ed., *Signs of Life: Bio Art and Beyond* (Cambridge, MA: MIT Press, 2009); Eduardo Kac, *Telepresence and Bio Art: Networking Humans, Rabbits and Robot* (Ann Arbor, MI: University of Michigan Press, 2005).

18. Shaw got inspiration from media arts history: "The history of the cinematic experience is a rich chronicle of viewing and projection machines. Before Hollywood imposed its set of ubiquitous formats, there were a myriad of extraordinary devices, like the Lumiere Brothers Photodrama, the Cyclorama, Cosmorama, Kineorama, Neorama, Uranorama and many more. The Kaiserpanorama – a stereoscopic cylindrical panoptic peepshow – is an especially relevant forerunner of a newly configured display system, Re-Actor." See Sarah Kenderdine and Jeffrey Shaw, "UNMAKEABLELOVE: Gaming Technologies for the Cybernetic Theatre Re-Actor," in *ACE 09 Proceedings of the International Conference on Advances in Computer Enterntainment Technolog*, Athens, Greece (October 2009).
19. See Jennifer Gonzales, "The Appended Subject: Race and Identity as Digital Assemblage," in *Race in Cyberspace*, ed. Beth Kolko, Lisa Nakamura, and Gil Rodman (New York: Routledge, 2000), 27-50; Victoria Vesna, "Under Reconstruction: Architectures of BodiesINCorporated," in *Veiled Histories: The Body, Place and Public Art*, ed. Anna Novakov (San Francisco: San Francisco Art Institute, 1998), 87-117.
20. See Monika Fleischmann and Wolfgang Strauss, "Staging of the Thinking Space. From Immersion to Performative Presence," in *Paradoxes of Interactivity: Perspectives for Media Theory, Human-Computer Interaction, and Artistic Investigations*, ed. Uwe Seifert, Jin Hyon Kim and Anthony Moore (Bielefeld: Transcript Verlag, 2008), 266-281; Monika Fleischmann and Wolfgang Strauss, "Extended Performance – Virtuelle Bühne, Selbstreprasentanz und Interaktion," *Kaleidoskopien* 384, no. 3 (2000): 52-57.
21. Hani Rashid and Lise Anne Couture, "Asymptote Architecture – NYSE 3D trading Floor (1998)," Asymptote's website, http://www.asymptote.net (accessed September 28, 2012).
22. Ingo Gunther, "Worldprocessor.com," in *Proceedings of ACM SIGGRAPH 2007*, San Diego (August 2007), 200.
23. Lovely Faces Dating Agency, www.lovely-faces.com (accessed September 28, 2012).
24. Johanna Dombois, "Master Voices: Opernstimmen im Virtuellen Raum. Fidelio, 21. Jahrhundert,'" in *Stimm-Welten: Philosophische, Medientheoretische und Ästhetische Perspektiven*, ed. Doris Kolesc, (Bielefeld: Transcript Verlag, 2009), 127-142; Johanna Dombois and Florian Dombois, "Op.72., II 1-5, 3D. Beethoven's 'Fidelio' in a Virtual Environment," in *Proceedings of the 5th World Multi-Conference on Systematics, Cybernetics and Informatics*, vol. X, Orlando, Florida (July 2001), 370-373.
25. Ernst Cassirer, *Philosophie der Symbolischen Formen* (Darmstadt: Wissenschaftliche Buchgesellschaft, 1954); Ernst Cassirer, *Individuum und Kosmos* (Darmstadt: Wissenschaftliche Buchgesellschaft, 1963).
26. Theodor W. Adorno, *Asthetische Theorien* (Frankfurt am Main: Suhrkamp, 1973).
27. Michel Serres, *Capaccio: Ästhetische Zugänge* (Reinbek: Rowohlt, 1981), 152.
28. The evolution of media art has a long history and now a new technological variety has appeared. However, this art cannot be fully understood without its history. See Rudolf Arnheim, "The Coming and Going of Images," *Leonardo* 33, no. 3 (2000): 167-168.
29. Bruno Latour and Peter Weibel, eds., *ICONOCLASH: Beyond the Image Wars in Science, Religion and Art* (Karlsruhe: ZKM, 2002).
30. Thomas Hensel, "Das Bild im Spannrahmen," *Gegenworte: Hefte für den Disput über Wissen*, no. 20 (2008): 39.
31. Donau-Universität Krems' website, www.donau-uni.ac.at/cis/mah (accessed September 28, 2012).
32. See the website of Media Art History, www.mediaarthistory.org (accessed September 28, 2012).
33. The content development of Re:fresh! was a highly collective process. It involved three producing partners, a large advisory board, 2 chairs for each session, call and review for papers, a planning meeting in 2004, keynotes, poster session and the development of application content over the time of two and a half years. Before Banff could host the conference, this was organised by the team of the Database of Virtual Art / Archive of Digital Art (ADA). The international planning meeting at Vigoni/Italy in 2004 (hosted by ADA) agreed that it is of importance to bring media art history closer to the mainstream of art history cultivating a proximity to film- cultural and media studies, computer science, but also philosophy and other sciences. After nomination and acceptance of the chairs, coordinated call for papers, review by the program committee and selection of speakers by the chairs organized and funded by the Database of Virtual Art – the conference brought together colleagues from the following fields: invited speakers (based on self description from bios) HISTORIES: Art History = 20; Media Science = 17; History of Science = 7, History of Ideas = 1; History of Technology = 1; ARTISTS/CURATORS: Artists/Research = 25; Curators = 10; SOCIAL

SCIENCES: Communication/Semiotics = 6; Aesthetics/ Philosophy = 5, Social History = 2; Political Science = 2; Woman Studies = 2, Theological Studies = 1; OTHER CULTURAL STUDIES: Film Studies = 3; Literature Studies = 3; Sound Studies = 3, Theatre Studies = 2; Performance Studies = 1; Architecture Studies = 1, Computer Science = 2; Astronomy 1.

34. Some of the conference results can be found in the anthology *MediaArtHistories* by Oliver Grau, ed. (Cambridge, MA: The MIT Press, 2007); recently: Andreas Broeckmann and Gunalan Nadarajan, eds., *Place Studies in Art, Media, Science and Technology: Historical Investigations on the Sites and the Migration of Knowledge* (Weimar: Verlag und Datenbank für Geisteswissenschaften, 2009).

35. See Oliver Grau, "New Images from Life," *Art Inquiry: Recherches sur les Arts* 2, no. 9 (2000): 7-25; Mitchell Whitelaw, *Metacreation: Art and Artificial Life* (Cambridge, MA: MIT Press, 2004).

36. See Oliver Grau, "Teleprasenz: Zu Genealogie und Epistemologie von Interaktion und Simulation," in *Formen interaktiver Medienkunst*, ed. Peter Gendolla et al. (Frankfurt am Main: Suhrkamp, 2001), 39-63.

37. Oliver Grau, *Virtual Art: From Illusion to Immersion* (Cambridge, MA: MIT Press, 2003); Jeffrey Shaw and Peter Weibel, eds., *Future Cinema: The Cinematic Imaginary After the Film (Electronic Culture: History, Theory, and Practice)* (Cambridge, MA: MIT Press, 2003); Sarah Kenderdine, "Speaking in Rama: Panoramic Vision in Cultural Heritage Visualization," in *Theorizing Digital Cultural Heritage: A Critical Discourse*, ed. Fiona Cameron and Sarah Kenderdine (Cambridge, MA: MIT Press, 2007), 301-332.

38. Oliver Grau, ed., "Remember the Phantasmagoria!: Illusion Politics of the Eighteenth Century and Its Multimedial Afterlife," in *Media Art Histories* (Cambridge, MA: MIT Press/ Leonardo Books, 2007), 136-161.

39. Oliver Grau, *Virtual Art: From Illusion to Immersion*.

40. Uwe Fleckner, BREDEKAMP, Horst Bredekamp and Martin Warnke, eds., *Der Bilderatlas Mnemosyne*, vol.1 (Berlin: Akademie Verlag, 2000); Hans Belting, ed., *Bilderfragen: Die Bildwissenschaft im Aufbruch* (München: Wilhelm Fink Verlag, 2007); Hans Belting, "Images in History and Images of History," in *Ernst Kantorowicz: Erträge der Doppeltagung*, ed. R. L. Benson and J. Fred (Frankfurt: Steiner, 1997), 94-103. And see also three recent works: L. Bader, M. Gaier and F. Wolf, eds. *Vergleichendes Sehen* (München: Wilhelm Fink Verlag, 2010); Hubertus Kohle, *Digitale Bildwissenschaft* (Glückstadt: Verlag Werner Hülsbuch, 2013); and Lev Manovich, *Software Takes Command* (New York: Bloomsbury, 2013).

41. While approaches of Media Archaeology by Zielinski or Huhtamo tend to focus on the media and instruments only, the MediaArtHistories approach investigates the arts and images as well and explores among other things the driving force the arts played historically for the development of the media. See Siegfried Zielinski, *Deep Time of the Media* (Cambridge, MA: MIT Press, 2006); Erkki Huhtamo and Jussi Parikka, eds., *Media Archaeology: Approaches, Applications, and Implications* (Berkeley: California University Press, 2011); and Oliver Grau, ed., *MediaArtHistories*.

42. Film Library, MoMA's website, http://www.moma.org/ explore/collection/film (accessed December 16, 2013).

43. A prophet of the virtual museum Andrè Malraux describes as "imaginary museum" or "museum without walls" collections of photographic reproductions comparing a large variety of ages and cultures in a virtual space that could never exist physically. André Malraux, *Psychologie de l'art: Le Musée Imaginaire – La création artistique – La monnaie de l'absolu* (Geneva: Albert Skira, 1947).

44. The International Virtual Observatory Alliance (IVOA) was formed in June 2002 with a mission to "facilitate the international coordination and collaboration necessary for the development and deployment of the tools, systems and organisational structures necessary to enable the international utilisation of astronomical archives as an integrated and interoperating virtual observatory." The IVOA now comprises 17 international VO projects. IVOA's website, www.ivao.net (accessed September 28, 2012).

45. The Millennium Ecosystem Assessment assessed the consequences of ecosystem change for human well-being. From 2001 to 2005, the MA involved the work of more than 1,360 experts worldwide. Their findings provide a state-of-the-art scientific appraisal of the condition and trends in the world's ecosystems and the services they provide, as well as the scientific basis for action to conserve and use them sustainably.

46. The Human Genome Project was an international scientific research project with a primary goal to determine the sequence of chemical base pairs which make up DNA and to identify and map the approximately 20,000-25,000 genes of the human genome from both a physical and functional standpoint. The mega project started 1990 with the collective work of more than 1000 researchers in

ESSAY

40 countries, the plan was to acchive the goal in 2010. A working draft of the genome was released in 2000 and a complete one in 2003. See International Human Genome Sequencing Consortium, "Finishing the Euchromatic Sequence of the Human Genome," *Nature* 431, no. 7011 (2004): 931-945.

47. Database of Virtual Art / Archive of Digital Art (ADA), www.virtualart.at (accessed September 28, 2012).

48. Oliver Grau, "For an Expanded Concept of Documentation: The Database of Virtual Art," in *Proceedings of ICHIM 03*, Paris, France (September 2003), 2-15. It was a long development since the classic text by Suzanne Briet, *Qu'est-ce que la documentation?* (Paris: Editions Documentaires Industrielle et Techniques, 1951).

49. Roy Ascott, Christiane Paul, Gunalan Nadarajan, Erkki Huhtamo, Jorge LaFerla, Martin Roth, u.a.

50. Oliver Grau, "Das Pionierarchiv der Medienkunst: Virtualart. at," *Kunstgeschichte aktuell* 1/09 (2009): 8.

51. See the website of Graphic Art Collection Gottweig Abbey, www.gssg.at (accessed September 28, 2012).

52. The digitization of the collection is a project developed by the Department of Image Science at Danube University and conducted in cooperation with the Göttweig Monastery. The collection of prints at Gottweig Monastery, which itself was founded in 1083, is based on acquisitions made by various monks since the 15th century. The first report of graphic art kept in the monastery dates back to 1621, with an archive record that mentions a number of "tablets of copper engraving" ("Tafelein von Kupferstich"). The actual act of founding the collection is attributed to Abbot Gottfried Bessel whose systematic purchases in Austria and from abroad added remarkably a total of 20,000 pieces to the collection in a very short span of time! Reaching to the present day, the print collection at Göttweig Monastery has grown to be the largest private collection of historical graphic art in Austria with more than 30,000 prints. The Department of Image Science's digitization center at the Göttweig Monastery uses technology to scan paintings and prints from the collection (up to 72 million pixels).

53. Oliver Grau, "Die Graphische Sammlung Stift Göttweig – Perspektiven der Erforschung und Vermittlung digitalisierter Druckgraphik" (paper presented at Kupferstichkabinett online Konferenz: Entwicklungen, Ergebnisse, Perspektiven / Internationale Tagung der Herzog August Bibliothek und des Herzog Anton Ulrich-Museums zu Graphik-Datenbanken im Internet), Wolfenbüttel und Braunschweig, March 14-16, 2011.

54. Although there are a number of promising case studies such as Caitlin Jones' "Seeing Double: Emulation in Theory and Practice, The Erl King Case Study," (paper presented at the Electronic Media Group Annual Meeting of the American Institute for Conservation of Historic and Artistic Works, Portland, Oregon, June 14, 2004), http://cool.conservation-us.org/coolaic/sg/emg/library/pdf/jones/Jones-EMG2004.pdf (accessed December 16, 2013). See also the websites of Inside Installations: Preservation and Presentation of Installation Art, www.inside-installations.org; Independent Media Arts Preservation, www.imap-preserve.org; CIAO – Conceptual Media Arts Online, www.bampfa.berkeley.edu/ciao/; Digital Art Conservation, www.digitalartconservation.org; and PACKED, http://www.packed.be/en/, (accessed September 28, 2013). All of those initiatives are fairly small.

55. See "Media Art Needs Global Networked Organisation & Support – International Declaration," the website of Media Art History, www.mediaarthistory.org/declaration (accessed December 16, 2013).

ESSAY

Interference Wave
DATA AND ART

> *The organism that would be the supposed subject and intentional origin of forces is an effect of impersonal potentials, and it is precisely the technical object that can expose the power of potentials to act beyond the organism's capacities.*
> — Claire Colebrook [1]

by

Adam Nash

adam.nash@rmit.edu.au

DATA, DISPLAY, MODULATION

The artist working in the digital medium must attend to the intrinsic qualities of the digital medium. Stiegler, Kittler, Manovich and Hansen, among others, have all meditated on what I characterise as the separation between digital data and its display. These writers tend, broadly, to characterise this separation in terms of technics and media. Such a characterisation owes much to the Platonic concepts of *amamnesis* and *hypomnesis*. Kittler takes the dichotomy to its extreme and posits that there are no longer any media: "with numbers, everything goes […] a digital base will erase the very concept of medium." [2] Kittler wants to move beyond the concept of the medium as a result of digital convergence because it transcends differentiation between media, a differentiation that is constitutive of the concept of media. Without differentiation between different media, there are no media, and since the convergence of all media into the digital removes any differentiation between media, in the digital era there are no media. Thus, when he concedes that there ostensibly still *are* media in our world,

This article investigates the nature of digital data as a medium for art. Specifically, what are the qualities and specificities unique to the medium of digital data, and how can artists working with this medium create work that cannot be created in any other medium? References are made to Friedrich Kittler, Mark B. N. Hansen, Marshall McLuhan, Gilles Deleuze, Anna Munster and Claire Colebrook to establish a bivalent ontological model of digital data. This bivalence is described in terms of 'data' and 'display,' where 'data' exists in an indeterminate state inaccessible to human perception until a determining operation is performed to modulate the data into a 'display' state, where 'display' does not necessarily imply visual display. Such a model suggests, in McLuhanist and Deleuzean terms, a medium that retroactively virtualises all previous media. This model is compared in detail to Gilbert Simondon's ontological model of transductive individuation. Finally, modulation - in the form of parameter selection - is presented as the defining work of the artist in the digital medium.

he sees them as comprehensible in McLuhanist terms, where the content of one medium is always another medium. The digital is singular, post-convergent, formless and plastic, and the differentiation that constitutes media occurs when digital data is modulated into some display state.

This way of thinking about the digital can be of practical use to the artist working with digital data. It has the advantage of unproblematically incorporating McLuhanist considerations - not only in what McLuhan calls the "rear-view mirror" operations that constitute so much of digital culture today, but also in the sense that McLuhan's concept of media-as-content itself becomes content in the digital medium. So, for this discussion of the role of art and interference in the digital era, it is important to recognise the distinction between plastic, formless, generic digital data and specific instances of display, where digital data is modulated from its state of data-as-data into a state of display, such as when a digital photograph is visually displayed on a screen, or a digital audio recording is audibly displayed through speakers. Before this act of modulation into display, there is no possible distinction between the photograph and the sound, since they are both generic, formless digital data. This act of modulation - between data and display - is the work of the digital artist.

ESSAY

Mark Hansen argues against Kittler's extreme version of the consequences of digitisation, seeing it as an overly literal, or formalist, reading of Claude Shannon's foundational work in information theory, where information is separate from meaning. Hansen is keen to show that the differentiation of media is a more complex assemblage involving what he calls *embodiment*, in the sense of being "inseparable from the cognitive activity of the brain." [4] In this, he relies partially on an alternative theory of information, contemporaneous with Shannon's, espoused by Donald McKay, where what we might call the non-technical interpretation of information is inseparable from its technical structure. But Hansen does not deny the technical fact of the levelling nature of digital data, and nor does he deny the subsequent generic translatability of digitised media. Rather, he is attendant to the framing, or subjectification, that he sees as a necessary driver of the consciousness that perceives the modulated display of digitised data. In some ways, Hansen's attitude can be seen as extreme as Kittler's, in that neither are prepared to consider the digital medium as a medium in its own right – a move that would allow them to consider the formal and intensive qualities and implications of the medium, using McLuhanist techniques to investigate what can be done in this putative new medium that cannot be done in any prior medium. Even though he, like Kittler, acknowledges that convergence into the digital renders all prior media undifferentiable, Hansen's privileging of the image is perhaps why he doesn't logically extend the McLuhanist gesture all the way to the conclusion that the digital convergence not only profoundly enacts W. J. T. Mitchell's assertion that "there are no visual media," [5] from the constitutive side instead of the "sensory modality" standpoint, but so totally incorporates all prior media as to subsume the very concept of differentiated media into a recursive subset of itself, and, *contra* Kittler, it does this as a medium, contributing operations in excess of all the media and semantic sources being digitized, constituting a whole that is comprised of all prior media plus the digital excess, a whole that completes McLuhan's project while offering a new medium that differentiates itself through its own constitutive, ontological, excess.

We can identify two elements and one principle that constitute the digital medium as a medium. The two elements are data and display, and the principle is modulation. Working with digital data is a constant process of modulating data back and forth between a display state and the state of data-as-data. Display does not necessarily mean *visual* display, but it may, and in this sense, 'display' may be thought of as 'expression', or perhaps even 'actualisation'.

Any distinctions between discrete media and any distinctions between discrete mediatic actions are collapsed in the digital. All media are virtualised in the digital, and then simulated in display, so that any distinction between them holds only in a nostalgic sense, in the rear view mirror. Precisely because the digital contains all prior media, virtualised as content, it is possible to analyse these media separately, but only nostalgically, in a McLuhanist manner, and only when modulated into a state of display, enacted as a simulation of media. As Justin Clemens and I put it in Thesis 4 of our *Seven Theses on the Concept of Post-Convergence*:

> 'All that is solid melts into data.' Alternatively: all is data. This is evidently an ontological thesis. What matters is data, but data isn't actually anything. Data is data. Data is absolutely not a phenomenological thing. It cannot be experienced as such, like Aristotelian prime matter. Unlike Aristotelian prime matter, however, we can manipulate data with ease; in fact, it is integrally available as manipulable. Marx claimed that human beings do indeed make history, but not as they please; today, we

make data and just as we please. Data is us. However, this is not the pure freedom that it may seem, nor does it lead to any triumph of the will. This is because data is only available to finite humans as filtered, as interpretation. These interpretations are, precisely, inscribed in display (whether audio, visual, haptic, what have you). Whatever is inscribed in display is always already modulated, and this modulation emerges from 'a formless soup of meaninglessness,' that is, a hyperchaos of data. [6]

The invitation, therefore, for the artist working in the digital realm, is to recognise that the work is modulation. A significant factor in the work of modulation is parameter selection. But this post-convergent medium virtualises everything, and so the concept of parameter selection itself becomes a parameter to be selected, at the same time as retroactively highlighting the latent cruciality of parameter selection in all prior media. This potentially overwhelmingly complex situation can elicit an extreme rear-view-mirrorism in practice, and such is the situation we often see with deterministic data visualisations and data-driven visual artworks.

VIRTUAL ART

In calling on the concept of the virtual, I am not equating it with technology or the digital, though of course in the contemporary era it rings with echoes of popular usage in the sense of a 'virtual friend' or 'virtual sex' or 'virtual environment.' Rather, I am evoking the Deleuzian sense that Anna Munster, in her book *Materializing New Media*, describes thus:

> [T]*he virtual dimension for corporeal experience evoked here lies in the way it poses the potential for* embodied distribution as a condition of experience for information culture *(original emphasis) by dislocating habitual bodily relations between looking and proprioception. Virtual forces are vectors that pulse through the contours and directions of matter.* [7]

In a fine study of the nature of the relationship between the digital and the material, and the virtual and the actual, Munster talks of these inter-relationships as "actualizations of virtual subjectivity," [8] and encourages us to see virtualisation as "an expanding and contracting field of differentiation." [9] This is a very useful tool for understanding the nature of the digital medium in relation to Kittler's proclamation of the movement beyond medium. Her convincing and nuanced argument can also be seen as extending McLuhan's famous extensions in a richer and more practical way than Hansen or Kittler, and is particularly useful for artists or practitioners of the digital attempting to come to terms with its intensive, and extensive, qualities and specificities. Her argument allows us to comprehend the ostensible contradiction between the collapsing, or levelling, nature of the digital and the specific differentiations required to interact with it. It does this by seeing all points of the digital - semantic sources, technical protocols and parameters, specific display instances and subjectification - as interdependently transformative negotiations of flows rather than assimilations of one thing into another. This may offer an approach to thinking the capacities of the immanently digital entity that differentiates both within and without its material manifestation, that both is and is not digital, without a semantic material provenance.

In a similar vein, but in specific relation to images and visual art, Claire Colebrook calls on Deleuze and Guattari's concept of *desiring machines* to understand the nature of the undifferentiated digital. She writes:

> It is naive and uncritical to see the analogue as a pure and continuous feeling or bodily proximity that is then submitted to the quantification of the digital, a digital that will always be an imposition on organic and vital life. There is, however, an inorganic mode of the analogue that is not a return to a quality before its digital quantification, but a move from digital quantities or actual units to pure quantities, quantities that are not quantities of this or that substance so much as intensive forces that enter into differential relations to produce fields or spaces that can then be articulated into digits. [10]

Both Munster and Colebrook are trying to think about the consequences of the digital in terms of Deleuze's concept of life beyond the organic. As Colebrook characterises it, Deleuze thinks of "a technical or machinic potentiality that enables organic life," [11] and both she and Munster can see a relationship between this and the operations of the digital, without equating the digital with this putative potentiality. In this, they (and Deleuze) are influenced by the thought of Gilbert Simondon, whose philosophy of ontogenesis requires us to "understand the individual from the perspective of the process of individuation rather than the process of individuation by means of the individual." [12] He talks of a preindividual state from which the individual being emerges but, in its individuation, not only "does not exhaust the potentials embedded in the preindividual state," [13] but continues to exist in a state of relations with its milieu, a milieu that includes the preindividual state.

Therefore, according to Simondon, being "does not possess unity of identity which is that of the stable state in which no transformation is possible: being possesses transductive unity." [14] This concept of transductive unity, or transduction, is crucial to Simondon's philosophy:

> By transduction, we mean a physical, biological, mental, or social operation, through which an activity propagates from point to point within a domain, which is operated from place to place: each region of the constituted structure serves as a principle of constitution for the next region. [15]

This aspect of Simondon's philosophy can be a useful tool for analysing the operation of the digital, particularly in the post-convergent terms of data, modulation and display. When existing as digital data, we can see a preindividual state from which a medium (e.g. a "photograph") individuates or, in the terms we are discussing, is differentiated by being modulated into a display state. This state of display, though, has a "relative reality, occupying only a certain phase of the whole being in question," [16] crucially in ongoing symbiotic relations with its digital milieu, comprised of all the conceptual (protocols, software, etc) and physical (electrical, ferromagnetic, etc.) interactions that go to make up a working digital system.

As alluded to above, in the quote from Justin Clemens and myself, what is of interest to artists (and philosophers) is that, with the digital, we are eminently able to manipulate these systems of relations and individuation. More precisely, we are able to actively engage with these systems. In this sense, we can see alignments between Simondon's concept of transduction and what I am calling modulation.

It is important to note that Simondon's philosophy is in no way a surrender to cybernetics or information theory, and by following Simondon we are able to avoid a crude reductionist view of the digital and its relation to life. As much as he was interested in the thinking of the first wave of cyberneticists, he was equally alarmed at their attempt to rationalise all life in terms of the working of the machine – such a mechanistic view entirely goes against Simondon who is, if anything, more likely to see a machine in terms of the working of an organism. But this would be a gross oversimplification of Simondon's ontological thinking, which entirely rejects any form of dichotomous thinking or substantialist division, along the lines of mind/body or human/machine, whilst still being perfectly capable of acknowledging the difference between these things. [17] Simondon sees no opposition between biology and technology, rather they are a continuation of each other. In this sense, there is a resonance with McLuhan's "extensions," but Simondon is far more egalitarian, seeing no hierarchy where human activity is more important or genuine than technological activity, a determinism which is perhaps implied in McLuhan's notion of extensions as applied to media.

Simondon's philosophy is very concerned with what we might call the recursive or even reticulated nature of systems, i.e., that transduction is a constantly co-operative process where elements influence and are influenced by each other and their milieu in interaction, which is a genuine *inter*action, rather than a one way line of cause and effect, each interaction both subject to and contributing to the nature of the system and thus the individual itself (and it is easy to see how such a philosophy appealed to Deleuze). So it is with modulation of digital data into a display state, a constantly recursive process of interaction between a myriad of physical (electricity, ferromagnetic particles, plastic, metal, silicon, nervous system, hand, eye) and conceptual (protocols, software, ideas, intentions) elements each engaging in a participatory process of individuation. Digital data is constantly being modulated into a display state in order to engage with another element in the system, whether that element be human or technical, then remodulated back into digital data, only to be modulated into another display state and so forth. With every modulation occurs a modification, of every element, of the interaction itself, of the modulation itself, a recursive, reticulated system of

de- and re-modulation, or what Simondon calls "recurrent causality," [18] crucially engaged with and engaging its internal and external milieu.

We might think of this, as alluded to in the title of this essay, as a constant process of interference, a standing wave of interference. The artist hoping to work with the digital, and hoping to effect some kind of interference with the received values and standards of their milieu, must attend very closely to this process of modulation since it is the only action available to them that can truly be called "digital," without rehearsing pre-digital notions of art that scan only in the rear view mirror, and therefore are more likely to confirm rather than question the contemporary hegemony of libertarian digital capitalism. Such a hegemony relies on pre-digital notions, particularly of the individual, and encourages users to see the digital through the rear-view mirror. This is in order to distract from the Simondonian processes the hegemony itself engages with to exploit its worldwide workforce of individual users, bewitching them into tirelessly labouring to produce its commodity (digital data), not only for free, but enthusiastically. This is of course exemplified by the so-called personalisation movement, a drive towards total solipsistic consumption-as-production. This shows that the processes that Simondon identifies, and that are mirrored in the digital, are not necessarily anthropocentric ideological processes, but can be utilised towards any pre-digital anthropocentric ideology by engaging with its processes to exploit Cartesian subjectivity or any other duallist or substantialist ideology that sees technics as external to the human experience. Such is the method employed mercilessly by contemporary global digital capitalists, with outrageous hegemonic success. Thus it is beholden upon artists, wishing to attempt to interfere with such hegemonies, to investigate the implications of genuine engagement with these Simondonian digital processes, inserting themselves by experimenting with parameter selection, thereby participating in the modulation process without succumbing to a subjectivist attempt to determine the teleology of the work.

In other words, since the digital opens up Simondon's concepts of technical beings and individuation, the artist must try to enter into relations with this digital process of modulation, allowing themselves, their ideas and their will to modulate – for example, through parameter selection – and be modulated. This means being mindful of avoiding any teleological impulses towards an artwork, rather opening up the work process to the recursive affectivity of the digital, so that the process of art in the digital is not formulated in terms of individual artworks. The process should be a part of the recursively relations-based nature of digital systems, engaged completely in the recurrently causal modulation process. In this sense, the artist's process becomes a node in the reticulated process of modulated individuation that characterises the digital process, constantly in changing, influencing and influenced relationship with the process and its milieu, which in this case, since the artist's process is an element within the system, includes both the internal and networked workings of the digital system as well as the artist's own milieu, which presumably includes the artist's social context, history and desires – desires both individual and social.

Colebrook's very important point about the inorganic mode of the analogue reminds us of the crucial difference between the digital and the numeric or mathematical. Kittler, Hansen and Deleuze all practice this conflation of the digital and the numeric. In fact, the digital is not numeric, it is purely binary, an enacted logic of switches. This widespread conflation is perpetuated by the popular misconception of the digital being constructed from "zeroes and ones," which is in fact simply a symbolic placeholder for the boolean logic of on/off or yes/no or is/is-not. Once we accept the numerical, or mathematics, as simply another parameter selection used to effect the modulation between data and display, we may be able to comprehend the move to pure quantities and even think the relationship between the contemporary technical interdependence of virtual/material and the Deleuzian interdependence of virtual/actual. In other words, we will have moved closer to Munster's exhortation to see the virtual as expanding and contracting fields of differentiation. In the digital, we as artists may see a tool for consciously or explicitly engaging with Simondon's transductive process of individuation where the individuated remains in dynamic interaction with the pre-individual, which is never exhausted.

IMMANENTLY DIGITAL ENTITIES

We have established that there is no longer any meaningful differentiation between discrete media, except as they relate to a display state. Now we can analyse the display of digitised entities that have a recognisable material (non-digital) provenance. For example, it is easy to see much contemporary data visualisation as a straight forward modulation of data into the visual display register using parameters selected along the lines of McLuhan's rear view mirror. Given that this act of modulation is already a formalised kind of interference, it is clear that to achieve the kind of interference that might also be considered an artist-led disruption (itself a rear view mirror kind of concept), the artist must take care to select parameters that cause the modulated display to visually question its own display. This might include questioning the veracity of the data's provenance or the assumptions made in the digitising of the data in the first place, or the scale of the data and so on.

But what of immanently digital entities? In other words, digital entities that have no recognisable semantic material source. This is the question that my colleague, John McCormick, and I are investigating in our ongoing project called *Reproduction*. The work involves experimentation in audiovisual, performative, evolving, virtual entities spawning and reproducing in virtual environments, capable of intercommunication with the material world via various systems of motion and data capture. Loosely based on principles of artificial evolution, the parameters that we as the artists initially selected are, rather than the standard artificial evolution parameters like strength and fitness, all audiovisual performative parameters like red, green, blue, opacity, rhythm, timbre, tempo, tone (pitch) and so on. The entities evolve, reproduce, live and die over thousands of generations according to a constantly emergent evolution of these crude parameters that is informed, but not determined, by both their interaction with humans in the material world and with their interactions with each other. In other words the original parameter set becomes, after the first generation, virtualised content for the next emergent generation. All the while, the entities are organising (or perhaps socialising) and improvising movements and "songs" amongst themselves, whilst observing and improvising with any human visitors to their "space." The space in this case means both their digital virtual environment (accessible by humans via an online multi-user environment) as well as the physical space of wherever the work happens to be exhibited. In the latter case, motion and data capture are used by the entities to perceive humans, while a modulated audiovisual display allows humans to perceive the entities. Our desire, as artists, is to engage - using sound, music, movement and dance - in what we might call a "genuine" improvisation with these digital entities, by which we mean the human and digital performers share equal responsibility and value in the emergence of the improvised performance, dynamically building a shared performative vocabulary by learning from each other's nuances, gestures and performative suggestions.

In this way, we are attempting to enact some of the possibilities raised by Simondon's ontogenetic philosophy of technical being that is in a recurrently causal, constantly evolving, relationship with human beings where, while remaining ontologically distinct, neither has primacy over the other.

We might be asking, at the insistence of Kittler, if there is life beyond the medium. The inter-relationships of flows investigated by Anna Munster, or the pure quantities posited by Claire Colebrook may be at work in the emergent and evolving persistent performance of *Reproduction*. Certainly, Munster calls very explicitly for media artists to move beyond what she calls "the twin premises of disembodiment and extension in space." [19] Accordingly, this work attempts to improvise in real time an enactment of these beyonds. And since we have established that the image cannot exist in the digital, perhaps we can leverage Colebrook's thinking when she writes "we might aim to think beyond the body as an extended substance receiving the world only in terms of its bounded actuality? An image can be experienced as such, not as a proper body or imperative." [20]

Of course it is possible to rationalise any interaction with or display of these entities in terms of the original human-selected parameter set, but this is no more meaningful than saying that any living material organism is nothing more than its originary DNA combination, and this is the potentially reductionist danger that informs some contemporary thinking around embodiment, framing and subjectification, especially in relation to the digital. This is where Simondon's philosophy, on its own and in relation to its influence over Deleuze, Colebrook and Munster, can come in very useful, so that there is a chance to rigorously examine the potential, in our interactions with the immanently digital, for the emergence of what Claire Colebrook calls "sense beyond the actual." [21]

REFERENCES AND NOTES

1. Claire Colebrook, *Deleuze and the Meaning of Life* (London: Continuum, 2010), 126.
2. Friedrich Kittler, *Gramophone, Film, Typewriter* (Stanford: Stanford University Press, 1999), 2.
3. Marshall McLuhan and Quentin Fiore, *The Medium is the Massage: An Inventory of Effects* (Corte Madera: Gingko Press, 2001), 75.
4. Mark B. N. Hansen, *New Philosophy for New Media* (Cambridge, MA: MIT Press, 2004), 3.
5. W. J. T. Mitchell, "There Are No Visual Media," *Journal of Visual Culture* 4 no. 2 (2005), 257-266.
6. Justin Clemens and Adam Nash, "Seven Theses on the Concept of 'Post-convergence,'" the website of Australian Centre of Virtual Art, http://www.acva.net.au/blog/detail/seven_theses_on_the_concept_of_post-convergence (accessed June 20, 2012).
7. Anna Munster, *Materializing New Media: Embodiment in Information Aesthetics* (Lebanon, NH: Dartmouth College Press, 2006), 90.
8. Ibid., 114.
9. Ibid.
10. Claire Colebrook, *Deleuze and the Meaning of Life*, 124.
11. Ibid., 125.
12. Gilbert Simondon, "The Genesis of the Individual," in *Incorporations*, ed. J. Crary and S. Kwinter (New York: Zone Books, 1992), 300.
13. Ibid.
14. Gilbert Simondon, *L'individu et sa genèse physico-biologique* (Presses Universitaires de France, 1964; Éditions Jérôme Millon, 1995), 30, quoted in Muriel Combes, *Gilbert Simondon and the Philosophy of the Transindividual*, trans. Thomas LaMarre (Cambridge, MA: MIT Press, 2013), 6.
15. Ibid., 30.
16. Gilbert Simondon, *The Genesis of the Individual*, 300.
17. Thomas LaMarre, "Afterword: Humans and Machines," in Muriel Combes, *Gilbert Simondon and the Philosophy of the Transindividual*, trans. Thomas LaMarre (Cambridge, MA: MIT Press, 2013), 90.
18. Ibid., 95.
19. Anna Munster, *Dematerializing New Media*, 179.
20. Claire Colebrook, *Deleuze and the Meaning of Life*, 128.
21. Ibid., 127.

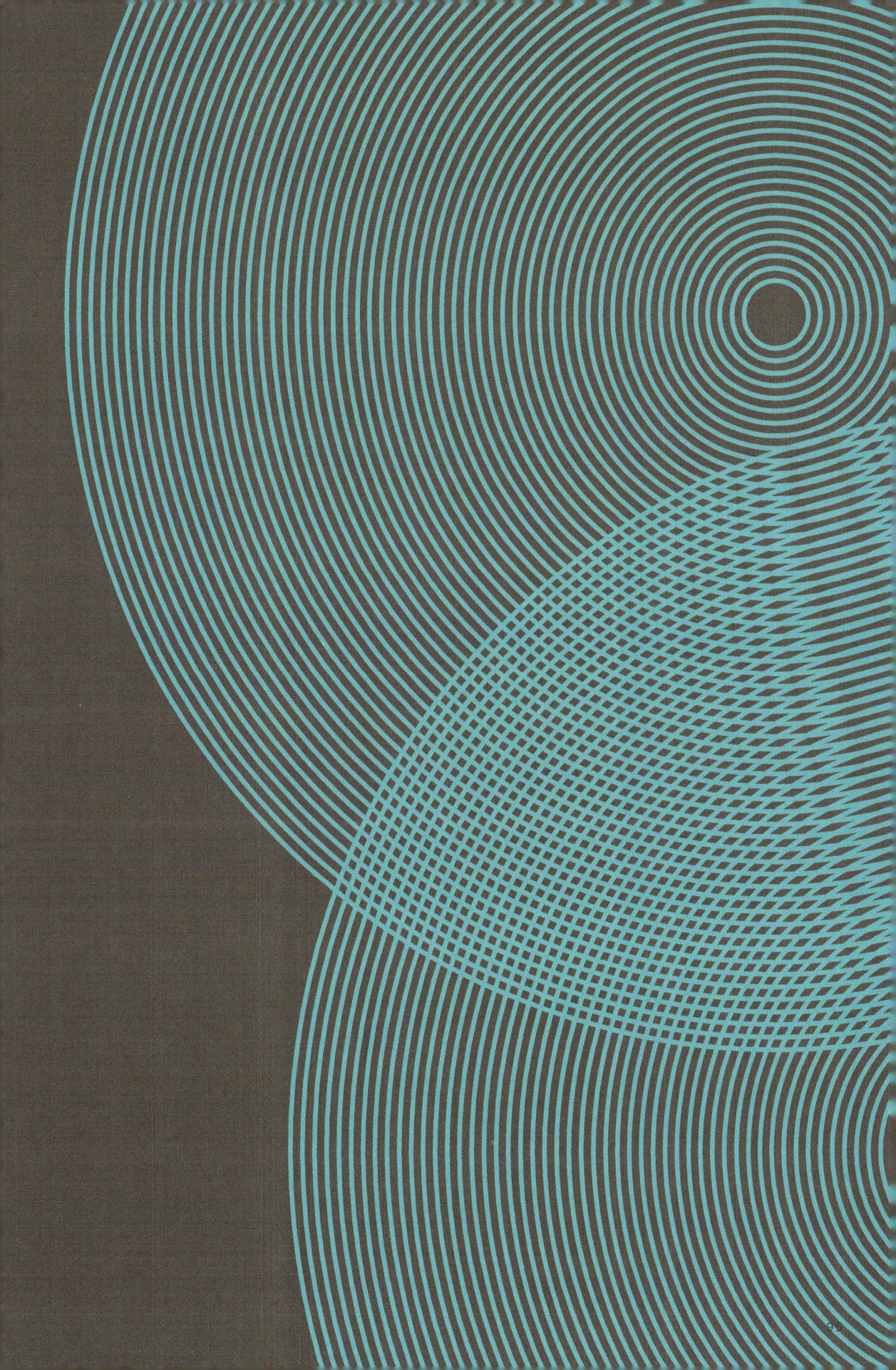

Interfering with the Dead

by

Edward Colless

ecolless@unimelb.edu.au

1. CORPUS CHRISTI

> *Jesus said, "Whoever has known the world has fallen upon a corpse."*
> — Logion 56.1, *Gospel of Thomas.*

To be worldly is to be dead. Falling upon something that you know: this is not like making a stumbling discovery; it is more like a plunge, more like leaping onto something than being accidentally tripped up by it. The corpse in this image is not the victim in a crime scene awaiting investigation, identification and justice. It is the sex object bidden by, succumbing to, and complying with necrophilic ravishment. Worldliness is a matter of life and death, of knowing that they will embrace, in a consummation devoutly to be wished. It might at first sound all too dour, but one can force a crazy twist of logic out of the timeworn death-drive in this odd remark of Jesus's. If to be worldly is to be dead, then to be unworldly is to be undead. But being undead is the most one can hope for by way of resurrection or salvation in this petulantly, huffy, pessimistic warning from a character who will later, in other venues, claim to be the Christ.

E S S A Y

An ancient library of what has become known, if contentiously, as the "gnostic gospels" was accidentally exhumed in 1945 from a monastic graveyard in Nag Hammadi in Egypt. Among these esoteric texts, most of which were lost to history since their hasty burial in the fourth century, the Gospel of Thomas *has an especially piquant pedigree. Cited throughout early Christian literature as an exceptionally heretical and prohibited text that had been purportedly composed in the first century CE, its cryptic (when not incomprehensible) apothegms are claimed to have been secret knowledge written by the twin brother of Jesus Christ. This claim, even taken as figurative, poses a modest predicament for the archaeology of Christian theology. However, taken as an artifact of media archaeology, this text – one of its verses, in particular, which proposes an equation of knowledge and death – extends a dark perspective on our own contemporary cultural imperatives with embodiment and performativity.*

This bizarre epigram is from an anthology of one hundred and fourteen non-narrative *logia* or sayings, allegedly direct from the mouth of Jesus, called the *Gospel of Thomas*. Almost two millennia after being written, this gospel – which evidently did not make it into the Christian *New Testament* canon – was discovered among a hoard of ancient manuscripts (twelve complete ones and the remains of a thirteenth) that was fortuitously unearthed in late 1945 by a goatherd, Mohammed al-Samman. He was poking about in among the clefts of the Djebel el-Tarif cliff, which skirts the farming fields of a hamlet called Nag Hammadi, on the west bank of the Nile near present day Luxor in Egypt. The manuscripts are fourth-century CE Coptic translations of what would have been formerly Greek and possibly Syriac texts. Although until this find they hadn't been seen for ages, many of these writings are mentioned in other authenticated literature of the early Christian Church; in fact, vociferously so in a famous diatribe against heresy by Irenaeus, Bishop of Lyons, written around 180 CE. [2] From these citations and cross references, it seems likely that the original versions of this Nag Hammadi library had been composed two, if not more, centuries earlier than their exhumed Coptic versions. This would place some of these texts – notably the *Gospel of Thomas* with this oddity from Jesus – in the latter part of the first century, and thus as close to the historical Jesus as the putative biographical accounts in the gospels of *Mark*, *Luke* and *Matthew*. Indeed, if not closer. [3]

ESSAY

Throughout the history of their various authoritative translations (from 1956 to 1988), the Nag Hammadi codices have collectively if contentiously become characterised as "the Gnostic Gospels" or "Gnostic Scriptures," the Gnosticism of which identifies a miscellany of purportedly separatist mystery cults dispersed across the eastern Mediterranean in the first to fourth centuries CE (Christian, Jewish and Graeco-Roman Pagan). The Nag Hammadi texts are pungently placed within the orthodox landscape of early Christian church doctrine, indicating sects in open or clandestine conflict with an emerging institutional apostolic Christian authority. [4] The *gnosis* featuring in many of these sectarian texts is a type of learning associated with initiation into an unspoken mystery distinct from philosophical wisdom (*sophia*) or intellectual comprehension (*sunesis*), and in this respect a learning distinct from the *logos* that provides an accountable ground of knowledge or, according to the famous opening of the *Gospel of John*, the ground of divine inception and incarnation. In the milieu of, for instance, the Hellenic Judaism of the Biblical *Proverbs*, *gnosis* (from the Hebrew *da'ath*) is identified, in chapter 2 verse 6, with the face of God. That's a pretty solid grounding. Many of the Gnostic sects acknowledged that such an exceptional exposure to *gnosis* would be a redemptive illumination, igniting an otherwise forsaken but soulful atom of divine light within the dark matter of the world and the bodies blindly banging around in it.

But the advent of the *gnosis* testified to in this Nag Hammadi literature had little to with the more common godly smiley-face benefactions, which might involve the reception of grace and the occasional epiphany, or to do with godly intercession, such as an Annunciation. The setting for a Gnostic illumination is too dark – and in the most creatively perverse cases too weird – to be accommodated within the relatively user-friendly devotional agonies and ecstasies of saintly visions. This is the sort of recondite and professionally specialist "learning" more suited to analyses of cloud chamber scans produced at the Large Hadron Collider than the sumptuous, illusionist quadratura painting that miraculously hoists a Baroque dome off its drum. One fine example of the quirky and vexing theology that Gnostic asceticism might lead to can be extracted from a hyperbolic doctrine developed by Marcion of Sinope, who – although from a modern viewpoint doesn't quite meet the Gnostic membership criteria – in 144 CE was excommunicated as a heresiarch. Ironically, Marcion was more doctrinaire than the bishops that judged him deviant: if he had his way, only Paul's writings would have qualified as true scripture.

The God of the Marcionist heresy was utterly alien to the creator God or demiurge who appears throughout the Hebrew Tanakh, the body of scriptures including *Proverbs* that will become known by Christians, when incorporated into their canon, as the *Old Testament*. This God, who permits no graven images of itself, is incongruously not only anthropomorphic in personality but tyrannical in temper: stubborn, conceited, jealous, and vengeful. For all his protestations that he is supreme and thus intolerant of competition, this God (who, in Marcion's tenacious anti-Judaic rage, is an inflated tribal Hebrew God) was a deceptive, indeed an abominable mask – just like the world he created, and like its creatures – obscured the true God who had disowned and retreated from the arrogant sordid theatre of creation. Marcion's dualistic doctrine bears only slight affinity with the vertiginously complex cosmogonies of contemporaneous Christian Gnostic religious systems, such as those of Valentinus, but is congruent with them in its insistence on the derogation of the created world. The redemptive *gnosis* offered by Christ in such religious topography would need to be pledged to an utterly faceless God: not an omniscient and omnipresent entity but an estranged absent divinity, both awfully remote to and alienated from the created world. And the world it has abandoned is not an illusion so much as it is a dreadfully real, terminal slave colony and abattoir: in short, death row. If there can be a Gnostic mystery extorted from Jesus's gnomic dictum told to Thomas, it would be that the created world is not just a dark world, but a dead world.

Today, when Gnostic spirituality is buoyantly promoted with the facile enthusiasm for New Age lifestyle therapeutics that include Wicca and Tantric sex and Kabbalah as a Hollywood hobby, the spiraling and even abyssal negative theology of these antique mystical schemes can be hilariously trivialized or trivially romanced. Popular Gnostic revivals are straw figures that deserve the ridicule brilliant polemicists like Slavoj Zizek hurl effortlessly at them. However, the liberty I am taking here with by this epigraph from *Thomas* is not to précis, revise or critique (let alone defend) Gnostic tradition (in some respects *Thomas* also eludes characterization as Gnostic), but to provoke the perverse trajectory of this particular motto as a morbid inversion of enlightenment. This provocation is not only a wanton wish to embellish *logion 56* with Gothicism, with a Doom House or a Death Metal timbre, even if it would wear each of those genres stylishly. It is also a reprimand against neutralizing the venom spat with each historical accusation of heresy and monstrosity delivered against it. (And just this sort of acquittal, or at least pacifying dismissal of those charges, accompanies the diplomatic, pluralist inclusion of the Nag Hammadi library into postmodern Gnostic exegeses of early Christianity.)

So let's take Irenaeus at his word when he levels against the *gnostikoi* the charge that their speculative cosmogonies and cosmologies are "an abyss of madness" and "a blasphemy against Christ." We might well deduce that this particular "Gnostic" cache which included *Thomas* was being hidden as a precious object when evacuated hastily from an archive in the desert monastery to be sunken into its graveyard; and that this provenance endows the Nag Hammadi artifacts with the patina of secret, forbidden literature interred for its own protection and clandestine preservation, with expectation of its eventual salvage and restoration. It was buried as treasure rather than as waste, but nonetheless it would have been hazardous material. Evidently, too, this library was not the exclusive testimony of a single cell or sect: the scope of metaphysical and mythographic speculation, as well as apocalyptic pronouncements, are too diverse and contrary to suggest anything other than that this was a miscellany of enigmatic heretical arcana. An illegal, underground, collection of prohibited knowledge. And the strange urgency to conceal these tracts back in the fourth century as much as the story of their twentieth-century discovery and passage into scholarship have the tantalizing drama – in the now idiomatic phrase – of a Dan Brown novel.

Illiterate and uninterested in his own Egyptian history, Mohammed al-Samman had hardly any idea of what he had discovered inside the large red earthenware jar in a cave that he had stumbled onto while digging for a natural fertilizer (known as *sabakh*) on the edge of the desert. Bitterly disappointed not to find any palpably recognizable treasure in the jar that he had broken open (despite the promising adjacency of a human skeleton), and regarding these old papyrus documents bound in leather as having negligible immediate value, the story goes that he tore a few up to trade for cigarettes with the camel drivers who were passing by at the time. Suspecting that objects of that vintage might sometimes be sold to city traders, he took the rest back to his house, although negligently throwing them onto a pile of straw in the open yard, where his mother resourcefully used some of them as kindling for the household clay oven. In addition to this archaeological fiasco, Muhammed himself was embroiled in an astonishingly gruesome family vendetta at the time. Shortly after the fertilizer expedition, he and his brothers attacked a man from a neighbouring village whom they believed responsible for the murder some months before of their father, dismembering the culprit, tearing the man's heart out of his chest and eating it! [7] Needing to lie low from police, Muhammed entrusted the remaining papyri to a local priest who, twigging to their possible historical significance passed a sample to a local Egyptian historian, who then contacted Cairo's Coptic Museum, initiating a consequent black market narrative of theft, extortion, curatorial ineptitude and smuggling involving postwar antiquities markets in Egypt, the United States and Europe (Zurich's Jung Institute, notably). Juicy as all this anecdotal intrigue is, and alluringly esoteric as much of the theological content and attribution of these codices has been, there is no fantastic conspiratorial history to their heresies, just as there was – despite Muhammed al-Samman's qualms at breaking open the jar with the mattock kept sharp to use on his father's murderer – no *djinn* let loose, no diabolical curse to carry away.

Well, not entirely.

Among the texts of this Nag Hammadi Library, the *Gospel of Thomas* has a particularly piquant genealogy. This gospel, thought to be lost until it appeared at Nag Hammadi, [8] is frequently cited (or at least its existence is testified to) in ancient literature from the early third century CE well into the early fourteenth century. [9] Since its modern discovery, *Thomas* has been placed among the *apocrypha*, those putative but suspicious sacred books which the early Christian councils considered to have dubious provenance, attribution, authenticity or authority and which were rejected from inclusion in canonical scripture. But the prototypical church historian and shrewd Constantinian publicist Eusebius, writing in the early fourth century, provides a singular warning that this judicious exclusion isn't nearly enough of an appropriate way to treat *Thomas*. Eusebius provided scriptural editors with a tripartite categorization of texts. Firstly, there were the "recognized books" (the undisputed new testament of Christian *evangelion*, which then contained the gospels of *Matthew*, *Mark*, *Luke* and *John*, with the *Acts of the Apostles*, Paul's correspondence, *1 Peter* and the *Revelation* of John the Divine); secondly, the "disputed" or apocryphal literature; and lastly, the "bastard" texts – outright counterfeit, fraudulent or spurious, that's to say illegitimate, works. Despite an initial effort by orthodox dogmatists to dispel it as an archaeological forgery, modern judgment since the Nag Hammadi discovery genially places *Thomas* into Eusebius's second category of apocryphal literature. For Eusebius, however, not only doesn't *Thomas* fit the designation of *apocrypha*; it doesn't even warrant the designation of being a bastard text! He needs to create a fourth category beyond the capacity of correction or expurgation, a sort of *oubliette* exclusively reserved for *Thomas*: a dark pit of prohibition and proscription, a sarcophagus like that around the Chernobyl nuclear reactor that sullenly entombs something too hot to handle…too contaminating even for alert, devout scholarship to cope with. Something poisonous, wicked, impious, evil. [10]

Some twenty-five years later, heeding the warning expressed by Eusebius, Cyril of Jerusalem in his *Catachresis* (possibly around 348 CE) predictably and generally declares false gospels to be harmful, but especially insists, "Let no one read the *Gospel of Thomas*." [11] In 367, Bishop Athanasius of Alexandria issues one of his *Festal Letters* with an inventory of the twenty-seven books which he asserts authoritatively constitute and foreclose the content of the Christian *New Testament*. (*Thomas* is markedly not among them.) It's a list later deemed canonical by the synods of Hippo Regius (393 CE) and then at Carthage (in 397 and 419). This ruling would not have been treated lightly by any officers of the churches and monasteries who came within the orbit of Athanasius's correspondence. He had some serious clout. At the Council of Nicaea, called by the converted Emperor Constantine back in 325, Athanasius had won a momentous victory against a faction led by a bishop of Alexandria named Arius. The Nicaean dispute had been over the 'substance' of Christ. Arius proposed that Christ was similar but not identical in substance to God the Father and thus Jesus, as the incarnate son of God, was son of Man with a mortal body. Seeing both a profound ideological scission looming from this disagreement as well as spotting a political opportunity, Athanasius countered that father and son were indeed identical in substance, and thus eternal. Suddenly, by denying what ought to be an incontrovertible belief in the divinity of Jesus, Arius sounded Satanic.

Athanasius's strident success in theological battle meant the denunciation of Arianism as heresy – a term derived from the Greek *airesis*, initially indicating a choice to disagree or dissent, but among early Christian apologists it assumed the judgment of a dangerously incorrect and misleading position on Church doctrine. Corrupted and corrupting. Arius lost his job (into which Athanasius stepped) and he and his followers were exiled. And Athanasius, during a checkered career with the church characteristic of an ideologue (requiring occasional flight from disfavor into the desert monasteries of North Africa), conducted further campaigns to clean up the speculative curiosities in Christian dogma: indeed, with a rhetorical style that would gain currency over the next thousand years as his legacy, heresies were regarded not only as misconceptions of doctrine but as unclean deviations, perversions, infections, which if not lanced and purged would spread like poxy contaminants. In one intriguing acerbic outburst in his thirty-ninth *Festal Letter*, Athanasius confirmed that "…we have made mention of heretics as dead, but of ourselves as possessing the Divine Scriptures for salvation…" [12]

Only those vigilantly compliant with the divine authority of orthodox scripture would be saved to live again. Unorthodoxy induced ontological doom as well as professional disaster: its perpetrators were already "dead," lost and rotting while yet living and spreading their filth. Heresiarchs were not only regarded as leprous outcasts, pollutants, carriers of contagion, but as the walking dead. It's a reasonable conjecture that – when delivered to a small monastic compound near Nag Hammadi, five hundred miles south of Alexandria – it was Athanasius's vitriolic letters that prompted the furtive, stealthy and secret burial of what must have seemed a damned or accursed book: the *Gospel of Thomas*. And the black mark against it persisted down the years. By the late tenth century, to read *Thomas* incurs anathema. Those who would dare open and respectfully scrutinize this by now legendary book, whether by deliberation or out of folly, are beyond redemption. Excommunicated, they are thus cursed by the church. The *Synodicon Orthodixiae* pronounces that, "To whomever who accepts or has affection for [*Thomas*]…and does not abominate [this book] and spit upon [it] as being worth only to be burned: anathema."

Why did this book – which we now know to be so slim and terse and such a puzzling volume – incur such animosity and contempt from orthodoxy for so many centuries? In part, this was due to a belief initiated by Cyril of Jerusalem that the gospel had been written by a Manichaean sect. That misconception was a boon to its notoriety. We owe the preservation of the citations of Thomas and their persistent sedition into the European Middle Ages largely to this guilt by association with the third-century CE Babylonian prophet and artist Mani and his heretical vision,

ESSAY

steeped in a millennium-old Zoroastrian legacy, of an irreconcilable cosmological dualism: a good God of spiritual light in fierce battle with its evil twin God of material darkness. A contrived joke against Mani's followers was how orthodox Christians referred to them as "Maniacs," spinning on the Greek words *maniakos* or *mainesthai*: to be mad. Delightfully inspired as this madness might sound, there is only a slim and opportunist relation between *Thomas* and Mani. Given the probable date of *Thomas* as a late first-century CE composition, it's improbable to think of it as having a Manichaean origin. And it is this putative date of origin that injects the *logoi* of this gospel with scintillating scandal, disclosed in the short prologue on the book's *incipit* or title-page: "These are the secret [or hidden] words that the living Jesus spoke, and which Didymos Judas Thomas wrote down." Two momentous dares accompany this parvenu's arrival, and it's little wonder that the guard dogs at the gates of canonical orthodoxy would fiercely rear up.

Firstly, were these esoteric, condensed "secret words" intended to be read only by the initiate? Well, not entirely. Almost half of the text, in the form of parables and more comprehensible maxims, correlate with passages in the canonical, synoptic gospels and which are hardly meant to be obscurely reserved for an inner circle. But other sayings manifest a mystifying and beguiling novelty and have little equivalence with the sentiments of the Christian *Testament*. *Logion 42*, for instance, laconically declares: "Be passersby." *Thomas* is often described as a sapiential text, yet this strange directive conveys no Confucian-like or proverbial wisdom, and also has nothing of the paradox lurking in Zen riddles. There's little consolation or ethical guidance in such a pithy admonition either, and so it doesn't accord with the rhetorical mode of the formulaic beatitude favoured by more familiar Christian moral aphorisms: "blessed are the meek," etc. Could the injunction in *logion 42* advocate for the virtue of an ascetic, itinerant, and presumably impoverished life? Not quite. In its curt economy, it doesn't sound pious so much as an almost slacker encouragement to be uninvolved, disconnected from the world, no matter how embroiled in its traffic. "Disengaged," notes one commentator, and distinct from the bonds of a community or *polis*. [13] One could add that, soliciting Jean Baudrillard's gyration of the libertine scenario of seduction, the passerby is also a spectator seductively "diverted." [14] The passerby cannot claim a mission: not as a pilgrim, not as a wandering mendicant sage, not even as a tourist. A passerby may be an onlooker, perhaps, but not an accredited witness, since they will have moved on. If anything, this *logion* has the rhetorical style of an invocation in a *memento mori*. Bentley Layton observes that the Greek verb *paragein* (to go past) was often used in epitaphs on graves, saluting the stranger who passed by (*parodites*) and petitioning "as though in the words of the corpse in the tomb." [15] As Jesus says, when one finds the world one finds a corpse; but if that corpse of the world speaks to you in secret words then it is no longer dead. But it is a corpse not saved from death, either. "Be passersby" is the motto of an unholy resurrection. The salutation of the undead.

A second, equally intriguing predicament, ensues with the attribution of authorship through a tripartite name which induces a cryptographic spin on the piquancy of this figure's connection with Jesus: Didymos Judas Thomas. Judas was a common name in the era of early Christianity, stigmatized among Christians through its association with the story of the betrayal of Jesus to Roman authorities by Judas Iscariot. Converts to Christianity born with the name of Judas usually added further names to mitigate this connotation. But the supplementary names of this gospel's author – who is, of course, in all likelihood a pseudonymous syndicate of scribes – hardly reduce or distract from the stigma. Instead they forge a multilingual, allegorical *nom de plume* that perversely overstretches the pseudo-apostolic relation with Jesus. The Greek component of the name, Didymos, means 'twin' and appears in the *Gospel of John* describing the apostle who, refusing to believe in the resurrection of Jesus until he places his fingers into the wounds of crucifixion, gains subsequent fame as Doubting Thomas. In the Greek version of *John* he's called 'Thomas the Twin,' as if it were a commonplace nickname, like Eric the Red. – The Syriac version of that gospel names this character as Judas Thomas; but in Syriac (or Eastern Aramaic) *t'oma* or *tau'ma* (transliterated in both Greek and Coptic as Thomas) also means 'twin.' Moreover, in another apocryphal if less problematic text, *The Acts of Thomas*, the apostle Judas Thomas is named as the twin of the messiah.

The signification of the authorship of the *Gospel of Thomas* is convoluted and abstrusely intertextual, perhaps deliberately to encrypt the author's prestigious but also audacious claim on being the twin brother of the "living Jesus." As with a nun's vow to become a 'bride of Christ,' Jesus's twin brother cannot be contained within a purely spiritual allegory. In Irenaeus's words this opens onto an abyss of madness: no longer a relation of apostolic deference, nor of mentorship, but of doubling. Entertain the dazzling blasphemy of this metaphor for a moment! Was Thomas conceived at the Annunciation at the same time as Jesus, and then disowned by the father as illegitimate, as his bastard progeny? Does this figurative illegitimacy shadow the spiritual imitation of Christ? But there may be another view onto this quandary that offers it as a negation rather than as a digression of parental accountability. It would take a strange adjective to describe this annulled relation, one that slurs categorial distinctions and invokes a mode of exclusion in the sly way that the word 'undead' does: the twin of Jesus Christ is 'unfathered.'

Salvation – the ultimate therapeutic treatment – comes to the world, it's announced in another Nag Hammadi text, the *Gospel of Philip*, "when the two become one and the outer become as the inner." This also is described in a ritual or ceremonial practice central to Valentinian Gnostic Christianity as the 'bridal chamber': an allegory of salvation in which spirit and physical matter are married into one (recycling the therapeutic union of opposites into an original unity, derived from Platonic philosophy). But the twinning of Jesus invoked by *Thomas* goes the other way. What happens to a world that turns against this pacific reconciliation of opposites; when, to use an odd recurrent autobiographical declaration of Nietzsche's, "the one becomes two"? Mani claimed to receive his Gnostic revelation from his suddenly manifested divine twin: in effect, what was revealed to him was a simulacrum of the divine, and with that the duplicity of his God who also was not one (the monotheistic persona of Abrahamic religions) but two (antagonistic but identical rivals). The heresy in Mani's prophecy – from which we derive any combative, destructive duality as Manichaean – was not just that there were twinned Gods (one, the substance of light; the other, the material of darkness) but that any God that divided from itself, who reproduced like this, would have to be a suspicious character and any world created by this God would be at best dubious, and more likely evil.

To understand such a world is to find a corpse. Not just a material, fleshly, down-to-earth world, but a dead one. But this is to be understood in the manner that the heretic is dead: living dead, anathema – in distinction to how the pious, the saved, live through the promise and provision of divine scripture. Let us think of this strange maxim uttered by a living Jesus as though it were in the words of the corpse in the tomb. A prophet speaking on behalf of the undead. Think of it as a defiance of the *logos* as holy word and in the Annuniciation: of word made flesh and disowned by

God in the way that Didymos Judas Thomas must be disowned. Not orphaned or cast out, but 'unfathered,' 'unmade.' To understand the world is to rot with it, to be its leper, be its grave; to be its black *gnosis* and black mass. Dead to the world.

2. CADAUER CHRISTI

> *Jesus said, "Whoever has known the world has fallen upon the body."*
> – Logion 80.1, *Gospel of Thomas*. [17]

What can we make of this tiny scribal alteration between *logion 56* and *logion 80*, which are identical other than for the substitution of "the body" (in Coptic transcription: *p-soma*) for "a corpse" (*-ptoma*)? Perhaps it was a slip of the pen, or of the ear. One commentator suggests that *logion 80* should be taken as the original because it implies a divine primordial body, and thus a far more positive image: "Whoever 'recognizes the world' in the Thomasine sense, a world permeated by the primordial light of the kingdom of God, finds the body and those who find the body are highly commended: they are superior to the ordinary world." [18] This would be uninterestingly pious stuff, except that it portrays *logion 56* as an astonishing impropriety and compelling corruption of the original, and thus far more interesting than its imputed correct version – particularly if it is indeed the result of a symptomatic slip. One should note that while *p-soma* could at a stretch be interpreted as the "corpus" (or proper scriptural body), *-ptoma* could readily be not only a "corpse," but also a "cadaver" or a "carcass." With such a tantalizing profile, this exquisite corpse – *symptoma* of the corruption of a Jesus-corpus – deserves more of our attention.

Corpses are not simply dead bodies. Corpses are problematic, reticent, and obstinate. The corpse may epitomize the entropic processes of self-digestion or autolysis, bloated decomposition and putrefaction in the steady, fateful slide into dank manure, slime and sewage; but the corpse also is paradoxically a ghastly icon of arrested rigor and ceremonial rigidity. As the problematic "stiff" in crime stories, the corpse has a colloquial phallic exhibitionism and obduracy, associated with awkward practical problems of disposal and with concealing guilt. And, of course, "stiffs" keep popping back up in these stories with the discomforting if not horrifying homecoming of a disavowed secret: floating to the surface in a black lake, exposed by accident in the boot of a car in transit, roused from a fetid tomb or clawing their way from an unholy grave. And sometimes, too, with blackly comic impropriety. Hitchcock's 1955 movie *The Trouble with Harry* plays wry sport with the embarrassing persistence of the guilty secret embodied in the well-dressed and forever immaculately neat male corpse lying in a meadow, whose death every member of the nearby tiny New England community separately believe they must have somehow caused, and whose corpse each person furtively drags from view in repeatedly failed attempts to cover up their complicity. The corpse in Ted Kotcheff's *Weekend at Bernie's* (1989) has a similarly stubborn and unspoiled conspicuousness. Bernie is the unscrupulous head of a corporation who has been murdered by a Mafia colleague at his beach house retreat. Two young innocent employees who have arrived for a weekend party at Bernie's witness the crime, and must keep the pretence of Bernie being alive in order to escape death themselves. Bernie's corpse is handled like a puppet, much to the maddening bewilderment of the hit-man who, despite repeated efforts, cannot put Bernie down.

Why insist on the implacable designation of 'corpse' for the protagonist in this sort of *danse macabre* rather than the more supple and chic term 'body'? It's not pedantry. The corpse is a residual indecency of life

ESSAY

that remains paradoxically unincorporated; that's to say, resistant to embodiment even as decay. A corpse is the atrocity, or perhaps the expletive of a body: the curse that diverts an oath from a pledge into a swearword, but it's also something that ludicrously or offensively sticks out of the form of the body. Stiff with erotic concentration but without the motivating surge of tumescence, the corpse stands spastically and forever at attention as a zombie soldier guarding a memorial flame of animate life or vitality, and attending this memorial in a hideous formal pantomime or pageant of the death it commemorates. Or, in another scenario, the corpse is the cadaverous 'lich' sustained by a curse, like the damned sailors of the legendary Flying Dutchman or Hector Barbossa's skeletal crew on the Black Pearl in *Pirates of the Caribbean: At World's End* (2007). Mummified or desiccated in a golden reliquary and in rotting lace or linen, the corpse is an enduring and magical artifact fabricated and maintained by a priestly caste or cult; an article so potent it must be locked away in secret; unseen, but guarded by spells and repeated rituals for the eternity it survives. Corpses are exquisitely blighted by an exclusion from both life and death. In the current popular jargon of vampiric and zombie fantasy, we would call this exclusion the protocol of the undead. Yet, as we intuitively acknowledge, corpses – certainly those farcical mannequins like Harry and Bernie – are worse than undead, more pathetic, less romantic. In comparison with any kind of corpse however, bodies are infinitely more flexible and inclusive, informal and mobile. They come and they go without ceremony.

Corpses may seem to be a subcategory of bodies; but where the corpse is a grotesque mockery, black magical ornament or irony of lifelessness, the body is anything and everything that is opposed to this specific state of the corpse. This is nominally so, because a 'body' can name structures of living as well as dead flesh, while also designating any extensive ensemble of things concrete (organic or inorganic) or abstractions becoming material or tangible. Embodiment involves incorporation: the constitutive formation of complex but unified substance. Compellingly, as a property of substances, 'body' always implies a volume if not fullness, a strength if not intensiveness, and weight if not ripeness...even in its morbid connotations. A body of water, a body of work, a body of evidence, even the bodies of plague victims piled in a cart: these have an agency and animation that the corpse – as the *cul-de-sac* of the *corpus* (which in its ancient and modern senses is a mass and massing together of working material, the stuffing of form) – no longer possesses. The Latin locution that the Vulgate *Gospel of John* renders for the dying Christ could be the nihilist slogan for all corpses: "*Consummatum est*," it is finished, my work is done. [19] But this has to be understood, however, not with the triumphal signification of Biblical concordances that identify this finish as consummation (fulfillment of passion), nor as consummate utterance (perfect in its fidelity to prophesies of the messianic mission). [20] Instead, we would treat the *Corpus Christi* as a black magic of the corpse, and the miraculous transubstantiation of the sacrificial body as an interference with death comparable to the putridly voracious, hellishly unfulfilled, unresurrected (unsaved) zombie. The paradoxical reticence of the corpse's consummation is an exquisite diabolical spell.

Bodies on the other hand are loquacious, even garrulous. They can be vivaciously original, sporting customized and unique aesthetic adornments and modifications, or can be subsumed in anonymous victimization or mass conformity. They can be tossed like debris within the fury of a tsunami; flow in ecstatic rage through streets or stadiums as inspired torrents; submit to masochistic objectification on grandly militaristic and on intimately tender scales of behaviour; they can entwine in rawness, hunger, affection and compassion with seeping volatility or with taut density and severity. Whatever they get to up or submit to, suffer from or are suffused with, however they may be interned or interred, bodies are garrulous, mutable and performative in ways that corpses are not. This is dramatically demonstrated in the ascendency of performance art through the second half of the twentieth-century, comfortably aligned with the emergence of the philosophical discipline of biopolitics and also strikingly coincident with the critical and pedagogical eclipse of the genre of the nude. By the mid 1970s the nude and the life classes that trained artists in this genre were politically noxious art historical relics, eclipsed by the bodily acting out of desires, sexual and gender identities, appetites, regressions, transgressions, perversions, sensualities, dietary or exercise regimes, therapeutics, and so forth. By the turn of the millennium, the polymorphous, polysexual, performative and performance-enhanced body had become the commodified core of lifestyle marketing as well as of the cultural studies industry.

It doesn't seem that surprising to encounter the hordes of the undead clamouring for enfranchisement within the liberal social and cultural policy that admits, emancipates or empowers this superabundant morphology and mutability and traffic of bodies. But the corpse doesn't quite meet any criteria for citizenship in a republic of bodies. Ironically, bodies are bound to their prolix properties. They multiply, proliferate and configure populations, demographic clusters, species and genera. Even in death their numbers accrue. In comparison, to this voluble if multifarious kinship of bodies, the corpse is an abhorrently exotic object, unassimilable, wretchedly hermetic. One might even go so far as to say that the corpse could be the enemy of the body. Its worst enemy. And it may be time to shut the body up by confronting it with its corpse. But if there is anything timely about putting a case for the corpse against the cultural cornucopia of bodies, it would be the use of the corpse as a means of interference with the effusive cultural studies of the body. This manoeuvre requires thinking of the corpse as an object that is 'un-embodied.' Yet this term is not as daunting, or as nonsensical as it might at first sound.

Such a weird, unembodied, object appears in Byzantine theology and aesthetics and is known to us by a now obscure Greek term as an *acheiropoieton*. This translates as 'not made by hand,' but its more beguiling meaning is literally unmanufactured. [21] *Acheiropoieta* were allegedly miraculous, indexical images of divinity, the most famous of these today being the Shroud of Turin: an alleged monoprint left on the funereal shroud of Jesus Christ, stained not by his corpse's blood loss nor by bodily secretions associated with putrescence of the cadaver (which would of course be a blasphemous explanation, since the corpse of Christ did not decompose), but deposited like a photographic print through the action of a divine, immaterial radiance. It's still postulated by stubborn apologists for the authenticity of the Shroud that rather than being a hoax produced with a fabric dye, the image may have been created by a mode of primitive camera-less photography, somewhere between a Rayogram and a Roentgen ray or X-ray. But there is a further point here that makes even this attempted explanation falter, and yet which shifts the theological doctrine into occult speculation. The theology of an *acheiropoieton* such as the Turin Shroud not only demands that the image cannot be made by hand (by human labour) but also it cannot be made by nature. [22] It cannot be a natural wonder, for instance, since a meteor shower isn't really an image other than when it is illustrated by hand; and it cannot be a wondrous sign, which can be accounted for as a natural phenomenon such as a burning bush through which a god presents itself. Hence the quasi-photographic technical explanation of the Shroud ends up attempting to be a secular and rather banal demystification or disenchantment of the occulted sign of the *acheiropoieton*;

banal, because what accords the *acheiropoieton* with its weird semiology as well as weird ontology is that it must be an un-made object, and an un-embodied portrait.

Let us treat the *acheiropoieton* as an artifact of media archaeology; granting that it is a provocation to speculate on what the medium of a 'miraculous' image might be and, further, that such an image – if we can call it that – would be an occulting of aesthetics and thus our media archaeology is a consciously fabricated crypto-archaeology. [23] Let us take this back to the complaint against the effusive performativity of the recent aesthetics of the body with a contrast to the aesthetics of the corpse. To do so, we should be just as anachronistic as considering the *acheiropoieton* as a media artifact. The *acheiropoieton* belongs with supernatural phenomena that were categorized as *eidola*, which were not generally or simply 'images' as the Greek is casually translated, but particular types of images that could be called 'double images' or spectres. In the Homeric idiom of pre-classical semiology, there are three cases of supernatural images like this: firstly, the phantom image (or *phasma*) which is a ghostly simulacrum created by a god in the semblance of a living person and which you encounter when you are fully awake (epiphanies or encounters with gods could fit this bill); secondly there is the dream image (*oneiros*), which is the apparition of a real being, perceived when you are unconscious, and sent by the gods as messenger or companion or tormentor (and which could, at a stretch, fit into Freudian and Surrealist topographies); and lastly, and most intriguing, the soul (*psuche*), which is the phantom of the dead – and which has the appearance of the living being but does not have its essential property: life. *Psuche* is the contradictory state of Being-without-essence, in other words of un-being rather than nothingness or non-being; and thus as un-being *psuche* is not a dissimulation or concealment of life but a dissimulation (or perhaps simulacrum) of nothingness. [24] We might say that, as with divinity mediated through the *acheiropoieton*, *psuche* is not non-existent so much as 'inexistent.' And, again comparable to the *acheiropoieton*, *psuche* is an image only insofar as it is a stain or blot that occludes the image of life. Inasmuch as un-being is an unidentifiable macula or blot rather than a hole or absence, we could say, that the corpse is a body seen against the transit of *psuche*. Sic transit. [25]

Obviously, in the Homeric world, *psuche* is not the soul as the animating life-force nor is it cause of the vitality of an organism (associated, for instance, with *pneuma*), such as it appears later in Aristotelian empiricism, and where it becomes a principle of generation or composition, of change, and also of decomposition or compost; and where it is necessary for a being to decay as much as grow in order to be of its own essence. Nor, evidently, is *psuche* in this archaic sense the flourish of an intelligibility of essence: of Being as the possession of an inalienable identity. [26] In the legends that are canonized through the Homeric stories, a living being does not possess a *psuche*; once dead they become a *psuche*. However, this becoming-*psuche* is not a process of living but the advent of unbeing and of life being undone, of being other than itself. Thus the Homeric, archaic *psuche* is neither an index to nor a potentiality of life since it plays no role in life and has no relevant relation to it, other than that it is identifiable in its rotting double, the corpse. [27] *Psuche* is outside this corpse as an unbeing, yet identified with it in the way that in a morgue a witness is asked to identify a dead body: duplicitously invoking the verb 'to be': "yes, this is so-and-so," but only if one adds "it is no longer this person." What is no longer is not pictured as a divorcing of life and body, or the subtraction of a living essence or ghost from the inert vehicle or machine, but as a wedding of body and corpse, an alchemical wedding in which the corpse is the blackening introduction of the catalytic bride;

in alchemical as well as Duchampian terms, a bride "stripped bare." This compromised recognition of the corpse could not occur if *psuche* were an immortal entity; what we identify as the archaic unbeing of a body – as *psuche* – is rather an un-mortal image of the corpse. *Psuche* is the image of a death in transit (not a life in transit, not life moving to another state of its being; nor the recurrent consoling benefaction of death as a further stage of life's way), and we construe this transit as an interference of images by occultation: we might say that *psuche* is a black cloud, and we might dub psychic images as 'clouding.'

But we must quickly add that this psychic image is not in any way an affirmation of life-after-death, not an evanescence of the animate spirit; nor, indeed, of any spirituality whatsoever. Outside but occulting that decaying and disappearing thing that it identifies, *psuche* is beside itself: sidelined, it is the literal ecstasy of the corpse. I'll borrow a phrase from Reza Negarestani – admittedly in a cavalier act, out of context – in his brilliant exposition of the mode of execution, mentioned in Virgil's *Aeneid* among other ancient sources as a practice of the so-called barbarous and piratical Etruscans, dubbed "the corpse-bride" in which a putrefying, blackening corpse is tethered to the living victim in an intimate face-to-face embrace, if not in actual copulation. [28] The amorous, sexual embrace of the corpse and living body occasions an exquisitely horrific image, and which desecrates not only the transfiguring sanctity of marriage but also those spiritualizing aspirations of the alchemical wedding recited in hermetic science, in which a blackening of substance in the alembic precedes the revelation of the philosopher's stone. Exploiting this desanctified miracle, I would describe the interference of the psychic black cloud (abducting the phrase from Negarestani) as "an epiphenomenon of necrophilic intimacy." [29] More bizarrely, if more technically, this ecstatic position of the corpse-bride could be a cypto-archaeological media artifact: an image of psychic blackening, which could in turn be dubbed, casually adopting a term of diverse mathematical and philosophical currency, a singularity. The singular, in my white-dwarf and perverted contraction of this usage, is a situation of the subject subtracted from any particularities, or from particular knowledge of the subject. A singularity, suggests Alain Badiou, is a situation of the subject as an "upsurge" or advent, an exception, rather than a condition of being or of predicated meaning. [30] We might think of this grammatically rather than in the more difficult logical terms of Badiou's remarks, and say that in a sentence that has a subject and a predicate, such as "the cat sat on the mat," the singularity is the subject subtracted from its predicated knowledge (that it is "the cat that sat on the mat"). Singularity is an interference with the ontological intelligibility of the sentence. Paradoxical as it sounds, the singularity will be universal since it excludes anything particular about the cat, but this is not the eternal essence of cat we are talking about, not 'catness' (since that essence can include the knowledge that "cats are beings that sit on mats"). Singularity (and here the term may have opportunistic coincidence with its use in astrophysics) involves not the revelation of essence but an exceptional disappearance or obscuring of it.

The singularity is the exceptional situation of the cat without its particular identifications that would identify and would make it appear as a being. In other words, that render it as unbeing. The singularity of the subject – and consequently, the image of *psuche* as an ontological interference – is beautifully eventful in the Cheshire's cat's ecstatic grin from Lewis Carroll's *Alice in Wonderland*; the grin which importunately and obscenely lingers beyond the disappearance of its predicate. The facetious obstinacy of this grin suggests the incomprehensible predatory unbeing of the living dead who don't stay within their graves or memorials, or the ghostly persistence of an importunate property

ESSAY

outside its body, as an afterimage with the aesthetic effrontery of a hallucination that haunts and horrifies. The Cheshire cat's smile is obscenely unworldly. In part, this is because that smile is sinister – in the way all cats' expressions seem elusively, disdainfully, deceptively enigmatic (captured expertly in Tenniel's original illustrations of the first publication of *Alice in Wonderland*, but not in any many other versions, such as the Disney animations). Partly too, this smile is also ominous. The Cheshire cat in Wonderland is an oracle: it tells the adventurer Alice, with mischievous unintelligibility, what will happen and which way to go. Yet – in a world where one's size telescopes and inflates like a concertina, where one must run as fast as possible to stay in the same place, where at the Mad Hatter's table it is tea-time all the time and one must celebrate unbirthdays – this advice about which way to go is not so much less than useful but more than useless. In its ecstatic state, extended beyond and yet subtracted from its nature and its being, does the cat's grin belong to it any longer? Is not the extent and the exclusion of this smile a hideous intimacy with the cat? Is not such a smile the very emblem of *psuche*, and thus a miraculous unworldly image? This smile is the mischievous horror of the corpse's un-embodiment and the eucharist of a blackening mass of the corpse. ∎

ACKNOWLEDGEMENTS

Research for this project was assisted by the Australian Government through the Australia Council for the Arts, its arts funding and advisory body, for their London Writers' Residency in conjunction with ACME Studios, London.

REFERENCES AND NOTES

1. The full verse continues "[...] and whoever has fallen onto a corpse, the world is worthy of him not." *An Interlinear Coptic-English Translation of the Gospel of Thomas*, 56i, http://gospel-thomas.net/splith.htm (accessed June 5, 2013). See also *Coptic Gnostic Chrestomathy: A Selection of Coptic Texts with Grammatical Analysis and Glossary*, ed. Bentley Layton (Leuven: Peeters, 2004). Other translations politely moderate the verbs, but in rendering a more familiar rhythm lose the brusqueness of the source's compounded syntax, and in some cases editorially enhance the source: for instance, "Whoever has come to understand the world has found (only) a corpse; and whoever has found a corpse, is superior to the world." Trans. Thomas O. Lambdin, *The Gnostic Society Library*, http://gnosis.org/naghamm/nhl_thomas.htm (accessed June 5, 2013), in which the parenthetical English adverb is an unjustified qualification; just as "worth," and the lack of it, suggests suitability rather than superiority. The Coptic term translated as "world" here is, appropriately grand and inclusive: "*kosmos*."

2. Irenaeus, *Adversus Haeresus* (Against Heresies) in *The Apostolic Fathers with Justin Martyr and Irenaeus*, ed. Philip Schaff (Grand Rapids, MI: Christian Classics Ethereal Library, 2001), 443-824. Two modern studies had in particular, if in divergent idioms, popularized this nomenclature for the Nag Hammadi library: Hans Jonas, *The Gnostic Religion: The Message of the Alien God and the Beginnings of Christianity* (Boston: Beacon Press, 1958); Elaine Pagels, *The Gnostic Gospels* (Harmondsworth: Penguin, 1982) with her sequel (focused on *The Gospel of Thomas*), *Beyond Belief* (New York: Random House, 2003).

3. The text authored as by "Mark" is presumed to have been composed between 60-70 CE; those attributed to "Matthew" and "Luke" 75-85 CE. The oldest fragment of the New Testament is the Rylands Papyrus dated at 130 CE (fragment of *John*, chapter 18) in the John Rylands Library, Manchester UK; the oldest extensive papyrus of the New Testament is The Chester Beatty and Bodmer Papyrus, dated between 180 and 225 CE in the Chester Beatty Library, Dublin, Ireland. Among others, *Thomas* scholar and

translator James M. Robinson has proposed that *Thomas* could be affiliated with the hypothetical *Q source* which, throughout the twentieth century has been theoretically postulated as a sayings compendium (partly oral, partly written but no longer extant) providing the source along with *Mark* for the canonical gospels of *Matthew* and *Luke*. Some suggested dating of the conjectural "layer 1" of *Q*, and by association *Thomas*, even precede the composition of *Mark* by thirty years.

4. The common noun *gnosis*, technical as it is, has a relatively benign and even banal affect compared to its more piquant adjectival use, both in antique testimonia and in modern usage. But the term 'Gnostic' as used today in an expedient summary of extremely diverse religious and metaphysical doctrines is an appellation that, with perhaps one exception, those antique sectarian movements would have been unlikely to recognize. The exception may be that of the faction led by Marcellina in mid second-century Rome. Her Christian sect, which allegedly practiced a type of communistic social code, is contemptuously mentioned by Irenaeus as publicizing themselves with the adjective *gnostikos*, although no testimonial of their own survives. (Iraneaus in Philip Schaff, ed., *The Apostolic Fathers with Justin Martyr and Irenaeus*, 503.) Irenaeus used the derogatory nuance of this word in the manner of Paul's usage for a reprimand against false knowledge (*1 Timothy* 6.20), with an evident Platonic pedigree. Modern scholarship has tended to employ this adjective and the proper noun of 'Gnosticism' anachronistically: derived from Irenaeus's derogatory jibe, it entered common English usage with Henry More's 1669 exegetical commentary on 2.20 of the *Revelation of John* (*An Exposition of the Seven Epistles*, no 99). In his *Antidote Against Idolatory* (which was printed with the *Exposition*), More alludes to "the old abhorred Gnosticism." See Bentley Layton, "Prolegomena to the Study of Ancient Gnosticism," in *Doctrinal Diversity: Varieties of Early Christianity*, ed. Everett Ferguson London and New York: Routledge, 1999, 106-122. (Specifically on More's terminology, see Bentley Layton, op. cit., 120-121.)

5. In her *Gnostic Gospels*, Pagels rhapsodically portrays Gnostic Christian communities of the late Roman empire as almost counter-culturally militant or renegade, in both their various ascetic as well as libertarian social and religious principles. In a more recent (1998) PBS education blog on *Thomas*, she associates *gnosis* with a Zen-like *satori* or insight, and also with a mode of Socratic self-knowledge instead of apocalyptic prophecy, situating the Jesus in *Thomas* in the tradition an enlightened religious sage figure rather than the rabbinical messiah of the canonical *New Testament*. "Jesus, in effect, turns one toward oneself, and that is really one of the themes of the *Gospel of Thomas*, that you must go in a sort of a spiritual quest of your own to discover who you are, and to discover really that you are the child of God just like Jesus." Elaine H. Pagels, "The Gospel of Thomas," *FRONTLINE* (blog), April 1998, http://www.pbs.org/wgbh/pages/frontline/shows/religion/story/thomas.html (accessed June 5, 2013).

6. Irenaeus, in Philip Schaff, ed., *The Apostolic Fathers with Justin Martyr and Irenaeus*, 449.

7. This anecdote is told by the Nag Hammadi scholar James Robinson from direct conversation with Mohammed al-Samman in James Robinson, "Nag Hammadi: The First Fifty Years," in *The Nag Hammadi Library after Fifty Years: Proceedings of the 1995 Society of Biblical Literature Commemoration*, ed. J. D. Turner and A. McGuire (Leiden Brill, 1997), 3-6; see also Bart D. Erhmann, *Lost Christianities: The Battle for Scripture and the Faiths We Never Knew* (New York: Oxford University Press, 2003), 51.

8. Fragments of it appear as the text *Sayings of our Lord* in the Oxyrynchus Papyri, discovered in 1897 by the Oxford scholars B. P. Grenfell and A. S. Hunt at an archaeological dig at the ancient Upper Egypt site of Oxyrynchus. Reconstruction and translation, Andrew Bernhard, "The Gospel of Thomas: Fragments from Oxyrhynchus," *The Gnosis Archive*, n.d., http://www.gnosis.org/naghamm/thomas_poxy.htm (accessed June 5, 2013).

9. Harold Attridge, "Appendix: The Greek Fragments," in *Nag Hammadi codex II, 2-7, volume 1*, ed. Bentley Layton (Leiden: Brill, 1989). For a much extended itinerary, with commentary, see Simon Gathercole, "Named Testimonia

to the *Gospel of Thomas*: An Expanded Inventory and Analysis," *Harvard Theological Review* 105, no. 1 (2012): 53-89.

10. Simon Gathercole, "Named Testimonia to the *Gospel of Thomas*: An Expanded Inventory and Analysis," 57-58.

11. Ibid., 58.

12. Quoted in Joe E. Morris, *Revival of the Gnostic Heresy: Fundamentalism* (New York: Palgrave Macmillan, 2008), 9.

13. R. Valentisis, *The Gospel of Thomas* (London & New York: Routledge, 1997), 118.

14. Jean Baudrillard, "Please Follow Me," in Jean Baudrillard and Sophie Calle, *Suite Vénitienne: Please Follow Me*, trans. Dany Barash and Danny Hatfield (Seattle: Bay Press, 1988).

15. Bentley Layton, *Gnostic Scriptures: A New Translation with Annotations and Introductions* (Garden City: Doubleday & Co., 1987), 387.

16. Paul Foster, *The Apocryphal Gospels: A Very Short Introduction* (Oxford: Oxford University Press, 2009), 32.

17. *An Interlinear Coptic-English Translation of the Gospel of Thomas*, 80i, http://gospel-thomas.net/splith.htm (accessed June 5, 2013).

18. Stevan L. Davies, "The Christology and Protology of The Gospel of Thomas," *Journal of Biblical Literature* 3, no. 4 (1992): 672.

19. *Gospel of John*, chapter 19, verse 30. The full verse is *cum ergo accepisset Ieusus acetum dixit consummatum est et inclinator capite tradidit spiritum*. (The King James Version translates as: "When Jesus therefore had received the vinegar [sour wine], he said, It is finished: and he bowed his head and gave up the ghost." The Revised Standard Version translates the last clause as "gave up his spirit.") The phrase *consummatum est* is derived from the Greek original, *tetelstai*, which invokes a stock term used in the completion of an economic, or financial, transaction equivalent to 'paid in full,' and which would in the gospel text would refer to a blood debt having been accounted for.

20. The Vulgate Gospel indicates the genealogy of the prophesied sacrifice in chapter 19, verse 28: *postea sciens Iesus quia iam omnia consummate sunt ut consummaretur scriptura dicit sitio* ("Afterwards, Jesus knowing that all things were accomplished, that the scripture might be fulfilled, said: I thirst." KJV).

21. The miraculous authority of *acheiropoieta* may have an analogy if not source in material practices such as the use of clay seals for authenticity of imperial proclamations and legal testimonials, or cast images in imperial coinage, as well as the indelible pattern left in dyed cloth after it has been washed. See James Trilling, "The Image Not Made by Hands and the Byzantine Way of Seeing," in *The Holy Face and the Paradox of Representation*, eds. Herbert L. Kessler and Gerhard Wolf (Bologna: Nuova Alfa Editoriale, 1998), 109-127. A startling extrapolation of the dyed image is the suggestion that the *acheiropoieton* known as Veronica's veil or the *mandylion*, bearing the face of Christ during the Passion, is associated with menstruation, thus identifying the Christian blood debt and sacrifice with the *mandil* as a menstrual towel. See Ewa Kuryluk, *Veronica and Her Cloth: History, Symbolism, and a Structure of a "True" Image* (Cambridge, MA and Oxford: Basil Blackwell, 1991). And in comparison see Avril Cameron, "The *Mandylion* and Byzantine Iconoclasm," and Herbert L. Kessler, "Configuring the Invisible by Copying the Holy Face," both in *The Holy Face and the Paradox of Representation*; and Jeffrey Hamburger, "Vision and the Veronica," in *The Visual and the Visionary: Art and Female Spirituality in Late Medieval Germany* (New York: Zone Books, 1998). On the signification of the untouched and the impure touch in manufacturing the image, see Marie-José Mondzain, "The Holy Shroud: How Invisible Hands Weave the Undecidable," in *Iconoclash: Beyond the Image Wars in Science, Religion, and Art*, ed. Bruno Latour and Peter Weibel (Cambridge, MA: Massachusetts Institute of Technology, 2002), 324-335.

22. Archeological and forensic assessments of the Turin Shroud are detailed in Robin Cormack, *Painting the Soul: Icons, Death Masks and Shrouds* (London: Reaktion Books, 1997), 89-132. On the centuries-long debates, generally called the iconoclastic controversy, over the possible iconolatry or idolatry of *acheiropoieta* in Byzantine

theology and aesthetics, see David Freedberg, *The Power of Images* (Chicago: University of Chicago Press, 1989), 392-399, and Moshe Barasch, *Icon: Studies in the History of an Idea* (New York and London: New York University Press, 1992).

23. For my own contribution see "Iconicity: The Medium of Miraculous Images," in *New Imaging: Transdisciplinary Strategies for Art Beyond the New Media* [special issue Column 7], ed. Su Baker, Melanie Oliver and Paul Thomas (Sydney: Artspace, 2011), 66-75.

24. On the distinctions between these three modes of supernatural imaging, see Jean-Pierre Vernant, "*Psuche*: Simulacrum of the Body or Image of the Divine," in *Mortals and Immortals*, trans. Froma I. Zeitlin (Princeton: Princeton University Press, 1991), 186-192.

25. *Sic transit gloria mundi* ("Thus passes worldly glory") is, of course the keystone to funereal homilies and valediction as well as having a ceremonial utterance in papal coronations, and is likely derived from Thomas à Kempis's *Imitation of Christ* (1418): *O quam cito transit gloria mundi*. My truncation of the phrase isolates the inevitability of the unpredicated passing as a crossing, an obscuring or an eclipse rather than a passing away or loss.

26. For a new interpretation of Aristotle's *psuche* as the entelechy or realization of essence of a body that "serves as its instrument," see A. P. Bos, *The Soul and its Instrumental Body A Reinterpretation of Aristotle's Philosophy of Living Nature* (Leiden: Brill, 2003).

27. Perhaps the most vivid and lurid manifestation of this bizarre identity is in the recurrent exquisite corpses of Edgar Allen Poe's fantastic premature burials and somnambulant revenants: Madeleine Usher clawing her way out of her coffin; Berenice's unearthly scream from the grave as her lover, in a fugue state, tears her teeth out with dental pliers; or Monsieur Valdemar, when released from his post-mortem mesmeric trance explodes into a puddle of putrescence.

28. " [...] The Lydians, / Renowned in war, in the old days settled there / On the Etruscan ridges, and for years /The city flourished, till an arrogant king, / Mezentius, ruled it barbarously by force. / How shall I tell of carnage beyond telling, / Beastly crimes this tyrant carried out? /Requite them, gods, on his own head and on / His children! He would even couple carcasses / with living bodies as a form of torture / Hand to hand and face to face, he made them / Suffer corruption, oozing gore and slime / In that wretched embrace, and a slow death." Virgil, *The Aeneid*, trans. Robert Fitzgerald (New York, London and Toronto: Alfred A. Knopf/Everyman's Library, 1992), Book VIII, lines 644-656. The reference to this practice occurs in several lost sources from antiquity: such as the florid oratory of Quintus Hortensius Hortalus (first century BCE), reported by Cicero in his lost dialogue *Hortensius*, and which St Augustine in turn reports on. Cicero also cites a reference to the corpse-bride in Aristotle as an analogy for the amalgam of body and soul; which in later Pauline language becomes the Christian soul shackled to the mortal flesh of the body.

29. Reza Negarestani, "The Corpse Bride: Thinking with Nigredo," *Collapse IV: Concept Horror* (May 2008): 134-135.

30. Alain Badiou and Slavoj Zizek, *Philosophy in the Present*, trans. Peter Thomas and Alberto Toscano (Cambridge: Polity Press, 2009), 26-48.

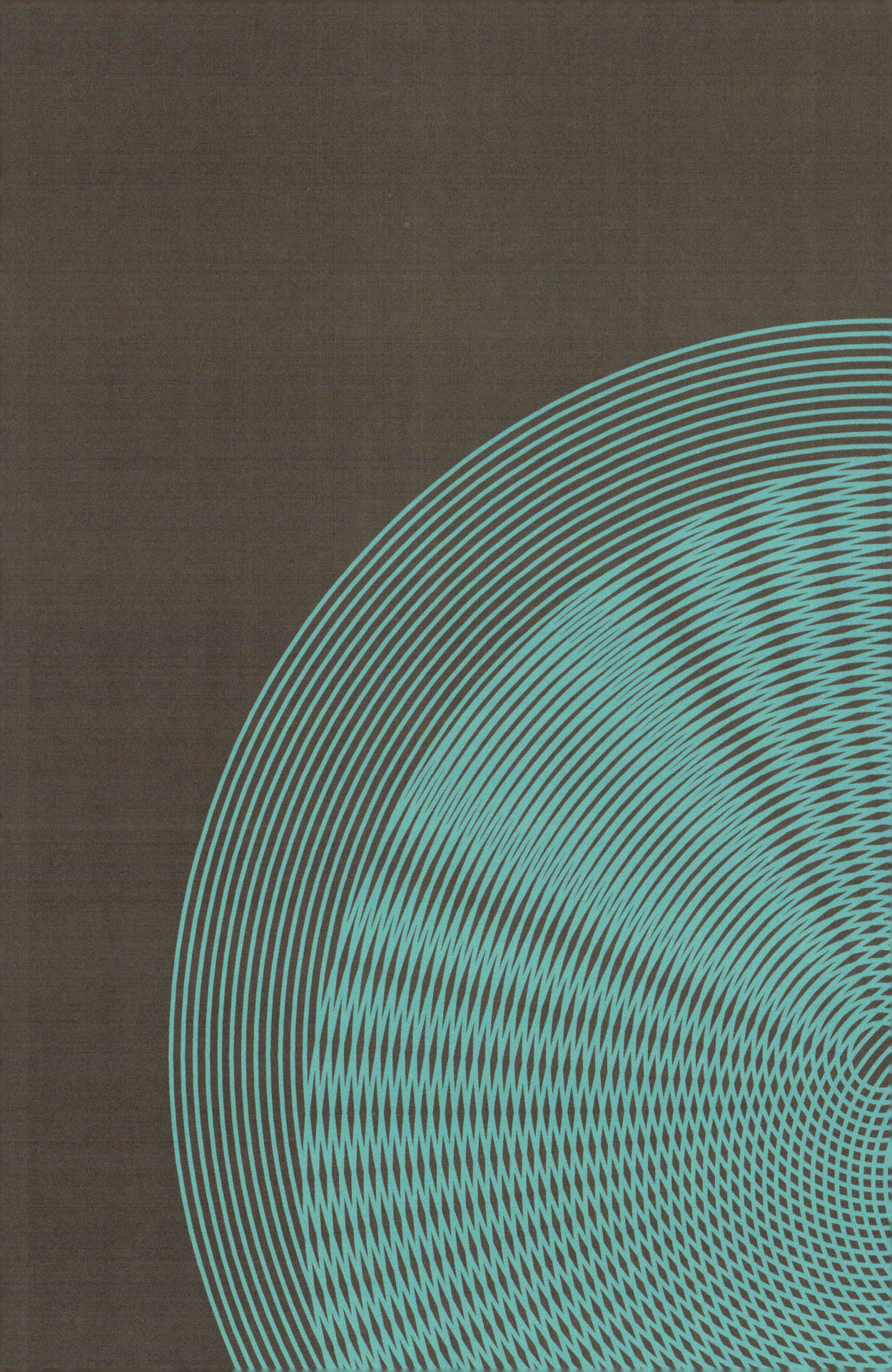

MERGE/MULTIPLEX

by

Brogan Bunt

Faculty of Creative Arts
University of Wollongong
brogan@uow.edu.au

INTRODUCTION

This paper addresses the issue of interference in another context. Not in terms of the spectre of a machinic economy of the image, in which visibility precisely is put at risk, but in terms of the aesthetic identity of socially engaged art. I am thinking of interference specifically as a form of blurring – the apparent obfuscation of identity. There is the conventional sense, for instance, in which contemporary socially engaged art blurs the lines both between art and ordinary social life and between art and other disciplines (ethnography, social work, etc.). Despite this specific focus, I am hoping that the issues I raise have more general implications, addressing not only the limits of art but also the limits of strategies of interference. Towards the end of this paper, my aim is to propose an alternative to the blurring of boundaries, to suggest the possibility of another way of drawing into relation multiple signals – not interference, but multiplexing. Multiplexing involves the spatial or temporal interleaving of multiple signals within an overall signal. The signals are combined but maintain their distinct identities and can at any time be separated into their component parts. This provides a means of conceiving socially engaged art practice differently, less necessarily as a site of aesthetic ambiguity than as one of unexpected clarification. Indeed these tendencies are not so easily opposed.

The tradition of modern and contemporary art seems to be characterised by an endless pushing back of the boundaries separating art and everyday life, art and the sphere of the social. This is typically interpreted in terms of a work of merging and blurring – an effort of interference that affects dimensions of both art and life. This paper suggests an alternative conception. Drawing upon the metaphor of electronic multiplexing, it argues that, while never simply absolutely distant from one another, art and the sphere of lived relations and social interaction are closely interleaved and yet retain a sense of distinct, differentiated identity. The energy of their relation, their potential to suggest new relations, depends upon an interplay of heterogeneous and always contingently determinable component signals.

EVERYDAY PRACTICE

The title of a recent book on socially engaged art practice, *Living as Form* [1] suggests a contemporary transition beyond ordinary artistic means and ordinary contexts of art. Life itself now takes shape as a form of artistic practice. Of course the danger here, in this specific context of blurring and interference, is the one-sidedness of the relation. Rather than equitably merging, life appears to be sublated within art. The title suggests a very conventional Hegelian dialectical framework in which art discovers a relation to its other, consumes its other and renders the other in its own terms. This issue of which of the two dissolves into the other, or how precisely they can find means to collapse together in a non-subsuming manner, is always fraught and never easy to resolve. Of course this title and the modes of social engaged art that concern it link to a very long tradition of utopian avant-garde practice that aims to disrupt the boundaries between art and everyday life and to foster new contexts for engaged living.

In his *Theory of the Avant-Garde*, for instance, Peter Burger argues:

> [t]he European avant-garde movements can be defined as an attack on the status of art in bourgeois society. What is negated is not an earlier form of art (a style) but art as an institution that is unassociated with the life of men. [2]

We can find all sorts of evidence for this in the manifestos of the early 20th century avant-garde, from the

ESSAY

Italian Futurist, Umberto Boccioni's, call for a "[l]iving art" that "draws its life from the surrounding environment" [3] to the Russian Constructivists, Naum Gabo and Anton Pevzner's, insistence that "[a]rt should attend us everywhere that life flows and acts...at the bench, at the table, at work, at rest, at play." [4] It is evident, as well, in French Surrealist, Andre Breton's, summoning of an "absolute reality, a surreality" [5] in which dreaming and living are combined, and in Romanian and French Dadaist, Tristan Tzara's, proclamation, "Freedom: DADA DADA DADA, a roaring of tense colours, and interlacing of opposites and of all contradictions, grotesques, inconsistencies: LIFE." [6] For my purposes, the interesting thing about these early examples is that they suggest less a seamless merging of art and life than an abrasive, energising interrelation. They acknowledge that life has its own richness and poetry. The relation, in other words, is not unequal, is not predicated on an assumed division between a dynamic, healing sphere of aesthetics and a moribund sphere of ordinary life. On the contrary, if anything, art risks its notional and disabling integrity to engage with a dynamism that exceeds and attracts it.

Later, of course, things appear a bit different as the initial integration of art and everyday life fails and, more generally, as the experience of vibrant industrial modernity passes into the experience of commodity capitalism. Theodor Adorno famously cautions against conflating art and dimensions of direct social existence, arguing that "art becomes social by its opposition to society, and it occupies this position only as autonomous art." [7] Art, in his view, necessarily inhabits a contradictory space – it withdraws in order to engage. Any effort to reconcile the distinction between art and life would only serve to obscure the genuine bases of antagonism, the genuine forces that make reconciliation impossible:

By emphatically separating themselves from the empirical world, their other, they [art works] bear witness that the world itself should be other than it is; they are the unconscious schemata of that world's transformation. [8]

But this hardly puts a stop to efforts at aesthetic intervention. In the wake of Henri Lefebvre's foregrounding of the sphere of everyday life, in which he portrays a profoundly elusive and ambiguous layer of experience, which figures as both a site of alienation (shaped by the spectre of consumption) and as a site of utopian potential (a realm of interference, in which the schemata of capitalist relations come unstuck as they are played out, as they are lived), [9] [10] Guy Debord emphasises the need for strategic intervention in the everyday. He begins by acknowledging its central importance, "Everyday life is the measure of all things: of the (non)fulfillment of human relations; of the use of lived time; of artistic experimentation; and of revolutionary politics," [11] but moves on to argue that, as a sphere of "separation and spectacle," everyday life lacks adequate means on its own to serve as a genuine site of resistance. There is a need for conscious, radical, critical agents to intervene within the everyday and transform it. The urgent task is to "replace the present ghetto with a constantly moving frontier; to work ceaselessly toward the organization of new chances." [12] While initially this was conceived in terms of artistic strategies of unitary urbanism, *detournement* and *derive*, the Situationists are famous for shifting beyond aesthetic intervention, for refashioning their critique and their modes of resistance in more explicitly political terms. Their work engages a tension between their commitment to pass away from the language of spectacle (whether cast in aesthetic, political or consumerist terms) into the realm of direct action and their awareness that every situation, every effort at subversion, is inevitably subject to recuperation (becomes an image, becomes distanced from its immediate, vital social energy). In this sense, despite serving as a continuing model for currents of activist art, the spectacle of the Situationist International disrupts any neat sense of subversive artistic agency. Art and agency are awkwardly configured, even opposed.

The 'activities' of Allan Kaprow, which involve the re-performance of everyday actions (brushing teeth, etc.) in an attentive, engaged manner, may seem very distant from Debord's more politically charged conception of the 'situation', yet they share a common assumption that the everyday requires active intervention, that it dissolves into habit and routine if left to its own devices. Although apparently emblematic of a concern to merge art and everyday life, his activities establish a tense and uncertain relation between the two. He describes his activities as having a paradoxical relation to art. They are performed, he argues, without any particular thought of art at all: "I could, of course, have said to myself, 'Now I'm making art!!' But in actual practice, I didn't think much about it." [13] What is it then that links the notion of the activity to art? Kaprow acknowledges its logical position in the tradition of historical avant-garde resistance to the field of autonomous art, suggesting that "developments within modernism itself let to art's dissolution into its life sources." [14] In this fashion, his non-art activities have a kind of inevitable relevance to art – they bear the imprint of art's own motion of self-critique. Yet there seems to be more to it than just this. The very act of re-performing the everyday has very evident aesthetic implications. It involves a work of making strange, of fostering heightened perceptual awareness. It follows a legibly conventional avant-garde critical model: life, the experience of life, has become empty and routinised; there is a vital need to renew it from within, to discover means to lead it to fully engaged reflective apperception. In short, the aim is to re-animate life, but this can only occur through a strategic withdrawal – if not via the traditional means of drawing, painting and sculpture then through the insertion of the slightest layer of difference within the texture of ordinary activities; the sense of re-performance rather than the blindness of action as such. Despite Kaprow's resistance to the field of art-objects, to the autonomy of images, he describes this layer of difference precisely in terms of the language of images:

This was an eye-opener to my privacy and to my humanity. An unremarkable picture of myself was beginning to surface, and [sic] image I'd created but never examined. It colored the images I made of the world and influenced how I dealt with my images of others. I saw this little by little. [15]

The metaphors are all of images. They all relate to a coming to visibility, as well as a shift away from the specific to the general. Kaprow recognises this. He catches himself slipping into the terrain of the aesthetic, so insists on bringing things back to the specific aesthetically alienated field of the activity itself:

But if this wider domain of resonance, spreading from the mere process of brushing my teeth, seems too far from its starting point, I should say immediately that it never left the bathroom. [16]

Overall, Kaprow struggles to position his activities beyond the frame of art, or just across its exterior threshold, but it could be argued that this alternation, this shift back and forth between interior and exterior, image and non-image, experience and reflective apperception, specificity and generality is the very motion of the aesthetic itself.

I lack the scope in this short essay to trace this history of ambivalent relation between art and everyday life, art and social action, convincingly through currents of conceptual, post-object, feminist, community and relational art to contemporary social engaged art and so-called social practice (the latter abandoning the mention of art altogether), but many of the main thematic contours are in place. It is worth mentioning, however, that different, less grand, conceptions of resistance have emerged. Apart from Nicolas Bourriaud's [17] social models and micro-utopias, there is also Jacques Ranciere's notion of an aesthetically grounded politics of "dissensus," [18] involving conflicts "between two regimes of sense, two sensory worlds," [19] which inevitably suspends dimensions of cause and effect, which, in a manner not altogether dissimilar to Adorno, brackets any simple, unmediated relation between art and the social. Also worth mentioning the efforts by critics such as Grant Kester [20] and Ben Highmore [21] to re-conceptualise the aesthetic, not as a terrain of separation and distance, but as fundamentally founded in the sphere of everyday experience and dialogic interaction. Finally, and most saliently for my purposes, is the Austrian philosopher, Gerald Raunig's, Deleuzian and Guattarian conception of the transversal relation between art and political activism; "[c]ontrary to models of totally diffusing and confusing art and life," Raunig "investigates other practices [...] in which transitions, overlaps and concatentations of art and revolution become possible for a limited time, but without synthesis and identification." [22] However, rather than pursuing these various debates in depth, it may be more useful to consider two contemporary examples of socially engaged art which demonstrate, as Claire Bishop suggests, that "art and the social are not to be reconciled or collapsed, but sustained in continual tension." [23]

GAME OVER

In March 2011 the Belgian-Mexican artist, Francis Alys, produced a short video entitled *Game Over*. [24] It documents the process of the artist crashing an old VW beetle into a tree at the botanical gardens in Culiacan, Mexico, then getting out of the car and walking off. This is followed by a brief inter-title explanation and a concluding statement: "Nature will do the rest."

The botanic gardens commissioned Alys to produce the work, which he conceived as a kind a road movie, in which he'd drive his car the entire way up to Culiacan only to crash it into a tree. He initially pitched it in terms of its capacity to establish "empathy between nature and culture": "[t]he plan was for the car to remain in the site and devolve into a sort of giant flowerpot for the garden's flora and fauna, becoming integrated with the local ecosystem." [25]

However, the absurdity and violence of the act clearly lends it wider implications. The town of Culiacan and Sinaloa state generally are notorious for drug-related crime. But even more than acknowledging this violent social background, the work emerges as a reflection on the dilemmas of socially engaged art. As he is driving intently towards the "wretched tree," Alys describes a sudden moment of realisation: "[i]t was as if I'd been punched in the chest by the absurdity and tragedy of this art mission in this lost town of Sinaloa. I don't know; a lot came to my mind..." [26] The work pointedly confronts an awkward and unresolved problem. It acknowledges that fond dreams of art-driven, ecologically inflected, social amelioration fail to adequately speak to the complex and intractable local situation. It interferes then precisely by suspending any ostensibly effective work of interference, by representing it instead as a moment of bathos and indirection. In this manner *Game Over* takes shape as a charged crystalisation of the contradictory forces that shape it. Rather than confronting the social field directly, the work is lightly and obliquely interleaved within it. This lends it a sense of separate, forlorn and impertinent identity.

Here, however, it is less a matter of multiplexing than of surreptitious action. *Game Over* is not so much a carrier of multiple signals - some positioned within everyday life, others within art – as it is a understated meditation on the limits of art, and the limits of arts critical relation to dimensions of everyday life.

SHELTER FOR DRUG-ADDICTED WOMEN

The work of Austrian art collective, *WochenKlausur*, is more clearly multiplexed. The group produce tactical activist work that aims to intervene within society and improve it. They have an unashamedly instrumental orientation, employing art as a means of achieving what they regard as socially useful ends. *Shelter for Drug-Addicted Women*, [27] one of their early works, was produced in 1994 in Zurich, Switzerland. As the title indicates, the work involved setting up a daytime shelter for Zurich's drug-addicted and typically homeless prostitutes. The role of *WochenKlausur* was to act as an innovative social catalyst. They arranged a series of meetings in boats on Lake Zurich, in which politicians, journalists, legal and medical professionals came together to consider practical ways of addressing this problem. In short, *WochenKlausur*, produced a novel context for social policy dialogue that led to the establishment of a women's shelter.

This would seem a clear example of a work in which the limits of art have become ambiguous, in which art has effectively merged into ordinary political activism. Yet the issue is not as straightforward as it seems. I would argue instead that *WochenKlausur* have discovered a very specific niche for intervening within society. They speak very clearly of taking advantage of the cultural prestige of art and its peculiar freedom to accomplish practical tasks. [28] So at the very same time that they are subverting the autonomy of art, they draw upon that autonomy for instrumental purposes. In this manner, they effectively play a trick on both art and society. This dimension of trickery, of employing all available means, whether in terms of adhering to the institutional demands of institutional art, publicising their actions in the media, manipulating local officials or conspiring with community groups, suggests a very different notion of interference. Not the interference of a pure and exterior form of artistic resistance, but the complicit, embedded interference of a tactically positioned cultural actor. Rather than fundamentally blurring the relation between art and the social, *WochenKlausur* suggest a new social identity for art and a new play of integration and distance. The gap between art and non-art is at once both exploited and rendered less pertinent. The important features now are skills, goals, tactical advantage and institutional authority. Within this context it is more important to pay attention to the multiple streams of differentiated social signals, to recognise their endless multiplexing and de-multiplexing, than to describe merging, blurring and ambiguity per se.

CONCLUSION

This paper has suggested that throughout the history of avant-garde art practice and even within the context of contemporary transdisciplinary and socially-instrumental art projects there is still a gap evident between the art signal and the signal flow of the social as such. It is not that art lies beyond the social – that it supervenes and intervenes from without – but rather that it preserves dimensions of distinct identity within an overall, complex and multiply stranded field. In saying this, however, there are always consequences in running signals so closely side by side. The art signal may not literally dissolve into the life signal or vice versa, but each of them is still integrally affected. Art discovers new institutional, political and discursive alignments. Everyday life once again reveals its profound, aesthetic implications. Within this context, socially engaged art obtains its critical force precisely in terms of the limit play it opens up between artistically marked social actions and social actions generally.

Multiplexing indicates not only an alternative way of conceiving the relation between art and the social, emphasising dimensions of interleaving and distinct identity, but also a specific artistic strategy that shifts away from notions of interference - whether conceived in terms of blurring or in terms of some capacity for integral subversion – envisaging, instead, a more discreet and cunning etiquette of attachment and separation, correspondence and sidelong glances. ■

REFERENCES AND NOTES

1. Nato Thompson, ed., *Living as Form: Socially Engaged Art from 1991-2011* (Cambridge, MA: MIT Press, 2012).
2. Peter Burger, *Theory of the Avant-Garde*, trans. Michael Shaw (Minneapolis: University of Minnesota Press, 1984), 49.
3. Alex Danchev, ed., *100 Artists' Manifestos: From the Futurists to the Stuckists* (London: Penguin Modern Classics, 2011), 11.
4. Ibid., 193.
5. Ibid., 247.
6. Ibid., 144.
7. Theodor Adorno, *Aesthetic Theory*, trans. Robert Hullot-Kentor (London and New York: Continuum, 1997), 296.
8. Ibid., 233.
9. Henri Lefebvre, *Critique of Everyday Life*, vol. 2 (New York and London: Verso, 2002).
10. Michael Sherringham, *Everyday Life: Theories and Practices from Surrealism to the Present* (Oxford: Oxford University Press, 2006).
11. Guy Debord, "Perspectives for Conscious Changes in Everyday Life," in *Situationist International Anthology*, ed. and trans. Ken Knabb, 90-99 (Berkeley: Bureau of Public Secrets, 2006).
12. Ibid., 95.
13. Allan Kaprow, "Art Which Can't Be Art," in *Essay on the Blurring of Art and Life*, ed. Jeff Kelley (Berkeley: University of California Press, 1993), 219-222, danm.ucsc.edu/~dustin/library/ArtWhichCantBeArt-Kaprow.pdf (accessed June 17, 2012).
14. Ibid.
15. Ibid.
16. Ibid.
17. Nicolas Bourriaud, *Relational Aesthetics* (Paris: Les Presses Du Reel, 2002).
18. Jacques Ranciere, *The Emancipated Spectator* (London and New York: Verso, 2009), 58.
19. Ibid., 56.
20. Grant Kester, *Conversation Pieces: Community + Communication in Modern Art* (Berkeley: University of California Press, 2004).
21. Ben Highmore, *Ordinary Lives: Studies in the Everyday* (New York: Routledge, 2011).
22. Gerald Raunig, *Art and Revolution: Transversal Activism in the Long Twentieth Century* (Los Angeles: Semiotext(e), 2007), 17-18.
23. Claire Bishop, "Participation and Spectacle: Where Are We Now?," in *Living as Form: Socially Engaged Art from 1991-2011*, ed. Nato Thompson (Cambridge, MA: MIT Press, 2012), 40-41.
24. Francis Alys, "Game Over," Francis Alys' website, 2011, http://www.francisalys.com/public/gameover.html (accessed June 17, 2012).
25. "Francis Alys," interview by Carla Faesler, trans. Camino Detorrela, *BOMB* 116 (Summer 2011), http://bombsite.com/issues/116/articles/5109 (accessed June 17, 2012).
26. Ibid.
27. WochenKlauser, "Shelter for Drug-Addicted Women," the website of WochenKlauser, n.d., http://www.wochenklausur.at/projekt.php?lang=en&id=4 (accessed June 17, 2012).
28. WochenKlauser, "Why Must a Sociopolitical Intervention Be Art? Can It Not Simply Remain What It Is?," the website of WochenKlauser, n.d., http://www.wochenklausur.at/faq_detail.php?lang=en&id=17 (accessed June 17, 2012).

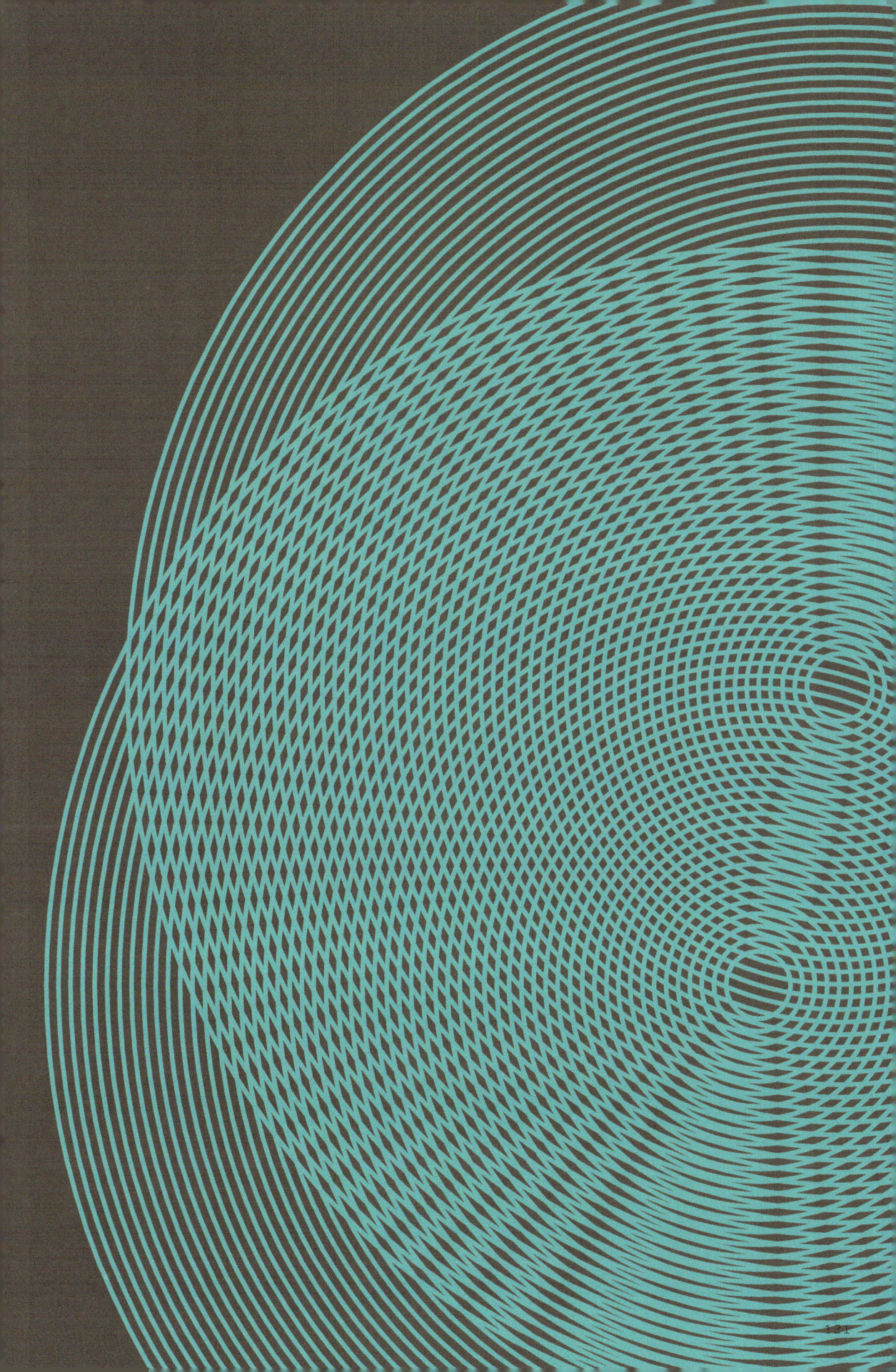

E S S A Y

A Robot Walks into a Room

Google Art Project, the New Aesthetic, and the Accident of Art

by

Susan Ballard

Senior Lecturer Art History and Contemporary Arts
Faculty of Law, Humanities and The Arts
University of Wollongong
sballard@uow.edu.au
suballard.net.nz

An art gallery is a public space, somewhere where almost anyone can walk off the street and experience something at a minimal cost. However, there are limits; not just to where we can walk, but to what we can look at, for how long and from what kind of distance. Galleries are social and transformational, but what if we no longer need to step through their doors? What if we let a machine do the walking, looking, and experiencing on our behalf?

A robot machine walks through an art gallery. Slowly over one evening it views the entire contents of an art gallery, not just the major art works, but everything: the fire hydrants, the exit signs, and the washbasins. To the robot, everything it sees is the same. It forms images that bear relationships to other images, which together will make a network of more images that will connect to other networks of images formed in other galleries, and then to viewers. Humans, not allowed into the galleries at night spend their evenings watching and reviewing what it is that the machine sees. The images the machine composes are the result of a long process, they are stitched together by another machine and checked for anomalies before humans

ESSAY

On the 1st February 2011 Google unleashed the Google Art Project, a new way to engage with the major collections of the world's art galleries. With the Google Art Project came a new way of viewing, not just art but the other objects that inhabit art galleries. Google Art Project depends on a robot looking machine. This aesthetic machine is a different form of digital material that has entered into what have for a long time been quiet still spaces for human, and not machine contemplation. With an equal focus on the spaces between things as much as on the things themselves, Google Art Project suggests a new way of understanding art, in the interval. Except it is not new at all. This essay draws a connection between the Google Art Project, James Bridle's new aesthetic tumblr log and Aby Warburg's Mnemosyne Atlas *in order to suggest that accidental encounters and ghost images formed in the spaces between things remain key to contemporary understandings of aesthetics.*

MACHINES THAT LOOK

can view them, some are astounding but sometimes errors occur. The machine encounters unexpected objects, and forms images of things that are not art, yet inhabit the spaces of an art gallery. These accidental encounters in the art gallery occupy a critical space that moves beyond established behaviours and expectations. The accidents both caused and caught by the machine are crucial to everyday encounters with art objects in the art gallery. These misunderstood moments offer up shared and transformative experiences, a nose can be pressed against a canvas, an exit sign or a glass toilet door with equal aesthetic pleasure.

The major public galleries of the world are now inhabited by robot machines that are capable of looking closer and in more detail than their human companions. With their wide-angle multiple eyes free to roam where even humans cannot go, the robot machines document the invisible, allowing anyone anywhere to see more and access more via the digital networks that now connect galleries and their collections to each other. Google Art Project has been live since 1 February 2011 when it opened with seventeen of the world's major art galleries. On 3 April 2012 it expanded to include a further 150 galleries from 40 different countries, and now is at the centre of the Google Cultural Institute. Interestingly, it has been met with general applause, particularly by curators of the galleries it has documented. For example, Beth Harris from the Museum of Modern Art says that Google Art Project allows visitors "to avoid the crowds, physical fatigue, and self-consciousness" that visitors to the museum struggle with. [1] Robin White Owen says "you can take as much time as you like, any time and place you choose." [2]

Trundling through art galleries opened specially for it in the early hours of the morning, the Google cameras have the space to themselves. They scan according to a predetermined path that gathers not just the ambient feel of the room, but generates a 360 degree panoramic immersion within the gallery spaces. Watching from our desktops we follow the eye view of a machine strapped into a trolley, standardised to an average human height of 170cm as if it is tracking an invisible adversary. It watches and scans the interior environment. However, StreetView technologies when moved inside create jittery and grainy images. The jerky movements replicate the hand held video camera footage favoured in horror movies from the late 1990s such as *The Blair Witch Project*. Alastair Sooke commented in *The Telegraph,* this is "a 'look' that is surely anathema to the carefully orchestrated clarity of the galleries in reality." [3] The smoothness of our journey is controlled by the precision of our scrolling hand and the speed of the stream we receive over the network. Every exhibition is viewed at an equivalent scrolling pace, works are apprehended from the same distance, video works are freeze framed, and there are moments where the camera zooms forward producing a rapid movement into the next room, when fragments are glimpsed out of the corner of the eye, yet stepping back renders them invisible. Not everything is equally visible. Google has not received copyright clearance for all images so they appear pixilated or bleached out, ghosts of their former selves. When this technique (usually used by Google as a protection of individual privacy when a face has been captured front on in StreetView) is applied to sculptures traces are left behind; a plinth seems strangely empty, or the reflection of a figure is captured in the glass of another image, yet when the view is rotated, the figure is gone.

When first opened to the public in the mid nineteenth century the art gallery enabled the general public to encounter the unexpected. Artworks were aesthetic tools able to transport people away from their everyday existence. This is not always the case when images are viewed inside Google Art Project. For example, Google described the inclusion of Hans Holbein the Younger's *The Ambassadors* as "tough." [4] This was due to the anamorphic techniques used to distort the image of a skull in the foreground of the painting. When looking at the original painting at the National Gallery in London, the depiction of the skull appears distorted until the viewer moves laterally to the side of the painting. Looking at the shape from the intended vantage point, the skull materializes in stunning 3D. Even in the gallery itself this is an unusual activity and met with stares and comments by other onlookers. To attempt to get side on to one's computer screen is even more challenging, and because the 'image' viewed via StreetView is made up of multiple fragments (the StreetView cameras see more like a fly than a human) the magic of distorted binocular vision is lost. In reality any unexpected encounter in Google Art Project is more likely to be with a blurred virtual force than something framed and labelled as art. Occasionally it is possible to catch glimpses of things reflected in mirrors and windows, objects that seem to have shadows but not presence. These documented accidental images become highly speculative objects within the gallery generating a new kind of aesthetic moment.

But with this new aesthetic must come a warning. To use Rancière's term, not everything a machine or a human sees is 'sensible.' [5] For Rancière the distribution of the sensible controls the laws by which things enter perception, or more specifically the conditions of possibility for seeing, hearing, thinking and speaking. Like any politics, Rancière says, the sensible is not available to everyone. In the late Eighteenth century it was the leisured classes who had time to hone their aesthetic judgements at public art galleries. In the early twenty-first century machines do a lot of looking on our behalf. This is more than a general cultural condition, but a combination of digital machines and the humans who watch and experience these machines and their outputs over time. It would be possible to continue this paper with a genealogy of moments in which machines have looked, or look: a camera obscura flipped the world into an upside down colour shadow of itself; as soon as the photographic camera was invented it was taken by balloon into the sky so it could see from above; and, in St Petersberg Dziga Vertov became one with his movie camera. "I am kino-eye, I am a mechanical eye, I, a machine, show you the world as only I can see it [...] my path leads to the creation of a fresh perception of the world I decipher in a new way unknown to you." [6] However this kind of listing does not offer many more tools to think about the robot we left exploring the art galleries of the world. For this we need to return to the aesthetics of the sensible and human relationships with the machinic environment.

A COLLECTION OF ARTIFACTS

The cataloguing of machine aesthetics reached obsessive proportions in April 2012, when Bruce Sterling wrote an article in *Wired* both critiquing and celebrating the work of James Bridle and the notion of the 'new aesthetic' as embodied in the Tumblr log: http://new-aesthetic.tumblr.com/. [7] Although Sterling labeled the new aesthetic as perhaps no more than a "glitch-hunt" Sterling's article lead credence to the Tumblr log and the activities of its collectors. Together, the collection of images seem to imply that there is a level of decision making, if not consciousness, to machines as they look. Bridle on the 'about' page describes it thus: "The New Aesthetic is not a movement, it is not a thing which can be *done*. It is a series of artefacts of the heterogeneous network, which recognises differences, the gaps in our overlapping but distant realities." [8] Dan Catt summarises the new aesthetic as the inspiration behind the cataloguing of computer vision; because the "digital and the physical are moving closer together." [9] Kyle Chayka describes the new aesthetic as not a revolutionary art movement out to shock society, but something operating in reverse. He says, it responds "to a shocked society." [10] Chayka continues "We will not just observe how machines act and perceive, but integrate how they act and perceive into our own sensory experiences and creative processes." [11] Chayka begins with something that sounds like an argument for digital materiality, but quickly slips into utopian imaginings for the future. Catt continues with the same approach: "As the digital and the physical move closer and closer, that combination will eventually look less like a hybrid and more like a united whole, the new aesthetic reality." [12] The new aesthetic, like Google Art Project, is the collection of artifacts that are already present rather than a movement for the creation of new aesthetic objects. Crowd sourcing moments of digital ephemera and convergences where glitch overlaps with the everyday, has made for a new and somewhat spectacular, cabinet of curiosities. After a premature closure and reactivation of the log, the new aesthetic remains a fast moving collaborative catalogue, made up of a Twitter feed, the Tumblr log, and a collection of blog entries that circulate around each other. What is sometimes lost among the flood of machine images is Bridle's original assertion that the new aesthetic is not a movement or an action, but a series of artifacts, which when viewed together encourage us (the humans, that is) to recognize differences and gaps.

It still seems easy enough to dismiss. Except, that as we look at the ongoing influence of Walter Benjamin's unfinished *Arcades Project* or Aby Warburg's also unfinished *Mnemosyne Atlas* it is worth considering if the image based gathering practices of the new aesthetic are more than an accidental convergence. [13] In the catalogue for his recent exhibition at Reina Sofia in Madrid and ZKM that examined the influence of early art historian Aby Warburg, Georges Didi-Huberman argued for a return to earlier methods of art history that involves piecing together "visual forms of knowledge" without teleological narration. [14] From 1924 to 1929 Warburg constructed seventy-nine wooden panels that he covered in black linen, each with groupings of reproductions, totaling over two thousand images. Labeling it the *Mnemosyne Atlas,* Warburg used the images to demonstrate the "iconography of the interval", an art history without the need for text. [15] The panels themselves are now lost, but Warburg's final arrangement of the Atlas survives as a series of 79 photographs. [16] Between and across the panels are aesthetic movements; sometimes patterns seem to flow out of one figure and into another, or grids overlap in a kind of invisible *moire*. In focusing on emergent points where ideas could be found to appear in-between the images on his panels, Warburg generated a diagram of gesture and energy. His methodology is described by Giogio Agamben as "an art of remembrance that shows the development of forms of expression." [17] And in this manner, Warburg's practice is often cited as core to the newly emergent discipline of art history that would initially focus on images and the connections that form between them in time and place. [18] However, Warburg's own work was not focused on the interpretation of the meanings of the images, but on their complex and autonomous inter-relationship and arrangement. [19]

Warburg described his relationship with images as a confrontation either lethal or vitalizing. [20] The atlas itself was a freeze frame of relationships. Brian Dillon describes the whole project as images held "in a paradoxical pose of frenzied immobility." [21] Art history was understood as a network of images within which there are stored enormous energies. For Warburg the art historian was someone who conjured up this energy from the past to give it a new life. Warburg activated dynamic properties, and following on from his research with German psychologist Richard Semon he argued that it is in the spaces between things that memory functioned. [22] Warburg did not concentrate on the movement of the images as a fluid construction of time and place but his focus repeatedly turned to the gaps. Agamben continues: Warburg's "'atlas' was a kind of gigantic condenser that gathered together all the energetic currents that had animated and continued to animate Europe's memory, taking form in its 'ghosts.'" [23] In between each image is a black field that serves to both isolate and frame the images. In these intervals Warburg saw faultlines. These irregular black spaces separated and isolated the images at the same time as they organised their relationships. Rather than links and nodes, Warburg produced a cartographic relief upon which the images floated, as if constellations of thought. [24] The panels do much more than juxtapose; they are productive and generative.

Bridle insists on the same approach for the new aesthetic Tumblr. This in-between activation of memory means that the new aesthetic will similarly never be finished, it is not a thing, movement, or process. It is the capturing of a series of interim possibilities and accidental convergences that only come into focus in the corner of our eye. We cannot yet remember the new aesthetic. For now, a machine collects and logs, and people are the contributors but not the keepers of the images. In some cases spaces between things generate new aesthetic moments as different pages spring up either in response to Sterling or to Bridle. [25] The majority of these are not yet dynamic or accidental (although many contain a superficial aesthetics of the accident as glitch or error).

Greg Borenstein was among the first to suggest that the new aesthetic resonates with other recent trends in speculative thought, and in particular with the philosophical momentum called object-oriented ontology (OOO):

> *The New Aesthetic is a visible eruption of the mutual empathy between us and a class of new objects that are native to the twenty-first century. It consists of visual artefacts we make to help us imagine the inner lives of our digital objects and also of the visual representations produced by our digital objects as a kind of pigeon language between their inaccessible inner lives and ours.* [26]

There is a tension here. The new aesthetic seeks to make digital objects visible, to suggest that within the accident or the glitch there are overlooked moments of literal and aesthetic 'beauty.' OOO suggests that objects have ways of apprehending the world that are not necessarily human, or defined by the human, and thus do not really need us to recognize them, but that we should leave them to their own nonhuman ways. I'm purposely reducing large and complex arguments here. The point is this: if the new aesthetic is to be a useful method for understanding nonhuman (and in particular *digital* objects) its objects need to remain invisible, they need to transform into the pieces of black linen peeping between Warburg's reproductions, and remain un-romanticized. Even un-aestheticized. To trace the (new) accident of art we need to return with much more certainty to Warburg's unnamed science, and rather than proclaim the visibility of machine aesthetics too quickly, spend some time looking at the intervals.

Philippe-Alain Michaud says that "The conception of the images in Mnemosyne, [is a] silent conception based in pure dynamic relationships and phenomena of visual attraction and repulsion." [27] In describing his exhibition Atlas, based on Warburg's work, Didi-Huberman says that the atlas is a visual tool, the links it makes are "not a link of similarity, but a secret link between two different things." [28] If it retains the sense of an atlas, of secret links – of moments of both attraction and repulsion that can only be apprehended obliquely – the new aesthetic Tumblr will take a new place beside the *Arcades Project* and the *Mnemosyne Atlas*. However, if it becomes a movement or even a single act of collection formed by filling in the gaps, it will become yet another redundant archive inhabiting the dark recesses of the Internet.

Where does this leave our robot in the gallery?

THE ACCIDENT OF ART

Trapped in a very different frenzy of the visible, yet also dealing with things caught in the corner of the eye, (but with a very different purpose) Google Art Project strives to eliminate the accidental. As more and more 'information' is fed into the Google machine, less and less accidental encounters are possible. Google Art Project aims for completion; when there are no more spaces between things, when there are no more accidents. Google Art Project aims to be an archive not an atlas. The images in an atlas are not located in time, as they are with an archive, instead there is a "confrontation and a co-existence of different times." [29] Currently Google Art Project allows viewers to form their own attractions and repulsions. Small dusty corners can meet with the same attention as the Mona Lisa. This confrontation is central to a journey through a gallery formed through images of images that do not discriminate but include the accidental as encounter. However, in letting more machines loose in the gallery, Google Art Project aims for a different form of reproduction, and a different process of accumulation to that undertaken by Warburg. Although at the moment Google Art Project is accidental and found in the intervals, as more images are rendered to multi-gigapixel scale, the intervals will become invisible and Google Art Project will form an archive of the world's museums where there can be no accidents.

Aristotle suggested that the accidental "does not inhere in the constitutive essence of a thing, being, or event." [30] The accidental is more a case of its relationships with other things, beings or events. This accident as relationship revealed the substance of something, what it could do. It is through the accident that the thing, being, or event presents itself to others. In the contemporary world, as both Google Art Project and the new aesthetics Tumblr show, machines bring their own accidents with them. Paul Virilio developed Aristotle's argument for a world where images and imaging have become one. Virilio says that the accident of art results from a proliferation of images that has lead to complex relations between seeing, knowing, and imagining a world: the accident is now generalized. [31] In identifying a shift from the accidental as caused by essential yet mistaken relations between bodies (the specific accident), towards the intended affects of that body, Virilio's generalised accident also elides the difference between accident and attack. The contemporary mediated accident of art is the eradication of these distinctions.

The lurking presence of catastrophe became the focus of Virilio's 'Museum of Accidents' project at the Cartier Foundation in Paris in 2002 in which the aestheticising of the events 9/11 resulted in a romantic sheen over the horror produced by accidental encounters between machines and architectures. [32] In Virilio's 'Museum of Accidents' images are placed together and archived in order to discover some kind of essential connections; links between the nodes. The problem is that the nodes are not in themselves positioned as transformative, but become fixed images. In harvesting machines or media into the service of accident, there is the risk of aestheticising extreme harm, and Virilio seems to tread on the wrong side of this line. The imaging machine itself cannot acknowledge the accident (all data is data, it is the human who distinguishes between information and noise) and despite what 'ooo' offers in its consideration of the non-human, it still seems a mistake to attribute some kind of agency to the machine independent of the human. In Virilio's museum the intervals become invisible rather than visible. A different kind of accident that escapes the catalogue is necessary.

THE NIGHT WATCH

As the accidents vanish from the corners of the Google Art Project we loose the opportunity to see them. These temporal artifacts are removed and smoothed over by the ever increasing 'resolution' of the digital image. Despite the best efforts of the contributors to the new aesthetic Tumblr, the new accident of art is the noise of the digital; only visible in retrospect when it is no longer there. Warburg's iconology of the interval suggests that the accidental encounter is the way to build an "unnamed science" from art history. [33] Both the Google Art Project and the new aesthetic Tumblr hold the potential for a new accident of art where the aesthetics of the sensible and those of the machine come together in the art gallery.

The robot that roams the galleries at night is not unlike the fox in Francis Alÿs' *Night Watch* (2004). The robot follows paths, maps routes, and does the walking for us. Like the fox it is always in motion, suggesting new forms of movement within gallery architecture. There is another connection though. Multiple surveillance screens track Alÿs' fox showing the many ways that the fox is a creature out of place, and reminding us that when we enter an art gallery we are always being watched. As I have said the Google Art Project depends on a robot looking machine. This aesthetic machine is a totally different form of digital material that has entered into what have for a long time been quiet still spaces for human, and not machine (or fox), contemplation. The digital matter the machine is formed from is flawed and what it sees is error-ridden. If, as has been argued by both Aristotle and Virilio, in its relations each machine contains an accident; encounters that recognise the interval between the image and instability might actually introduce new affective productions within the gallery space. This means that rather than archive and document the gallery, while it retains the blurred and the grainy, the invisible and the somewhat visible, the Google Art Project is constructing an atlas of the spaces between things. Google Art Project picks up objects that misbehave and in the process maps the transformation of both machines and architectures. Agamben describes the spaces between the images in Warburg's Atlas as "the dark demon of an unnamed science whose contours we are only today beginning to glimpse." [34] There is a surprising similarity between Warburg's careful atlas of relationships where accidents emerge in the interval, the new aesthetic Tumblr, and Google Art Project's gathering together of invisible interferences, visible only to those who choose to look. Rather than collate and archive images, the new accident of art traces the unnamed science of the interval with care. Warburg called his atlas a "ghost story for adults" [35] – the images currently produced by Google Art Project are also a ghost story: a machinic aesthetics formed in accidental intervals. And like ghosts they will soon vanish at the hands of a rational smoothing of time and space, where everything is captured and rendered into a perfect deception fit for human eyes. ■

REFERENCES AND NOTES

1. Nancy Proctor, "The Google Art Project: A New Generation of Museums on the Web?" *Curator: The Museum Journal* 54, no. 2 (2011): 215.
2. Robin White Owen, quoted in ibid.
3. Alastair Sooke, "The Problem with Google's Art Project," *The Telegraph*, February 1, 2011, http://www.telegraph.co.uk/culture/art/art-news/8296251/The-problem-with-Googles-Art-Project.html (accessed August 14, 2013).
4. Philip Kennicott, "National Treasures: Google Art Project Unlocks Riches of World's Galleries," *The Washington Post*, February 1, 2011, http://www.washingtonpost.com/wp-dyn/content/article/2011/02/01/AR2011020106442.html (accessed August 14, 2013).
5. Jacques Rancière, "Aesthetic Separation, Aesthetic Community," in *The Emancipated Spectator* (London and New York: Verso, 2009), 51-63.
6. Annette Michelson, ed., *Kino-Eye: The Writings of Dziga Vertov* (Los Angeles: University of California Press, 1984), 17.
7. Bruce Sterling, "An Essay on the New Aesthetic," *Wired*, April 2, 2012, http://www.wired.com/beyond_the_beyond/2012/04/an-essay-on-the-new-aesthetic/ (accessed August 14, 2013).
8. James Bridle, "about," The New Aesthetic, http://new-aesthetic.tumblr.com/about (accessed August 14, 2013).
9. Dan Catt, "Why the New Aesthetic Isn't about 8bit Retro, the Robot Readable World, Computer Vision and Pirates," revdancatt.com, July 4, 2012, http://revdancatt.com/2012/04/07/why-the-new-aesthetic-isnt-about-8bit-retro-the-robot-readable-world-computer-vision-and-pirates/ (accessed June 26, 2012).

10. Marius Watz, Kyle Chayka, Jonathan Minard, Greg Borenstein, James George, and Kyle McDonald, "In Response to Bruce Sterling's 'Essay on the New Aesthetic,'" The Creators Project, April 6, 2012, http://www.thecreatorsproject.com/blog/in-response-to-bruce-sterlings-essay-on-the-new-aesthetic (accessed June 26, 2012).

11. Ibid.

12. Dan Catt, "Why the New Aesthetic Isn't about 8bit Retro."

13. Susan Buck-Morss, *The Dialectics of Seeing: Walter Benjamin and the Arcades Project*, 6th edition (Cambridge, MA: MIT Press, 1996). See also Philippe-Alain Michaud, *Aby Warburg and the Image in Motion*, trans. Sophie Hawkes (New York: Zone Books, 2004).

14. Georges Didi-Huberman, *Atlas: How to Carry the World on One's Back* (Reina Sofia and Karlsruhe: Museo Nacional Centro de Arte Reina Sofia and ZKM, 2011).

15. Philippe-Alain Michaud, *Aby Warburg and the Image in Motion*, 262.

16. Brian Dillon, "Collected Works: Aby Warburg's Mnemosyne Atlas," *Frieze*, no. 80 (2004), https://www.frieze.com/issue/article/collected_works/ (accessed August 14, 2013).

17. Giorgio Agamben, "Aby Warburg and the Nameless Science," in *Potentialities: Collected Essays in Philosophy*, ed. Giorgio Agamben (New York: Stanford University Press, 1999), 93.

18. Philippe-Alain Michaud, *Aby Warburg and the Image in Motion*, 278.

19. Ibid., 252.

20. Ibid., 77.

21. Brian Dillon, "Collected Works: Aby Warburg's Mnemosyne Atlas."

22. Philippe-Alain Michaud, *Aby Warburg and the Image in Motion*, 253-255.

23. Giorgio Agamben, "Aby Warburg and the Nameless Science," 96.

24. Philippe-Alain Michaud, *Aby Warburg and the Image in Motion*, 253.

25. Marius Watz, "In Response to Bruce Sterling's 'Essay on the New Aesthetic.'"

26. Ian Bogost, "The New Aesthetic Needs to Get Weirder," *The Atlantic*, April 13, 2012, http://www.theatlantic.com/technology/archive/2012/04/the-new-aesthetic-needs-to-get-weirder/255838/ (accessed June 26, 2012).

27. Philippe-Alain Michaud, *Aby Warburg and the Image in Motion*, 246.

28. "ATLAS Entrevista con Georges Didi-Huberman," YouTube video, 3:44, posted by museoreinasofia, December 21, 2010, http://www.youtube.com/watch?v=WwVMni3b2Z0 (accessed June 26, 2012).

29. Ibid.

30. Hillel Schwartz, *Making Noise from Babel to the Big Bang and Beyond* (New York: Zone Books, 2011), 547.

31. Paul Virilio, "The Museum of Accidents," in *The Paul Virilio Reader*, ed. Steve Redhead (New York: Columbia University Press, 2004), 255-262. Sylvere Lotringer and Paul Virilio, *The Accident of Art (Semiotext(e)/ Foreign Agents)*, trans. Mike Taormina (Cambridge, MA: MIT Press, 2005).

32. Sean Cubitt, "Unnatural Reality: Review of Paul Virilio The Vision Machine," *Film-Philosophy*, no. 3 (1999), http://www.film-philosophy.com/vol3-1999/n9cubitt (accessed June 26, 2012).

33. Giorgio Agamben, "Aby Warburg and the Nameless Science."

34. Ibid., 90.

35. Philippe-Alain Michaud, *Aby Warburg and the Image in Motion*, 260.

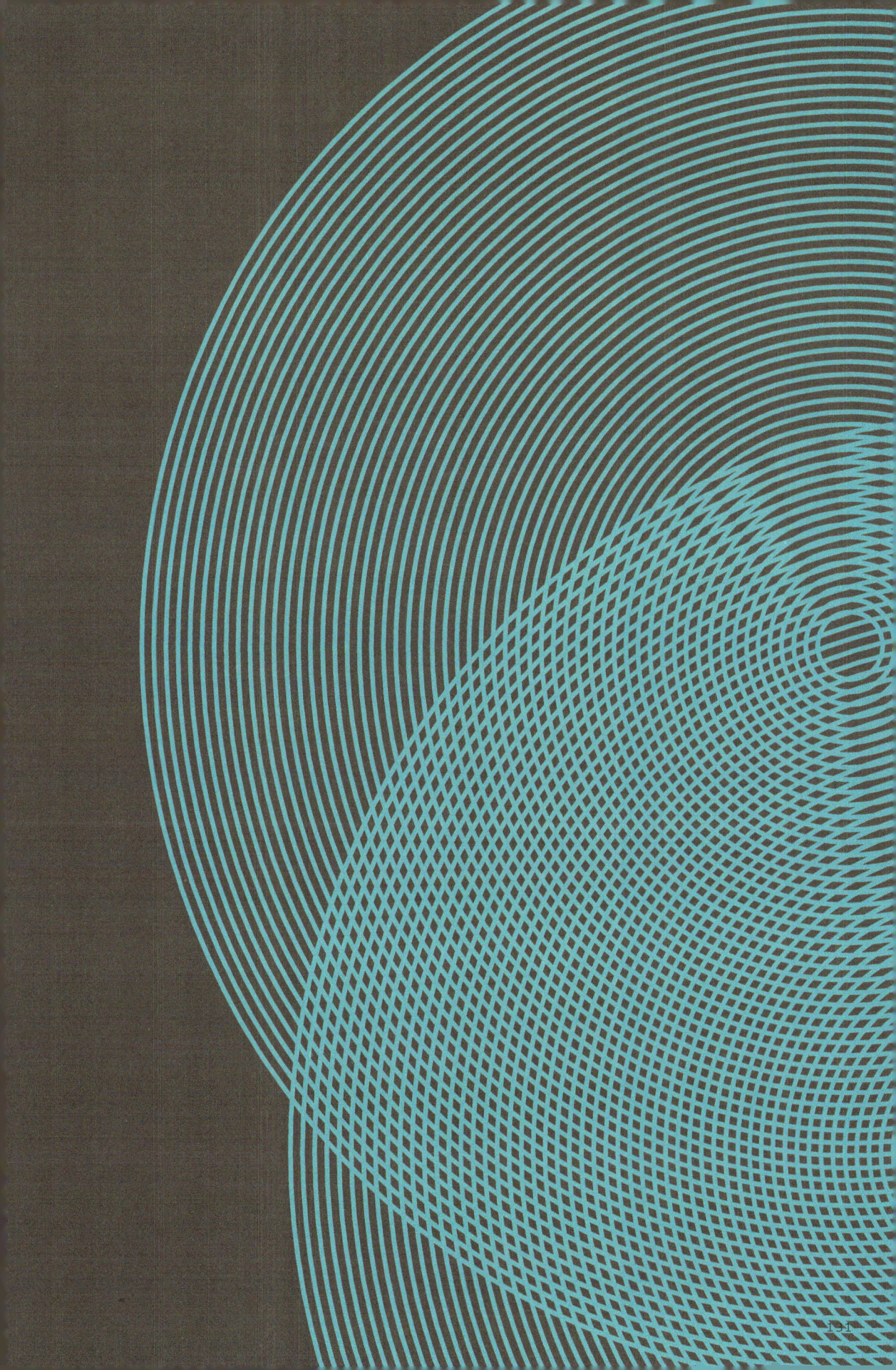

Towards an Ontology of Colour in the Age of Machinic Shine

by

Mark Titmarsh

University of Technology, Sydney
mark.titmarsh@uts.edu.au
www.marktitmarsh.com.au

Colour is a very familiar experience, we are always already immersed in it, but when it comes to speaking or writing colour, something else happens, that is neither colour nor language. The more we talk about colour the more we talk about language and its limitation at the phenomenal edge of perception.

Because of this, as David Batchelor demonstrates in his book *Chromophobia*, [1] we tend to live in a world of colour prejudices and cultural taboos against colour, that align good taste and cultural sophistication with a severe restriction on the use of colours. As such the West is inherently chromophobic, equating taste and sophistication with clothes, houses and paintings that are black, white, grey, or brown. This is to be contrasted with chromophilia, [2] a wantonness of colour which erupts in the excessiveness of the "feminine, primitive, infantile, vulgar, queer or pathological." [3] This apartheid of colour is also reinforced by the ancient argument between colour and line, dating back to Aristotle who argued that the "repository of thought in art is line, the rest is ornament." [4] Ever since then colour has been understood as superficial, an ephemeral occurrence on the surface of things, whereas line and the under-coloured is permanent, structural and meaningful.

This paper argues that the enduring mystery of colour, in particular its elemental effusiveness, has been tamed and managed by notions of good taste and chic that equate cultural maturity with a limited palette. Yet colour in all its post industrial forms continues to break free of constraints in an audacious display of autopoiesis. The science of colour based on image, mimesis, and the physiology of the eye has missed the phenomenon of colour altogether because it takes place at the incalculable level of shine and radiance. Ontologically colour makes things manifest by revealing them in their unique presence rather than merely facilitating communication, representation or spectacle. Before colour is seen, before light can facilitate a look, colour looks back in such a way that looking and seeing are provoked.

Using Thierry de Duve, David Batchelor and Martin Heidegger it will be shown that these ways of being with colour are extended by a formal evolution in painting whereby expanded painting addresses everything in the everyday world that carries colour from data screens to plastic utensils and even paint itself. Ultimately, the medium of painting however deconstructed or expanded, has become the entity to 'whom' the work of colour is addressed.

Despite some of the prohibitions against immodesty in colour, the meaning of the most basic term in this discussion, namely "colour" itself, is poorly understood. The slipperiness of colour has been sometimes held in place by symbolism that ties some colours to specific social purposes and meanings. For example the Sumptuary Laws of Elizabethan England mandated that only royalty could wear purple attire. Into the 20th century, various modern artists attempted to develop a grammar of colour linked to music or emotions. Kandinsky developed a primary polarity of yellow and blue that suggest active and passive perceptual sensations. Johannes Itten a colleague of Kandinsky at the Bauhaus, developed a complex colour theory that linked colours to certain emotions and spiritual states.

Colour is verifiable, it surrounds us at all times, but the words we use to divide the spectrum of colour into functional divisions is quite arbitrary and untranslatable between different cultures and ages. The Inuit supposedly have a vast array of terms for the single colour we call white, the French use brown and purple as interchangeable in certain situations, Russians see two colours where we just see blue, and Hindus don't differentiate red and orange. The word 'red', or any colour term in any language, has no inherent chromatic value and is only an arbitrary signifier shifting under cultural and historical differences.

Colour is there, but it continually slips through the grasp of linguistic possession.

Batchelor cites Plotinus [5] to show us why. In short, there is an incommensurability between colour and language because colour is indivisible, there are no breaks in the rainbow, while language is based on divisions and conceptual units that contradict colour's natural tendency to "spread, flow, bleed, stain, soak, seep, and merge." [6]

Because of this, the difference between the perception of colour, the social experience of colour and the history of colour terms, has produced a bewildering set of possibilities. At various points physics weighed in as the most authoritative voice, but due to an unresolvable uncertainty between wave and particle theories it has resulted in "one of the worst muddles in the history of science." [7]

COLOURISM

Colour is a constant challenge to our understanding. It challenges the scientist to quantify light, the thinker to bring colour to language, and the painter to embrace it elementally. It is the indeterminacy of colour in its movement between physical presence and modes of understanding that leaves us with a bewildering array of colour strategies in art. In 20th century art whenever there was a struggle between concepts as pure idea, unadorned by colour, and perception embodied in colour, idea always won out. Consider the different status of Conceptual Art and Cubism versus Op Art and Fauvism.

The polarity of colour and concept is a lingering Platonism that favours the immortal realm of ideas over the temporary and sensuous. [8] Colourist artists are usually associated with a kind of anti-realism, breaking with the natural colours of things, to make colour an expressive, affective or formal element as in impressionism, abstraction, and colour field painting. The nature of colour for a colourist changes with time and according to the presence of pigments and how they are harnessed and made available. Before the 20th century colour came from earthly pigments sometimes captured in a tube, later on synthetic colours were produced in tins and made from laboratory concoctions, now colour is largely pixel based. The demand for colour in various non-art situations, as in house paint and industrial surfaces, saw the creation of new industrial paints and related products. This in turn pushed the nature of art making away from the accurate representation of flesh to the seductive presentation of colour that might somehow compete with the spectacular materials and facades of the modern world. To be a colourist in the 21st century means thinking colour anew, specifically in terms of the ubiquity of coloured plastics and the plasticity of colour on an electronic screen.

As Batchelor points out the tension between these two worlds of colour is symbolised by the difference between the colour wheel and the colour chart. The colour wheel is historically steeped and scientifically justified in its hierarchies of colour, that rationalise the visible and makes it ready for representation. Whereas the colour chart is a "disposable list of readymade colour" in a "grammarless accumulation of colour units" that strips colour free from colour theory and places it in an entirely autonomous zone ready for abstraction.

We might take a further step from the colour wheel through the colour chart to the colour cell, that is, the picture cell or pixel of the video and computer screen. These are the colours of any screen we might use for domestic entertainment, telephony, global location, gaming platforms, video art or media facades.

The pixel that makes up the LCD screen on a phone or the plasma screen that hangs in a gallery is electronically endowed with a colour more intense than any painting. As Jeremy Gilbert Rolfe puts it, these kinds of screens

> *make the world more than it is, more colourful and more defined ... offering painting another surface to which to refer ... brighter than any that preceded it, unimaginably thin, a surface without depth.*

What permits the impossible brightness and thinness of electronic colour is plastic itself, the plastic of the surface of the monitor and the plastic components that hold the screen elements together. Plastic, the ultimate technological agent has also become the agent provocateur of colour, transmitting a new kind of colour while also challenging painting to find ever new intensities that can match it. In the history of colour, pigments were originally refined by hand from natural materials such as ochre, beetle eggs, flowers and crushed shellfish. Later industrial science and the petrochemical industry produced synthetic pigments that were more intense and not reliant on expensive exotic biomass. Today the colour cell has no origin in material substances at all, shining out from the interior of electronic light itself. The colours of a digital screen have moved beyond the materiality of pigment towards something like structural color. Structural colour occurs in nature without pigment through optical effects such as interference, refraction, and diffraction. It happens when the arrangement of physical structures interacting with light produce a particular iridescent colour as seen in peacock feathers, mother of pearl shell, beetle shells and butterfly wings.

Many things today aspire to the condition of structural colour whether it is made of plastic or pigment, whether it is material or electronically immaterial. The challenge is taken up in the laboratory where new synthetic chemicals attempt to reach the colour intensity of a data screen through fluorescent paint or the integration of LED technology into wearable fibre and building exteriors.

As such the electronic monitor and painting reach out to each other through the medium of colour and the format of the screen, alternately embracing and exceeding each other.

If Pollock and Newman engaged wide angle cinemascope screens and in response Technicolour film stock aspired to the intensity of painterly expressionism, then contemporary painting refers to the digital monitor in its luminescence and multimodal forms while small digital screens show complex visual presences mimicking miniature painting and postage stamp design.

This change in the nature of colour involves refiguring the presence of paint and the object of painting itself. The matter of paint in this new environment of colour can no longer be constrained by coloured stuff gathered from a tube, but must also include any object that has been invested with colour such as string, clothing, furniture, cars, data screens and buildings. Similarly the object of painting can no longer be confined by a flat surface but must include works that spread out across space and time encroaching on other media like sculpture, installation, performance and video. Riffing on painting, mixing colour in different painted materials, some things are left out of the painters repertoire, such as brush and easel, and new things are introduced, such as anodised aluminium, coloured smoke, and architecture. These works are not nameable as painting but nevertheless originate within the differential field of colour.

In the current situation there is nowhere that colour cant go, there are green stripes on toothpaste as it is extruded from the tube, cars and cleaning utensils have an infinite array of tones, human limbs as well as everything plastic can be injected with myriad colour variations. Wherever colour is, in commodities, on screen interfaces, in experiential environments, painting can take a stand, addressing colour as that which is environmentally all around.

COLOUR IS

One thing is certain at this stage, colour is, but the nature of its presence has not yet been captured or named [11] since it is essentially resistant to nomination. [12] Colour invokes a series of nested questions, how does it present, how is it experienced and how can it be spoken? Experientially colour rains down from the sky in the warmth of the sun and erupts up out of the earth as raw pigment and the hues of nature. Colour is awesome and ubiquitous in its presence, it is in everything, on everything, everything is shot through with colour, colour shines out from a world of things, and in its shining brings a world into existence. Colour is not a solitary separate thing or event, it is always the colour of something. The whole world is coloured and so to some extent the world is

colour. Everything is in colour, colour emerges from the obscure ground of things, it is all around like air, things are always already coloured. In the everyday we are so immersed in colour that it is taken as granted, it becomes un-thought, a background phenomenon, until a sunset or work of art shocks us into remembering its uncanny way of being surprising, awesome, astounding. As Michel Haar puts it, "[c]olours are all at once the ground, 'the secret soul of what is below', the surface, and what sublimates the surface, 'the ideas', substance, figure, and 'general harmony', 'the life of God'." [13]

Colour is not just seen, it is experienced in depth, through and through. It is an unfolding encapsulation from sensation to perception, to affect, to my sense of being in the world. In this movement from perception to being, "colour cracks open the form-spectacle." [14] Thus colour is not a spectacle or an element of form, but a necessary precondition to both. Colour is more than my affective or sensory experience, it moves me to a place of ecstatic embeddedness. Through the sensation of colour I am of the world.

Colour, like the act of thinking, can be forgotten and at times must be forgotten, so that performance and experience can take place. One way of remembering the forgotten of colour is through painting. In painting, touching colour as a maker, or being touched by colour as a viewer, is much the same thing. It begins with seeing colour, then really seeing colour, then touching colour, then feeling colour, then knowing colour, then being in colour, then in colour, being.

This kind of language is an attempt to find another way of talking colour that honours and justifies the new ways we walk with colour today. I find some help in this process from the German philosopher Martin Heidegger. Heidegger was not known for his chromatic sensibility despite the fact that he was a personal friend of modern masters such as George Braque and Paul Klee. His writing does briefly mention colour as lighting or shining out, in an ontological sense, without relying on any scientific theory of colour or light.

In "The Origin of the Work of Art" he mentions stone, colour and language as various materials that can be used to set forth a work of art, such that "rock comes to bear and rest; metals come to glitter and shimmer, colours to glow, tones to sing, the word to say. All this comes forth as the work sets itself back into the massiveness and heaviness of stone, into the firmness and pliancy of wood, into the hardness and lustre of metal, into the lighting and darkening of colour, into the clang of tone, and into the naming power of the word." [15]

All these types of work from sculpture, to painting to poetry rest back into a material element. If we try to understand the work by analysing the materiality of stone, metal, colour, tone and word, the material itself simply withdraws. Thus for example "if we attempt a penetration by breaking open the rock, it still does not display in its fragments anything inward that has been opened up. The stone has instantly withdrawn into the same dull pressure and bulk of its fragments." And similarly with colour, "colour shines and wants only to shine… when we analyse it in rational terms by measuring its wavelengths, it is gone. It shows itself only when it remains undisclosed and unexplained." [16]

It is the work of art that allows us to see the shine of colour as opposed to a more direct physiological and scientific understanding of vision. Art, particularly painting reveals an ontology of colour in which shine and radiance is experienced as "showing self-showing." [17] The artwork introduces what is undisclosed about colour into the world, while a scientific grasping of colour simply dims it down as explanation or calculation. The shining of the earth through the material of colour radiates through the world as a sense of manifest meaning. "The world stands as the medium through which the shining of the earth distributes itself through relations of significance." [18] Colour as an aspect of earth, presents a radiance that penetrates or 'juts' into the world as pure shine or shimmer. Kenneth Maly describes it as a

shimmering that shines with a certain unsteadiness where it is always at something like a boundary, it can never cross that boundary, even as it is always moving 'across' the boundary. [19]

At that point, colour casts an ontological light rather than an optical presence, moving closer to the movement of thought and away from the physiology of vision.

In this moment colour and light become one and the same issue, each resting within the other, neither existing without the other.

ONTOLOGY OF LIGHT

In everyday experience for something to show up as substantially present to our awareness it must be apparent, that is, have some aspect of accessibility. The current understanding of visual access relies on a model of perception based on the laws of representation and the physiology of the eye. However other ages, notably ancient Greece, had no such conceptual structure. For them vision was more laterally democratic in that "the one who looks shows himself and appears" [20] in the act of seeing. Thus objects seen and those who look "emerge in the double sense that the object rises in self showing and the essence of the looker is collected in the look." [21] Looking is then the way humans come into presence with other beings, all sharing the commonality of appearance, each drawing out and revealing something of the other in the moment of appearing.

By treading around the extreme edges of what is currently understood about the eye, light, and subjectivity, old certainties begin to give way. New possibilities beyond the scientific quantification of light and its lens based metaphors begin to take shape. A significant move in this context is Heidegger's contrast between modern representational looking and pre-modern apprehension of presence:

> That which is, does not come into being at all through the fact that man first looks upon it, in the sense of a representing that has the character of subjective perception. Rather man is the one who is looked at by that which is, he is the one who is – in company with itself – gathered towards presencing, by that which opens itself. [22]

At first instance apprehension might seem to be a passive mode requiring only a certain openness and availability on the part of those who look. However Heidegger does go on to define both active and passive poles of apprehension. Passively the looker lets something come to be seen so that what appears can show itself out of itself. On the active side apprehending is a dynamic claiming, similar to the legal understanding of apprehending a witness who is held for detention and interrogation.

> Apprehension in this double sense denotes a process of letting things come to oneself ... [and to] take up a position to receive what shows itself. [23]

Thus apprehension is not simply a passive absorption or active consumption by a knowing subject, since it takes place beyond any mode of sensory perception.

> Apprehension is not a way of behaving that the human being has as a property; to the contrary, apprehension is the happening that has the human being. [24]

Apprehension actively creates an appropriate receptivity in the moment of looking. It is "fundamentally a de-cision ... and thus a confrontation *with* seeming." [25] The 'de-cision' to be made is not a conscious choice but a separating that establishes the possibility of a new meeting place between self showing and a welcoming invitation. It requires a certain touch since if it is too soft then nothingness reigns as an "unseeing gaping," [26] and if it is too hard then deception rules as a form of self referentiality, seeing the world only as an anthropomorphic mirror. As Merleau Ponty put it,

> since the seer is caught up in what he sees it is still himself he sees: there is a fundamental narcissism of all vision. And thus, for the same reason, the vision he exercises, he also undergoes from the things, such that, as many painters have said, I feel myself looked at by the things, my activity is equally passivity – which is the second and more profound sense of the narcissim: not to see in the outside, as the others see it, the contour of a body one inhabits, but especially to be seen by the outside, to exist within it, to emigrate into it, to be seduced, captivated, alienated by the phantom, so that the seer and the visible reciprocate one another and we no longer know which sees and which is seen. [27]

In apprehension the seer is seen by what appears, and what appears settles back into itself through the action of shining out. Apprehension is the moment of shine, a moment of encounter between looking and being seen.

Unusual support for the counter intuitiveness of this idea comes from the world of science, in particular quantum physics where a reversal of the dynamic relationship between seer and seen has been documented. The Heysenberg uncertainty principle, [28] suggests that by simply looking at something causes it to change its behavior. This was based on the observation that sub atomic particles, beings that do not have sight or emotions, were effected by the act of human inspection regardless of the accuracy of the technology being used. The uncertainty principle was found to be inherent in all wave-like systems of which light is one. The uncertainty principle is one of many theories that shows a fundamental limit to the precision with which certain basic physical properties, like position and momentum, can be known. The more precisely position is known, the more mysterious is its momentum and vice versa. The uncertainty principle in quantum physics is a variation of the observer effect in traditional physics, where simple acts of observation interrupt the phenomenon being observed. For example when I am pumping up the tyre on my bike to the recommended level of 6ohpm, as I release the pump a certain amount of air always escapes leaving the precise measure of pressure unknown. However this error can be reduced to almost insignificant levels by using better instruments or different observation techniques. This cannot be done in quantum mechanics because things observed are at a sub atomic level, at the limit point where energy and matter become indistinguishable. Quantum systems are infinitely vulnerable to the presence of observational technology showing that observer and system cannot be separated, that the observer must be considered part of the system being observed.

Even in psychoanalysis the act of looking is made problematic and reversible in a similar manner. Freud initiated this discussion when he identified *Shaulust* (scopophilia), the pleasure of looking, as a major component of human sexuality. [29] Laura Mulvey applied this idea by suggesting that there was a particular kind of sexualised male looking in modern cinema that subjected women to "a controlling and curious gaze." [30] In this kind of thinking looking is the seer's shoot, a shot of power coming out of the eye that intentionally holds what is seen in a willful and self-serving manner. The cinema became a unique situation for analysing the nature of human looking or the gaze as a kind of extromission theory. [31] Accordingly there are three types of look in the cinema, that of the camera recording the event, the looks between characters on the screen and the viewer watching the completed film. Sitting in the cinema the viewer has little to do but sit still in a seat. There is no need to move their eyes since attention is fixed strait ahead on an immobile screen placed at a convenient distance. The viewers look has been laid down in favour of a screen that looks back at the viewer with the omnipresence of an all seeing eye. "I not only look at the point of fixation (the screen), it looks at me." [32] The same uncanny sense of being looked at by the object of our gaze was an important issue for Jacques Lacan the most important psychoanalytic theorist after Freud. In his discussion of the development of the human ego, looking into mirrors, specularity and the gaze were of paramount importance. For Lacan looking was not a one way street, the look existed in a field of looks whereby what is looked at is also an active looker. "I am not simply that being located at the geometrical point from which perspective is grasped." [33] "In the scopic field [...] I am looked at, that is to say, I am a picture" [34] looked at by the world. Žižek notes that from a common sense point of view Lacan's concept of the gaze is easily misunderstood as indirectly belonging to the subject. However "it is crucial [...] that it involves the reversal of the relationship between subject and object, as Lacan puts it there is an antinomy between the eye and the gaze, ie the gaze is on the side of the object." [35]

Some of this counter intuitive play between human looking and objects that see is played out in the film work of Andy Warhol. Warhol is most well known for a series of paintings that capture the post war moment of industrial production and mass media through images of movie stars like Marilyn Monroe and consumer culture products like Coca Cola. His personal presence in this work seems driven by a desire to step out of the mundanity of everyday existence into the glowing presence of stardom. Being a 'star' is to generate light and attraction based on the kind of fame associated with success in the world of popular film and music. As Stephen Koch puts it, it is about "the obliteration of the self, the unworkability of ordinary living. Warhol proposes the momentary glow of a presence, an image--anyone's, if only they can leap out of the fade-out of inexistence into the presence of the star." [36] The star in nature shines in the night sky as a source of light and visual fascination. In popular culture the star is a person who has acquired the cultural status of a heavenly body, capturing the look of ordinary consumers who drift and dream under a virtual firmament. In shining, the star activates a certain kind of enchanted look that draws the looker towards a phantasmatic presence. The star captures and transforms the look, offering a certain glow as a bestowal on those who look. In this way the star looks back, not with an intentional gaze but through the marvellous shine of a hypnotic presence. Warhol in his own experimental 16mm films, inspired by his love of Hollywood stardom, demonstrates a way of looking at the world that is both actively voyeuristic and passively immobile, as if an inert object was initiating or imitating a look. His camera gazes at people and things but refuses to follow the action, it is "an inattentive camera [...] that will not give the spectacle its full concern." [37] As a director, as an individual with human choice, he absents himself and takes a certain distance, while at the same time drawing out an exhibitionistic display from those who appear in front of his camera. Paradoxically it is Warhol who becomes the star, not the performers who strut on his temporary stage, but Warhol as the one who shines from an untouchable distance.

In separate ways, from vastly different disciplines, Heysenberg, Lacan and Warhol, take us out of subjective gazing into a primordial encounter with shining light, where there is a loss of the division between subject and object, where "looking is the primordial way of coming into the light." [38]

MOMENT OF VISION

Human beings are intrinsically oriented towards sight and visibility as way of knowing the world. "All human beings strive to see, …. to existence there belongs a pursuit of seeing, of being familiar with." [39] Any action in the world requires a moment of deliberation and decision in the face of the unknown, an orientation toward the unknown for the sake of future familiarity. In the moment of action, such as taking a journey, conducting an experiment, making a work of art, a view ahead is established. It is suddenly seen as a "catching sight of the here and now." [40] Something is determined in "that moment at which talking and deliberation come to a standstill." [41] In that moment the doctor makes a prognosis, the craftsmen picks up a tool, and the artist makes a mark. Something has been sighted, it is now in view and all action is aimed towards it. Yet it is also the moment of having been looked upon. That which has been sighted has the looker in its hold and guides them towards its light. It is the moment of apprehension, "the moment of having-seen, in the sense of having been looked upon [...] removing any [...] connotations (of) an 'active' or 'perceptive' seeing that would belong [...] to (an individual's) own originating accomplishment." [42] It falls outside the contemporary understanding of "modern looking in which we direct ourselves to an object of representation and thereby 'grasp' it." [43] In being looked at, an ability to look is activated, and in the act of looking I show myself as engaged and orientated towards the world and all its possibilities. Thus it is "only because we are already addressed, looked upon by beings themselves, can we respond to them in the manner of looking 'at' them." A grasping look is a fallen kind of looking that crushes what is seen with a predetermined intention, while apprehending is "not yet a 'looking at' but is a more subliminal and pre-discursive 'catching sight' of something." [44] In the moment of apprehending the seer is no longer the one who sees and knows, "in having seen there is always something else at play other than the completion of an optical process. From there [...] seeing is not determined by the eye." [45]

Various modes of looking, not determined by a physiological eye, can be found in the historical records. Modern theories of sight and understanding date back to classical Greece in particular Plato's allegory of the cave that sets up a division between shadows and reality. However even further back in the age of Homer there is a different and more primal sense of non-visual radiance. This is demonstrated in a passage from the Odyssey where the goddess Athena appears in the form of a beautiful woman. Ulysses sees her but his son Telemachus does not, "for it is not to all that the gods appear *enargeis*." [46] Under Plato's influence the Romans translated *enargeis* into *evidentia*, a mode of becoming visible, literally visual evidence in the form of an outward appearance. However for Homer *enargeis* meant "a brilliance, a shining, a lighting up, a radiance proceeding from things themselves as they presence." [47] This kind of etymology detects a double valence of light, lost in layers of historical usage and translation, latent with potential for strategic reactivation. Since Ulysses saw and Telemachus did not, *enargeia* and radiance need not have a necessary relationship to light or outward appearance. This aspect remains latent in the English word 'light' and its two contemporary usages. Light's primary meaning refers to the registration of brightness and optical presence. It has a secondary meaning to lessen a burden or lighten a load, that is "to push aside whatever resists, to bring it into a realm without resistance, into a free realm." [48] The free realm is radiant in the sense that it liberates the eye and all the senses in a moment of self-showing presence. It is the simultaneous moment of seeing, enacting the bodily capability of seeing and being seen. It suggests a brief experience, where there is sight, insight and something out of sight, something that has not been created by the actions or thoughts of any individual. In this way the visible world has us rather then we having it. Consequently the so called primacy of perception is made secondary to the opening of presence. [49] Perception is no longer an original relation to being or things since it already "presupposes a world to be given and understood." [50] The sense of the world, is not created through an accumulation of perception nor a totality of sensible impressions. "Perception, although it seems to arise at first glance, is late-born, derived." [51] What we mistakenly call perception is the concretion of a world whose essence is to appear, in it "the visible has a relation to itself which traverses me and constitutes me in seeing." [52] Once again arriving at a situation where "I can feel looked at by things." [53]

Even at the most basic level of biology we understand photosynthesis as a kind of non human looking, whereby the look of the sun as perceived by plants generates the building blocks of life. The sunflower, an aptly named representative of plant life, returns a look without eyes by orienting itself towards the compelling gaze of the sun. The result is the transformation of light into energy and the dehiscence of seeds into new generations of life. From here it seems no coincidence that the birth of human vision is linked to photosynthesis in the earliest forms of life on earth. Four billion years ago, microscopic single cell organisms, had no eyes but photoreceptors, that were receptive only to light direction and intensity. They had no vision for objects, they could not see each other, but they sensed the light from the sky. In the middle of the day, the light was too harsh so they swam down, while at twilight they swam to the surface to turn light into energy. The same molecule that was used in their body to photosynthesise, to give them life, is the same one that facilitates vision in creatures with developed eyes. [54]

The sun, as the source of light grants the possibility of sight as a donation from one that does not see to those who cannot yet see. The sun in its generous looking attracts the gaze of the sunflower and the dehiscent splitting open of the seed pod, returning the gaze as the movement of life from one generation to the next. In the light and warmth of the sun humans are open to a similar process of looking as dehiscence. "Dehiscence opens my body in two, [...] between my body looked at and my body looking, [...] there is overlapping and encroachment." [55]

This kind of thinking about looking and light momentarily disturbs the current understanding of a self sufficient subject who grasps the world through a calculating gaze. It is no longer possible to say "we [...] have on the one hand, things identical to themselves which would afterwards give themselves to sight and on the other hand, a vision, at first empty, which would then open itself to the visible." [56] Something more primordial than an optical mechanism enables an encounter with things in the form of a shining out, where the one who looks is more correctly looked upon by what is seen. What shines comes into sight by virtue of an opening, where presencing, can take place. The seer can only see what appears because they have already gotten out of the way to some extent. The seer, in the moment of shine, has laid down a nominal subjectivity for the sake of a captivating absence, namely the immediate withdrawal of that which appears in favour of a shining out. "It is the prevailing absence in which the seer is held [...] responding to that which presences in its very withdrawal, in its unfathomable and multiple concealments." [57] It is literally and metaphorically a hole in vision, a blindness that is a pre-condition to sight, occurring at the point where the optic nerve connects with the retina, requiring a second sight to occult its absence. [58] The withdrawal from opticality coincides with the flash of radiance, occurring in that brief instant before presence is dulled down to a functional availability. It remains only as a lingering hint, an after image, that is strangely fascinating and 'enchanting.' As such, it "comes to radiance (Schein) in the fullness of its enchantment." [59] It is as enchanting as the twilight glow is for a single cell organism, holding the promise of the fullness of life. Further down the human evolutionary chain, but in the same lambent glow, it shimmers and irridesces, constantly showing different facets of appearing and being. [60]

As such light has the character of excess and unknowing, moving beyond scientific readability into the realm of the incalculable. It is both the light of our understanding and the shadow that surrounds us as an unthinkable limit, that defies being pictured. Art and expanded painting in particular, indicates this in its apprehensiveness, in the apprehension of being looked at by colour, caught up in its shine, shining out in the midst of being, an open place where colour, light and meaning occur.

CONCLUSION

The enduring mystery of colour has led to a scientific muddle, a linguistic aporia and an unspoken prejudice against its apparent excessiveness. Just in case it should overwhelm us in its elemental effusiveness colour is restricted by good taste that equates cultural maturity with a limited palette. Yet colour continues to break free of its constraints, it bursts out of the earth and sky in an audacious display of autopoiesis, tempting poets and painters to reveal, but not capture, its power. The science of colour based on image, mimesis, physiology of the eye and individual subjectivity has somehow missed the phenomenon of colour altogether. Colour rather than being seen and calculated, shines out, shimmers and reveals a world in much the same way that thinking does. This new understanding of what colour 'is' is exemplified by shifts in emphasis from the colour wheel in its rationality, to the colour chart in its availability, to the pixel in its shimmering intensity.

The ontology of colour and the phenomenon of shine stand apart and are incommensurate with the science of light, the psychology of seeing and the subject of vision. Understood phenomenologically colour makes things manifest by revealing them in their unique presence rather than merely facilitating communication, representation or spectacle. Before colour is seen, before colour can be looked at, colour looks at us in such a way that looking and seeing are provoked. In its ordinariness colour is captured and quantified by the grasp of scientific technical rationality. In its extraordinariness colour demands a certain attentiveness, a responsive lingering on the edge of the visible and invisible.

All of these ways of being with colour are enabled by a formal evolution in painting whereby expanded painting addresses everything in the everyday world that carries colour. Expanded Painting, unlike painting, no longer addresses an audience directly, an audience that might validate it through critical and financial response. Instead Expanded Painting addresses a non-human respondent, the medium of painting itself. By analogy, the medium of painting however deconstructed or expanded, has become the entity to 'whom' the work of colour is addressed. ■

REFERENCES AND NOTES

1. David Batchelor, *Chromophobia* (London: Reaktion Books, 2000).
2. Ibid., 21.
3. Ibid., 22.
4. Ibid., 29.
5. Ibid., 85-86.
6. Ibid., 86.
7. Umberto Eco, "How Culture conditions the Colours we See," in *Colour*, ed. David Batchelor (Cambridge, MA: MIT Press, 2008), 178.
8. Jacques Ranciere, *Aesthetics and it Discontents* (Cambridge: Polity Press, 2009), 71.
9. David Batchelor, *Chromophobia*, 104-105.
10. Jeremy Gilbert-Rolfe, "Cabbages, Raspberries and Video's Thin Brightness," in *Painting in the Age of Artificial Intelligence, Art and Design* 11, no. 5-6 (1996): 14.
11. Jacques Derrida, *The Truth in Painting* (Chicago: University of Chicago Press, 1987), 169.
12. Stephen Melville, "Color Has Not Yet Been Named: Objectivity in Deconstruction," in *Deconstruction and the Visual Arts*, ed. P. Brunette and D. Wills (Cambridge: Cambridge University Press, 1994), 33-48.
13. Michel Haar, "Painting, Perception, Affectivity," in *Merleau-Ponty: Difference, Materiality, Painting*, ed. Veronique Foti (Atlantic Highlands, NJ: Humanities Press, 1996), 185.
14. Ibid., 188.
15. Martin Heidegger, "The Origin of the Work of Art", in *Basic Writings* (New York: Harper & Row, 1977), 171.
16. Ibid., 172.
17. Kenneth Maly, "Imaging, Hinting, Showing," in *Kunst und Technik: Gedachtnisschrift zum 100 Geburtstag von Martin Heidegger* (Frankfurt: Klosterman, 1989), 201.
18. A. J. Mitchell, *Heidegger Among the Sculptors* (Stanford: Stanford University Press, 2010), 12.
19. Kenneth Maly, "Imaging, Hinting, Showing," 197.
20. Martin Heidegger, *Parmenides* (Bloomingtom, IN: Indiana University Press, 1992), 103.
21. Ibid.

ESSAY

22. Martin Heidegger, "The Age of the World Picture," in *The Question Concerning Technology and Other Essays* (London and New York: Harper & Row, 1977), 131.
23. Martin Heidegger, *Introduction to Metaphysics* (London: Yale University Press, 2000), 147.
24. Ibid., 150.
25. Ibid., 179.
26. Sophocles, quoted in Martin Heidegger, *Introduction to Metaphysics*, 185.
27. Maurice Merleau-Ponty, "The Visible and the Invisible," in *Basic Writings*, ed. Thomas Baldwin (London and New York: Routledge: 2004), 256.
28. Werner Heisenberg, "The Physical Content of Quantum Kinematics and Mechanics (1927)," in *Quantum Theory and Measurement*, ed. J. A. Wheeler and W. H. Zurek (New Jersey: Princeton University Press, 1983), 62-84.
29. Sigmund Freud, *On Sexuality: Three Essays on the Theory of Sexuality and Other Works* (London: Penguin, 1991), 109.
30. Laura Mulvey, "Visual Pleasure and Narrative Cinema," *Screen* 16, no. 3 (1975): 8.
31. First proposed by Empedocles that light is emitted by the eye, as opposed to modern intromission theory that shows that vision is based on light entering the eye.
32. Claude Bailble, "Programming the Look," *Screen Education*, no. 32-33 (1979): 102.
33. Jacques Lacan, *Four Fundamental Concepts of Psychoanalysis*, (London: Penguin, 1979), 96.
34. Ibid., 106.
35. Slavoj Zizek, *The Fright of Real Tears* (London: BFI, 2001), 34.
36. Stephen Koch, *Stargazer* (New York: Praeger, 1974), 12.
37. Ibid., 77.
38. Martin Heidegger, *Parmenides*, 107.
39. Martin Heidegger, quoted in William McNeill in *The Glance of the Eye* (Albany: SUNY, 1999), 21.
40. William McNeill, *The Glance of the Eye*, 44.
41. Ibid., 46.
42. Ibid., 301.
43. Ibid., 307.
44. Ibid., 311.
45. Ibid., 320.
46. Homer, quoted in William McNeill, *The Glance of the Eye*, 332.
47. William McNeill, *The Glance of the Eye*, 332.
48. Martin Heidegger, quoted in William McNeill, *The Glance of the Eye*, 334.
49. Michel Haar, "Late Merleau-Ponty's Proximity to and Distance from Heidegger," in *Merleau-Ponty*, vol. 1, ed. Ted Toadvine (London and New York: Routledge, 2006), 353.
50. Ibid., 354.
51. Ibid., 355.
52. Ibid., 356.
53. Maurice Merleau-Ponty, quoted in Michel Haar, "Late Merleau-Ponty's Proximity to and Distance from Heidegger," 356.
54. Simon Schaffer, "Let There Be Light," *The Light Fantastic*, episode 1 (London: BBC, 2004), DVD.
55. Maurice Merleau-Ponty, quoted in JacquesTaminiaux, "Phenomnelogy in Merleau-Ponty's Late Work," in *Merleau*-Ponty, vol. 1, ed. Ted Toadvine (London and New York: Routledge, 2006), 289.
56. Jacques Taminiaux, "Phenomenology in Merleau-Ponty's Late Work," 289.
57. William McNeill, *The Glance of the Eye*, 326.
58. Martin Jay, *Downcast Eyes* (Berkeley: University of California Press, 1993), 8.
59. Martin Heidegger, quoted in Veronique Foti, *Heidegger and the Poets* (London: Humanities Press, 1992), 11.
60. Jeff Malpas, *Heidegger's Topology* (Cambridge, MA: MIT Press, 2008), 37, 249.

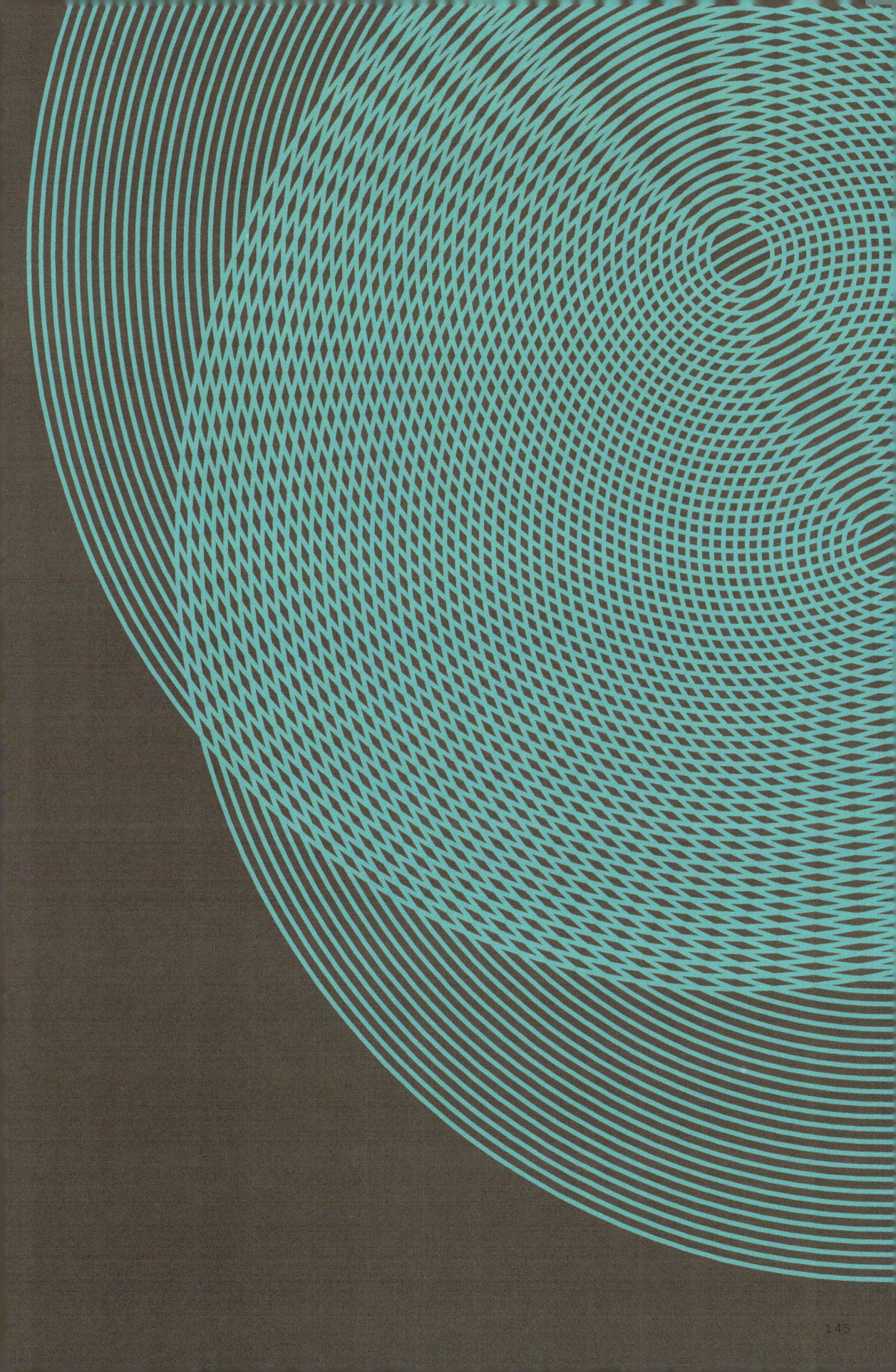

TRANSVERSAL INTERFERENCE

by

Anna Munster

National Institute of Experimental Arts
School of Art History and Art Education
University of New South Wales
a.munster@unsw.edu.au
http://sensesofperception.info

Texts have recently shown themselves to be inaccessible. They don't permit any further pictorial mediation. They have become unclear. They collapse into particles that must be gathered up. This is the level of calculation and computation, the level of technical images.
— Vilem Flusser, *Into the Universe of Technical Images* [1]

Inserted into *The Pencil of Nature* (1844) and *Sun Pictures in Scotland* (1845) – collections of the first commercially published photographic plates – William Henry Fox Talbot placed an inscription, which called for a jump cut in the perception of recorded images:

The plates of the present work are impressed by the agency of Light alone, without any aid whatever from the artist's pencil. They are the sun-pictures themselves, and not, as some persons have imagined, engravings in imitation. [2]

In effect, what Fox Talbot added in *after* publication was a modulation of the *pre*conditions for facilitating the emergence of a photographically entangled visual perception. His insertion attempted to immediately

ESSAY

Increasingly, the images we regard as authoritative – those with a seemingly direct relation to the 'truth' of our brains, profiling our identities, or mapping our universe – are not generated optically. They are composed out of other media, notably sonic and electromagnetic materialities, and other processes, primarily algebraic and statistical transforms. In actuality they are transmaterial assemblages. *Yet such heterogeneous image entities continue to command the epistemological privilege of indexicality that light-based images previously claimed. If the scientific, authoritative image is already constituted 'transgenically,' what implication does this have for interference as a viable aesthetic strategy? To what extent can artists and cultural producers visually interfere with the politics and ethics of such imaging practices? This article suggests that we should abandon the strategy of interference* as intervention *in favour of a better understanding of interference as pattern, indeed fabric, subtending many contemporary non-visual imaging practices. I argue for a transversal* diagrammatic *approach to the nonvisual image; to diagramming as both a holding together* and a dynamic deformation of images into new assemblages. In turn, such diagrammatic practices reflexively remind us that what we see as fixed and authoritative images are instead processual, virtual and speculative modes of 'viewing' and engaging life.*

condition this modality so that perceptual distinctions would be made in relation to the different materialities deployed in the inscription/recording of images.

Fox Talbot was a component of – both engaged with larger machine flows and actualising through various techniques – the event of technical images. He became enmeshed with what was to become a new 'diagram' of visuality, co-extensive with the socio-historical field that, among a number of novel inventions, helped to create scientific photography. As I will argue, building on recent work that I have published on diagrammatic events and functions, especially as these unfold in a technical dimension, a diagram is

ESSAY

an abstract assemblage of relations. [3] Abstractly, this relational assembling pulls together the conditions under which nonhuman and human elements conjoin, play out historically, and inflect across social, aesthetic, political (and more) registers. A diagram is also always open to and conditioned by an 'outside.' Outside-in, yet crucial to its capacities to differentially transform, the diagram's tensors are its potential to deform, explode, shift or inflect toward indeterminate conjunctions. Today that diagram, which once conditioned the event of the technical image and the experience of a photographically inflected visual perception, is undergoing palpable encounters with its outside, now exceeding what was within and resulting in new conjunctions. We are experiencing images that are no longer visual and visual perception becomes a process of composition that is fundamentally transmaterial and transmodal. The technical image is now diagrammatically traversed by an intensive *interference* that arrives from elsewhere.

But if this interfering outside were somehow already insinuated in technical images (the interfering immanent materiality of those "sun-pictures themselves"), what does this say about the curious diagrammatic onotogenesis of technical images? Although Fox Talbot's phrase "the pencil of nature" has become synonymous with an understanding of the indexical relation between the world and optical photographic processes, this phrase, at least in its usual indexical deployment and understanding, curiously elides these diagrammatic events conditioning images. Yet what we also sense from his after-insertion is something more direct that must be expressed: the page lit immediately by the sun image. Plates, which have the capacity to be materially affected by light travelling cosmically as both or either waves and particles; metal plates that, at a molecular level, have conjoined with the sun itself. And in this conjunction we have something novel, something gloriously aesthetic – albeit a nonhuman aesthetics – a base metal to cosmological directness of the photographic image, making a machine for expression without requiring the artist's hand. Yet as is often argued, Fox Talbot's "pencil of nature" and photographic plates were intended to demonstrate the deep and objective coalescence between the new means for recording and making images and that new instrument of science, the photographic camera. [4] What to do, what to say, about all this intensity, then, that seems to offer something more than objectivity yet not at all subjective?

Quite dramatically the sun-picture, the camera, the plate diagram cobble together the rudiments of an assemblage, a machine for producing an aesthetic-technics at once artistic and scientific. This art-science proximity – sometimes loosely hanging out, sometimes in tension – nonetheless accompanies the descent of imaging, from photography onward, into what Vilem Flusser has called "the universe of technical images." [5] It is not the case, then, that the technical image breaks away from an aesthetic register – as Fox Talbot's supplication to "sun-images" all too poetically attests. Instead, the relations between the scientific and aesthetic have to be constantly renewed with respect to the question of indexicality, as if the imprint of the world – the affective proximity of materialities and their forces – will always threaten to interfere with the image's claims to either science, on the one hand or art, on the other.

What Flusser makes clear is that what the technical image ushered in – not with the optics of photography but via the programmaticity of the camera as apparatus – was a new mode of dealing with the relational forces of different materialities con- and disjoining domains such as art and science. Images came to be semiotized through the process of their (eventually) endless recording – the camera a kind of program that both enabled and sequenced that recording. Eventually the sun-picture would become so recordable that it has come to almost shoot itself, holding up a back camera to itself as its own source of light. The contemporary plethora of imaging of the image-itself results today in a purely nonhuman technicity for the entire visual field, where the data/image relies on code and program for any semiosis whatsoever. We see this nowhere as clearly as the transcoding of data through scientific and medical visualization. Yet as Flusser also suggests, this does not mean that materialities of the image or text disappear. Instead, as the relations between texts, images, code and symbols historically mutate, so too do they materially transform. Encoded through binary semitotizing regimes, the new materiality of text implodes into zero-dimensionality. Surprisingly, it is on the zero-degree plane of the electronic encoding of image as data that visuality now pins its hopes. Its index, and 'authority' is no longer the natural world but a universe of pure mathematics.

With this broader deformation and sense of the image's aesthetic, sociotechnical diagramming and transformation in mind, I want to approach this newer 'technical' indexicality of the image now via a series of propositions. First, that the fabric of the image within scientific and medical arenas while seemingly abstracted from the natural world's 'pencil' is nonetheless fundamentally transmedial and transmaterial. Second, that we are undergoing a seismic shift in optics, which cannot simply be understood chronologically as an historical shift from optico-chemical techniques of recording light's properties to computational encoding. Rather the visual field itself is undergoing a re-orientation driven by sensing *invisible* phenomena. This is not captured by the common conception that the invisible is being made visible, as is often claimed when data visualisation is explained, lauded or marketed. Instead, invisibility itself has become an *optical phenomenon* within the domain of the visible. In turn, this suggests that optics has undergone radical and fundamental

transmaterial, transmedial and *amodal* transformations. I want to spend some time grappling with at least some of the scientific aspects of such changes.

Caught up with both these propositions are certain consequences for how artistic practices will need to strategically reposition themselves in this new domain of technical invisible phenomena. A common tactic of artistic intervention into data-based or data generated material has been to 'interfere' with the smooth encoding of the image, often by seeking to introduce, unearth or trigger corruption and/or noise within the data. If data generated images somehow suggest the presence of a perfectly functioning objective and scientific program or machine numerically crunching away, then the artist must bring the image back down to earth or so it goes: "Glitch art is process art: the artist's hand intervening in digital data leaves its mark in the visual essence of the image." Thus the image bears the trace of material aesthetic presence as an interference performed at the level of a "glitchy" gesture. We seem to be in inverse Fox Talbot terrain: the data-generated image is so abstracted from the material world that now the artist's body must materially intervene.

We see a return to a certain kind of indexicality via a strategy of interference/intervention, here weighing in on the side of the aesthetic, body and process against the digital, numerical order. But, as I will argue throughout this article, interference can no longer be aligned with the aesthetic, and is not easily available as an artistic tactic in the contemporary universe of data-generated technical imaging. And, moreover, the data-generated image is already deeply traversed by nonhuman *material* patterns of interference. My third proposition concerns these states of affairs and consequently asserts that interference is already incorporated as a condition of the event of the (scientific) contemporary technical image. In this context, interference provides a diagnostic ordering – an interpretative structuring pattern – responsible for generating a range of contemporary scientific imaging from the very near to the very far; from biological microscopic interaction and development through to astronomical images of plasma nebulae emitted by black holes.

I want to spend some time with these propositions, stepping through the ways in which each of these are unfolding in the domains of scientific and medical visualization. It is important to become 'practically' familiar with these monumental changes in the material and relational fabric of imaging today. It is important to gain a sense, especially, of the taken for granted transmateriality of the image and of interference patterns as foundational for images as they are produced throughout the sciences. Tracking both transmateriality and interference seems a necessary first step in tweaking or even resetting aesthetic strategies and tactics in terms of the ways in which scientific images gain authority as they circulate through aesthetic and cultural domains. If we take into account the shift I have signaled toward an optics of the invisible, along with the role of interference as diagnostic ordering, then we will inevitably also raise questions about the status and politics of whole areas of aesthetic endeavour such as 'practices of visualization' and even 'visual studies.' Much art-science and even much nonscientific contemporary discourse about the visual misconstrues a number of the directions taken by scientific imaging, taking, for example, 'visualization' to be one of science's main aims. Concomitantly, aesthetic discourses come to adopt a program, which actually miss what the sciences might more radically offer. That is, they miss a kind of speculative imagistic trajectory that inhabits many visual scientific endeavours oriented toward a fading of visibility, indexicality and illustration as imperatives for the scientific image.

Interestingly though, a range of cross-media art practices are also engaged in loosening these imperatives rather than in shoring up the materiality of the artist's presence in an immaterial informatic domain. Indeed some practices that specifically engage with the authoritative status of the scientific image amplify or intensify the transmaterial and transmedial relations permeating scientific imaging. This is a deliberate aesthetic strategy for unknotting the authoritative status within scientific imaging and needs to be tagged. Other aesthetic practices are concerned with the non-visible but have displaced it, transversally, so that the dominance of the visual begins to fade. I will gesture toward some of these aesthetic practices in tandem with my unfolding of the above propositions about transformations to the scientific image. I hope to signal that a different aesthetic event – not movement or genre but more process – is emerging, which I will call 'diagrammatic'. To be open to this aesthesia, we might have to re-orient entirely…away from the 'visible' *per se* toward something I will tentatively name the imperceptible. This is already coming into expression diagrammatically through the transversality of such cross-media artistic experiments.

First a note on my use of the term 'transmateriality'. By this, I do not mean innovative 'materials' from plastic through to digital fabrications that bring about transformations in culture or society, as is suggested by, for example Blaine Brownall. [8] The problem with this elaboration of the 'trans' is that materiality itself remains unaffected by its 'trans'ing; its movement across and between itself and the socio-technical, ethico-aesthetic components with which it conjoins and separates to form and deform. In Brownall's account, 'material' seems to possess properties *to innovate*. Yet we are more likely to find that the material properties of the image such as 'light' considered as wave and/or particle are in fact already *transformed* by very material movements. Such movements are not slides across but rather transductions between different energetic forms. It is precisely by transducing

ESSAY

that 'an image' such as a Magnetic Resonance Scan is produced. Hence what I am referring to as transmateriality operates *prior to* any individuation of 'a' material. The transmaterial image is an image whose optical qualities are not so much properties but rather artefacts of the transduction of nonvisual materialities and relations. As we shall see, 'relations' here are to be taken seriously in the functioning of materialities – in their *materialization*. For it is the various relations that dynamically hold between and across ('betweenness' and 'acrossness' *are* relations) light, sound and algorithmic transform, for instance, that crystalize to become the transmaterial scientific image. Transmateriality, then, is a metastable process that *precedes* any given material individuation. It exists virtually, in the Simondonian sense, signalling the potentialities that certain materialities might become, might actualize as, as a result of a transformation of those potentialities in the direction of a structuration. But it is also processual, actual – the movement toward materialisation, individuation, singularity. The relations engaging and engaged by transmaterial processes, then, are both the metastable, virtual ones of pure difference *and* the actualizing ones of a 'thingness' as it assembles. We could develop a conception of transmateriality as a general condition of imaging itself but that is beyond the scope of this article. Instead I intend to be more concrete with respect to the transmaterial conditioning of authoritative scientific images.

Let's begin by probing a little into one of those familiar scientific images of interiority that claim to index the biological basis of human behaviour: the fMRI of the human brain. What does an fMRI actually visualize? The areas of 'color' converted from the original grayscale image are a 'capture' of cerebral hemodynamic response – we are looking at the surplus of oxyhaemoglobin (oxygenated blood) remaining in the veins as a ratio of the increase to decrease of cerebral blood flows. Before asking 'what,' we should ask 'how'

does an fMRI visualize? We should be clear on one thing – an fMRI is not a *visually generated* image. In fact, in order to become image, what is required is the conversion of non-visual data into image space. Like MRIs, fMRIs measure the combination of magnetic signals emitted from hydrogen nuclei in water from the area of the body being imaged (magnetic resonance). Magnetic field gradients are captured in the scanning process, and their frequencies and rate of change are related to the position where the signal is picked up by the scanner. The magnetic signals captured – in fMRIs these are emitted over time as the cerebral blood flow changes in response to stimuli – are composed of a series of sine waves, with individual frequencies and amplitudes. These frequencies and amplitudes are computed using a process called the Fourier transform, which converts signal from the time domain into the frequency domain. The frequencies are then separated out and their amplitudes are plotted as an image. A number of manipulations in the Fourier transform space that allow for smoothing of the final image data, elimination of noise via, for example, high pass filters and so forth, take place before the 'image' of an fMRI is generated. What is being scanned and then what is done computationally to the signal captured are in fundamental ways non-visual and the image/s we eventually see map the *rate of change as a function of time*. What we are looking at, then, is first and foremost a temporally imputed imagescape. As Joseph Dumit has suggested, functional brain imaging at its constitutive level should not be confused with morphological images of the brain, even though such images appear to generate a sense of the brain's topography.

The areas of 'colour' we often see are converted from gray scale in the original imaging, map a 'capture' of cerebral hemodynamic response. We see the surplus of oxyhemoglobin (oxygenated blood) remaining in the veins, measured as a ratio of the increase to decrease of cerebral blood flows. Active neurons require both glucose and oxygen in order to fire and an fMRI traces the flow of blood transporting glucose and oxygen through the vascular system necessary for firing. But are we seeing the trace of the activity of neurons themselves, for example, or are we seeing the trace of activity caused by neurotransmitters, which likewise require cerebral blood flow? An fMRI cannot distinguish these substantially – it is a mapping of oxygenated blood flow; that is, of process not substance. So, we are looking at a mathematically inflected (the ratio of increase to decrease), re-coloured, afterimage selected out of dynamic processuality. Interestingly, the more the fMRI becomes visual artefact (and especially when it is framed as 'an' image or even two comparable images), the less visually indexical it can be said to be, given that its initial data comprises signal generated by electromagnetic waves. As 'an' imaging of the brain, then, we need to understand the final startling brain 'images' of so-called located emotions or as evidence of rewiring less as things being imaged and more as temporally inflected (data)sets made up of cross-processed transmaterialised signal. What is important in this cross-processing is that relations between data variables such as frequency, amplitude and position are maintained.

But the fMRI corralled into 'demonstrating' neural correlation of behavior has become rigidly indexical, losing the potential for the brain to again change in response to, for example, less exposure to media, exposure to noise in the street, a quick decision to not lie or just to *change ad infinitum*. It has instead actualized according to a regime of truth, which is *held together by a particular diagram of power*. [11] A diagram – and here I am following the concept of the diagram laid out by Michel Foucault, especially in his work on disciplinary societies – that continues to hold together the relations of force of our visual regime. These relations are co-extensive with an entire social field of securitization and control – relations such as correlation, identification, visibility and so forth. What we need, then, is a way to perceive such neuro-images as part of that diagram of relations of force – relations that are co-extensive with a visual regime connected to securitization and control but also to sense that those relations are open to deformation. [12]

My second proposition asserts that a shift in optics is occurring re-orienting that field toward invisibility as an optical phenomenon in and of itself. [13] For many of us, this seems to suggest a kind of paradox insofar as our optical devices – eyes – deal with the visible spectrum of light behaviour, which in terms of wavelength, sits in the range of about 380 to about 740 nanometers. But there are also ranges of nonvisible (for the human) electromagnetic radiation. We are of course already familiar with optical devices such as night vision glasses that generate visibility for humans under normally nonvisible conditions. We have been experiencing a steady increase in technical applications that render the 'invisible' visible. But my proposition here concerns a vector in the opposite direction – the generation of visible invisibilities.

Contemporary art practices are likewise engaged with rendering the nonvisible through inventive techniques and explorations of media. But perhaps the focus for artistic activity in this sphere is less rendering the invisible and more a shift toward non 'optico-centric' contemporary aesthetics. In David Rokeby's *Dark Matter*, first exhibited in 2010, a sonic sculpture permeates a completely darkened space, waiting silently for participants to activate it. [14] Participants must reach out with their hands to shape or sculpt the sound so that it comes into existence through the space. The experience of the work is entirely nonvisual – participants engaged in auditory-kineasthetic-tactile and proprioceptive relations throughout the piece and darkness envelops them.

Interestingly enough, though, *Dark Matter* does not reject the visual; we get a sense of this through its composition and design. Infrared video cameras are positioned within the gallery space at four points. They gather positional data based upon a software division and mapping of the space into thousands of three-dimensional zones. Rokeby has selected a range of these zones and has attributed sound behaviours to them. The data from the cameras is cross-referenced, calculating which zones are experiencing the greatest physical activity by participants at any given moment and then the installation plays the sounds linked to those zones throughout the speakers in the space. At both the level of the system hardware and at the level of artistic composition, Rokeby provides us with relations to visuality, all the while composing a work that is fundamentally nonvisual.

Throughout the corpus of his work, stretching back to the early 1980s, Rokeby has been interested in nonhuman vision systems especially infrared cameras and their potential to "survey" an audience involuntarily. [15] In thinking about such vision, he invokes the ancient Greek notion of the eyes beaming "rays of perception" outward to the world rather than receiving images onto the retina. Additionally, he comments upon the design process of attributing sound behaviours to various zones in the room: "They were 'painted' into the space by hand. Starting with an empty space, the artist placed the sounds in the space by selecting a sound then waving his hand in a particular area to locate the sound." [16] Rokeby reconnects the optical via gesture to painting and its permeation by the haptic. This resonates too in participants' experiences of the space as they reach into the "painted soundscape" to "touch" the invisible sculptural curves and dimensions. Furthermore, the title of the work refers to that ineffable, unknown astrophysical phenomenon, which can only be inferred from its gravitational effects on *visible matter*.

Rokeby works to expand and dissipate the visual field in order to push us into an arena in which visuality loses its hitherto privileged status based in part on the socio-political anthropomorphism that holds between visuality and the hierarchy of the senses in human perception. In Rokeby's installation, visuality becomes instead a field in flux: a property of the machine; something to be evoked in a transdisciplinary relational manner; and ultimately only inferable. As we participate with *Dark Matter*, we come to inhabit a space in which by taking away visibility the visual field relaxes, taking on a more relational, diagrammatic feel where it can be modulated and inflected via multimodal and multisensorial deformations. This points to a really radical opening of contemporary aesthetics toward a direction quite different from that prescribed by, for example, a "visual culture approach," which, despite its claims for interdisciplinarity, still argues for the determining role of the visual in the wider culture to which it belongs. [17]

Rokeby's aesthetic invention of a diagram for a sonic-haptic space, which nonetheless holds itself in relation to the visual, is light years ahead at the level of a sociotechnical diagrammatic shift than the shift into invisibility optics currently gathering speed in scientific research. Research into 'metamaterials,' for example, has intensified around phenomena such as invisibility cloaking. [18] Metamaterials are artificial materials that can only be described in terms of the system of relations that adhere between atomic or sub-atomic elements rather than the properties inherent or attributes of the materials themselves. Some materials are characterised by their 'periodic structures' for example; that is, their system is formed through self-impositions of the material elements that generate displacements. Such displacements can exhibit optical properties not found naturally. An electromagnetic metamaterial affects electromagnetic waves by having structural features smaller than the wavelength of the respective electromagnetic wave. Metamaterials sit over or around an object, guiding or scattering electromagnetic waves around or away from it, creating an illusion or cloak of invisibility. Currently, experiments have only been successful with the microwave spectrum and at a very small scale so actual *visible light* invisibility is still some way off but researchers are hoping to break the light barrier soon.

Although we might applaud this kind of research as it seems to signal an exciting shift toward the invisible, we have only to look at the major applications (and of course funding institutions) at the core of such innovation: the US military and NATO. The military fantasy surrounding these new materials lies with the dream to build entire ships, planes and spy satellite systems enveloped by invisibility. In the meantime, both institutions are already developing applications for remote sensing devices, antennae, cloaks for counter-detection and electromagnetic shielding applications among a growing host of surveillance and missile related projects. [19] This is hardly surprising but it does provide a clear signal that the diagram of power relations to which an invisible optics continues to belong is still one of securitization and control. As it turns out, then, invisibility is as much bound up with the socio-political forces of a regime of force relations that organise to maximise opportunities for societies of control. If, as Kevin Heggarty and Richard Ericson' observed in 2000 that a new surveillant assemblage had emerged functioning around the "disappearance of disappearance," then we are now experiencing its flipside: a *reappearance of disappearance*. [20] The scientific shift to invisibility within optics participates in a diagram of force relations in which perception is also captured and redistributed, oscillating now between the visible and the hidden. This diagram is co-extensive with an entire social-technical field of techniques for pervasive profiling and sensing. But Rokeby's aesthetic uptake of the *non*visible finds a different inflection point in this diagram and moves it somewhere else. While the visual continues to play a role in cross-media art works such as Rokeby's *Dark Matter* for example, a different sensing of the visual is also made available that takes into account nonhuman vision systems and a redistribution of the usual hierarchization of human senses.

But the emerging optics of invisibility within scientific research into metamaterials also raises another aspect of the composition of imaging. This aspect holds equivocal possibilities for the political and social directions of both art and science and hence impacts upon the ways in which both come to participate in a particular diagram of power. The (meta)materialist effect of cloaking an object in 'invisibility' works because the materials are themselves comprised of components that have small inhomogeneities. The differential summed response across these components allows the parameters of the electromagnetic wavelengths hitting the object to be variably manipulated. In general, then, (and I am being quite reductive here for the sake of brevity), metamaterial-cloaking produces *interference patterns* across the spectrum of electromagnetic waves, resulting in an 'image' of invisibility. Furthermore, the actual generation of metamaterials themselves out of components often takes place as a result of processes that deploy interference patterns such as "interference lithography." [21]

Put briefly, interference is a physical phenomenon where waves superimpose to form a resultant wave of greater or lower amplitude. Without spending too much time cataloguing and explaining the importance of this phenomenon for the production of a wide range of scientific images, I do want to note at least a few of these: astronomical interferometry (used in, for example ,Very Large Array telescopes to increase the strength of the electromagnetic signal received), bio-layer interferometry, which I alluded to at the beginning of the talk, used in differential interference contrast microscopy to look at *in vivo* cell structure and development; interferometric techniques used in software to adjust imaging the motion-tracking of three-dimensional objects.

Physics, it can be surmised from this range of applications, conceives interference more generally as a phenomenon and then technique for generating a diverse range of scientific imaging from the mid-twentieth century onward. Here interference is understood as pattern rather than as subversion or intervention. We need to at least take heed of this understanding if we are to seriously engage with the composition of the contemporary image. That does not imply simple acquiescence to the scientific framing of interference as orderly rather than ordering. In other words, we do not need to adopt the orderliness of pattern as *the necessary value* to be derived from interference phenomena. There is a tendency by both artists designing for interaction and in the current discourse around interactivity to want to resolve machinic or participatory interference phenomena in the direction of harmony or co-operation, that is, a kind of 'order.' To return to *Dark* Matter, for instance, Rokeby speculates that when multiple participants are present within the *Dark Matter* space, the cacophony of sound produced will lead to a situation where no one knows who or what is controlling the sound. [22] Rokeby speculates that order will emerge form this situation as a result of co-operative interaction between participants, who will tend to work toward the creation of a "resolved," orderly, sound sculpture. Yet anyone who has watched participants engaged in artistic interactive installations will quickly note that co-operation is a learned behaviour not a naturally recurring result; chaos, surrender and sometimes futility are quite often more common.

What I am suggesting is that higher-level homogeneity or equilibrium is not the necessary outcome, especially not a required or desired *aesthetic* outcome, of

component inhomogeneous interactions or, to adopt a more sympathetic socio-political term, heterogeneous relationality. In terms of potential aesthetic strategies for dealing with the growing importance of interference as a scientific diagnostic and imaging technique, we might steer a more interesting course than to fall into one or other side of the pattern versus disruption debate. In *Interference*, a web work made in 2008 by Michael Kargl (now inactive), the aesthetic premise starts with a questioning of the homogenising tendencies of interference as pattern within the domain of networking. [23] The image which loads for the start-up page of the work immediately directs us to a scientific representation of waveform interference indicating that we should take interference phenomena seriously as they general phenomena from pharmacological interactions to linguistic transformations. Interference as a generalised experience of concurrence and overlap is the premise, then, for Kargl's work. The point of creating such a work *online* is precisely to deal with online networks as participants in just such a concurrent mode of making and consuming the visual and the aesthetic. To place art online is exactly to make it available for interaction everywhere and for everyone concurrently. But should we accept this as the necessary condition for viewing, Kargl's work asks? What is viewed, the visible of the work, in fact disperses and dissolves itself back into its inhomogeneities. Or in terms more familiar to network thinking and cultures, *Interference* is distributed heterogeneously. Launching the site turns out not to be a concurrent or similar viewing experience at all but a unique and solitary one. Only one person can gain access to the work at a time; should another participant try to engage, the script driving the page view launches "a placeholder page...and the viewer has to wait." [24] Each instance of *Interference* plays out uniquely as a kind of 'netfilm' for that participant alone. In a rather quiet and noninterventionist manner, Kargl tackles the diagram of the network in which ubiquity and homogeneity come to be the imperatives toward which its relations of force, hijacked by media and techniques of convergence, stratify into a diagram of network pattern, a network diagram. *Interference* instead makes us wait in line (an undecidedly non-networked experience), returning watching and interacting with the web to a myriad of singular, constitutive viewing instances. We are sifted back, systematically, into our inhomogeneities, producing a kind of emergent nonvisible yet singular networked audience. This kind of interference that refuses to hold itself to the increasing predominance of pattern formation – at its core an aesthetic-political diagram co-extensive with a society of control – touches upon a transversal interference:

> *Transversality..tends to be realized when maximum communication is brought about between different levels and above all in terms of different directions.* [25]

The ethical imperative for aesthetics that interferes with contemporary scientific imaging will be to 'lay down a path in walking' (as Francisco Varela once suggested) between and across the radical empirical possibilities of science's transmaterialism and an ongoing artistic commitment to what is indeed radical in the empirical. Heterogeneity. ■

REFERENCES AND NOTES

1. Vilem Flusser, *Into the Universe of Technical Images*, trans. Nancy Ann Roth (Minneapolis: University of Minnesota Press, 2011), 7.
2. William Henry Fox Talbot, quoted in Helmut Gernsheim, *A Concise History of Photography* (Toronto: Courier Dover Publications, 1986), 40.
3. Anna Munster, *An Aesthesia of Networks: Conjunctive Experience in Art and Technlogy* (Cambridge, MA: MIT Press: 2013), 28-30.
4. Mary Warner Marien, *Photography: A Cultural History* (London: Lawrence King Publishing, 2006) 30-32.
5. In *Into the Universe of Technical Images*, Flusser was already arguing in 1985 (the date of the book's original German publication) that we were inhabiting an informatic world comprised of photographic, televisual, cinematic and computational images. See Vilem Flusser, *Into the Universe of Technical Images*. For Flusser, then, the media support of the image is not what is at stake in understanding the cultural, aesthetic and social impact of images. Instead, what must be analysed and critiqued are the epistemological conditions under which images come to *ontologically* organise our broader ecologies of perception. The technical images that pervade contemporary culture, and of which the photograph was an initial instance, are a computationally produced mosaic of information compiled textually but without meaning. They alter our relation to the linear unfolding of meaning, previously generated by the sequential flows of information in text. Hence they change our relation to history and to previous dimensions of meaning-making such as linearity and the two-dimensional surface properties of representational images (like the painting or illustration).
6. Vilem Flusser, *Into the Universe of Technical Images*, 6.
7. Hugh S. Manon and Daniel Temkin, "Notes on Glitch,," *Wrong: World Picture* 6 (Winter 2011), http://www.worldpicturejournal.com/WP_6/Manon.html (accessed July 9, 2013).
8. Blaine Brownall, *Transmaterial: A Catalogue of Materials That Redefine Our Physical Environment*, vols. 1-3 (Princeton: Princeton Architectural Press, 2006).

9. Gilbert Simondon, "The Genesis of the Individual," in *Incorporations*, ed. J. Crarey and S. Kwinter (New York: Zone Books: 1992), 24-25.
10. Joseph Dumit, *Picturing Personhood: Brain Scans and Biomedical Identity* (Princeton: Princeton University Press, 2004), 189.
11. Michel Foucault, *Discipline and Punish: The Birth of The Prison* (New York: Knopf Doubleday Publishing Group, 1977), 205.
12. In my book, *An Aesthesia of Networks* (2013),143–145. I look at the way in which a cross-media art work by Daniel Margulies and Chris Sharp, *Untitled* (audiovisual and participatory installation, 2008), gives us just this transversal relation to the transmaterial 'authoritative' image of the fMRI of the brain.
13. This argument is to be distinguished from the more usual and widely argued point that we are in the midst of an aesthetics of invisibility, where what is impossible to see, touch and so forth is being visualised by computational processing. For more on an aesthetics of invisibility, see, for example, Daniel Black, "An Aesthetics of the Invisible: Nanotechnology and Informatic Matter," *Theory, Culture & Society* 31, no. 1 (2014): 99-121.
14. Documentation of Dark Matter can be accessed on David Rokeby, "Dark Matter," the artist's website, 2010, http://www.davidrokeby.com/Dark_Matter.html (accessed August 15, 2013).
15. See the blog post uploaded after a workshop with Rokeby at Baltan Laboratories: "Poeme Numerique Masterclass: Days 5 and 6 with David Rokeby," the website of Baltan Laboratories, October 30, 2010, http://www.baltanlaboratories.nl/?p=2499 (accessed August 15, 2013).
16. David Rokeby, "Dark Matter."
17. See Nicholas, Mirzoeff, *An Introduction to Visual Culture* (London: Routledge, 1999), 4.
18. For example, see Ulf Leonhardt, "Metamaterials: Towards Invisibility In the Visible," *Nature Materials* 8, no. 7 (2009): 537– 538.
19. RTO Task Group, "Metamaterials for Defense and Security Applications,", the website of Nato Research and Technology Organisation, 2011-2013, http://www.cso.nato.int/activities.aspx (accessed August 15, 2013).
20. Kevin Heggarty and Richard Ericsson, "The Surveillant Assemblage," *British Journal of Sociology* 51, no. 4 (2000): 619.
21. Wenshan Cai and Vladimir Shalaev, *Optical Metamaterials: Fundamentals and Applications* (New York: Springer, 2009), 42.
22. "David Roskeby Explains 'Dark Matter,'" YouTube video, 2:51, posted by THEMUSEUMtv, November 16, 2011, http://www.youtube.com/watch?v=QE9NE9n3HTI.
23. Michael Kargl, "Interference," artist statement, the artist's website, 2008, http://michaelkargl.com/?p=137 (accessed August 15, 2013).
24. Ibid.
25. Felix Guattari, *Psychanalyse et transversalité* (Paris: Maspero/La Découverte, 2003), 80.

www.ingramcontent.com/pod-product-compliance
Lightning Source LLC
Chambersburg PA
CBHW041930240526
45473CB00034B/683